Revit Structure 2013 Basics:

Framing and Documentation

Elise Moss

ISBN: 978-1-58503-740-7

Publications

Schroff Development Corporation

www.SDCpublications.com

Schroff Development Corporation

P.O. Box 1334

Mission, KS 66222

(913) 262-2664

www.SDCpublications.com

Publisher: Stephen Schroff

Trademarks

The following are registered trademarks of Autodesk, Inc.: AutoCAD, AutoCAD Architectural Desktop, Revit, Robot Structure, Autodesk, AutoCAD Design Center, Autodesk Device Interface, VizRender, and HEIDI

Microsoft, Windows, Word, and Excel are either registered trademarks or trademarks of Microsoft Corporation.

All other trademarks are trademarks of their respective holders.

Moss, Elise

    Revit Structure 2013 Basics: Framing and Documentation

    Elise Moss

ISBN: 978-1-58503-740-7

Examination Copies:

Books received as examination copies are for review purposes only and may not be made available for student use. Resale of examination copies is prohibited.

Electronic Files:

Any electronic files associated with this book are licensed to the original user only. These files may not be transferred to any other party.

The authors and publisher of this book have used their best efforts in preparing this book. These efforts include the development, research, and testing of material presented. The author and publisher shall not be held liable in any event for incidental or consequential damages with, or arising out of, the furnishing, performance, or use of the material herein.

Printed and bound in the United States of America.

Acknowledgements

Thanks to the following Autodesk employees: Gary Hercules, Kevin Durham and Brian Johnson.

Thanks to Daniel Stassart and Bill Brown Construction for the use of portions of one of their projects.

Thanks to Stephen Schroff and Mary Schmidt, who work tirelessly to bring these manuscripts to you, the user, and provide the important moral support authors need.

My eternal gratitude to my life partner, Ari, my biggest cheerleader throughout our years together.

Elise Moss
Elise_moss@mossdesigns.com

Preface

This book is geared towards users who have been using Revit and are familiar with the basic Revit interface: Project Browser, how to navigate around a project and use the ribbon.

I advise my students to do each exercise two or three times to ensure that they understand the user interface and can perform the task with ease.

I have endeavored to make this text as easy to understand and as error-free as possible…however, errors may be present. Please feel free to email me if you have any problems with any of the exercises or questions about Revit in general.

When you install Revit, only the templates and libraries for the default units are installed. If you want to have access to both metric and imperial libraries and templates, you need to select the Configure button during the installation process.

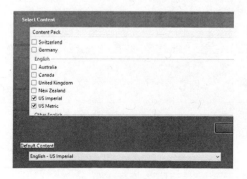

Place a check next to the templates and libraries you want to be able to use.

If you forget to install the libraries and templates you need, you can add them using the Modify/Change option in the Control Panel.

TABLE OF CONTENTS

About the Author

Notes:

Lesson One
Structural Columns and Walls

After completing this lesson, you will be able to:

- Load structural columns
- Create structural column types
- Create openings in structural columns
- Use AutoCAD profiles to create a structural column family
- Add and modify structural columns
- Edit a wall profile
- Add an opening in a wall

➤ Pin columns in position to prevent columns from moving.

Command Exercise

Exercise 1-1 – Load a Structural Column

Drawing Name: **i_columns.rvt**
Estimated Time to Completion: 10 Minutes

Scope

Load a structural column

Solution

1. 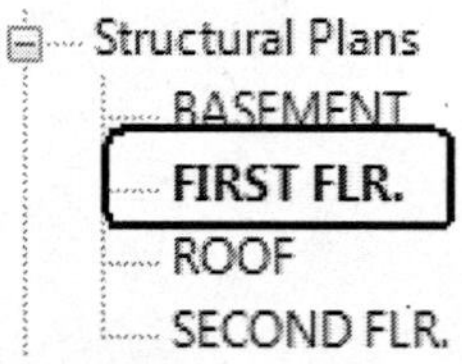 Activate the **FIRST FLR Structural Plan** in the Project Browser.

2. 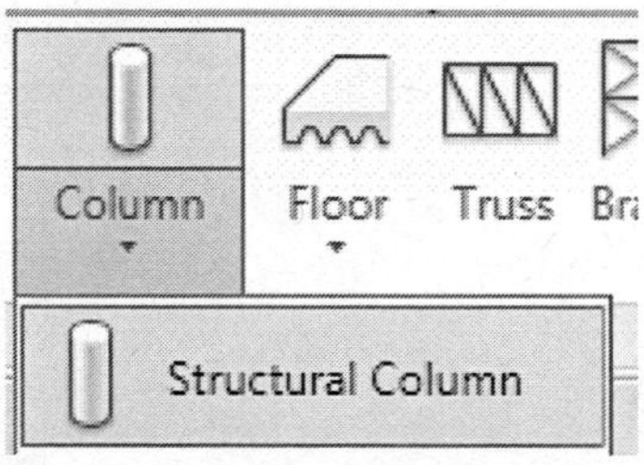 Activate the **Structure** ribbon.

   Select **Column→Structural Column**.

3. 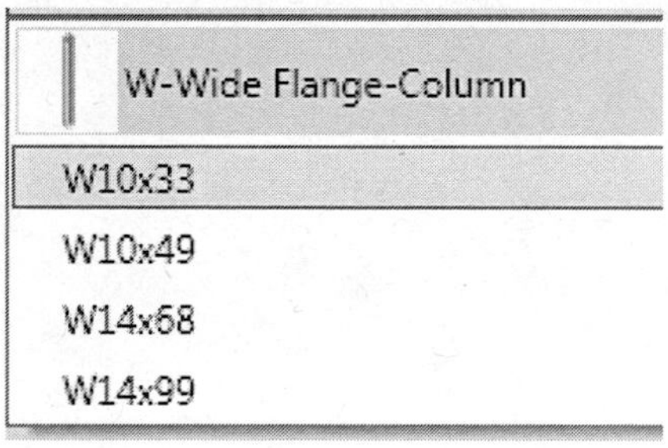 In the Type Selector, note that there are several Wide Flange- Columns available.

4.  Select **Load Family** on the Mode panel.

5.  Browse to the *Structural Columns* folder.

6. 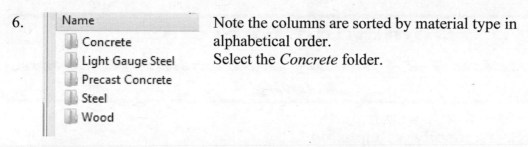 Note the columns are sorted by material type in alphabetical order.
    Select the *Concrete* folder.

7. Highlight the *Concrete - Rectangular Column with Drop Caps*.

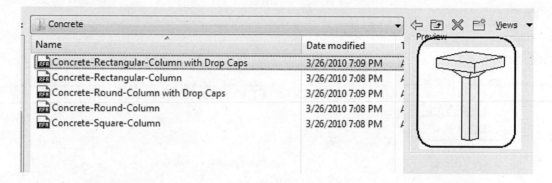

Note that you see a preview of the family in the Preview window.

8.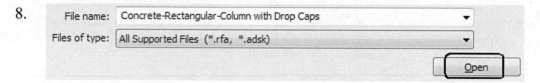

Press Open to load the the *Concrete - Rectangular Column with Drop Caps* family.

9. You are trying to load the family Concrete-Rectangular-Column with Drop Caps, which already exists in this project. What do you want to do?

    If you see this dialog, select the second option.

    → Overwrite the existing version

    → Overwrite the existing version and its parameter values

10. 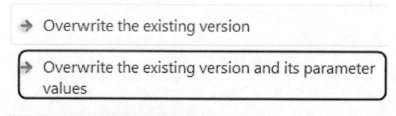 On the Properties Pane:

    Select the Type Selector to see the different sizes available for that family.

11. Close without saving.

Command Exercise

Exercise 1-2 – Modify a Structural Column Family

Drawing Name: **modify_columns.rvt**
Estimated Time to Completion: 10 Minutes

Scope

Modify a Wall Profile

Solution

1. Structural Plans
   BASEMENT
   FIRST FLR.
   ROOF
   SECOND FLR.

   Activate the **FIRST FLR Structural Plan** in the Project Browser.

2. 20' - 6"

   Cancel

   Repeat [Load Family]
   Recent Commands

   Detach From Plane
   Reset Analytical Model to Initial Positi

   Hide in View
   Override Graphics in View

   Create Similar

   Edit Family

   Select Previous

   Select the column located at **A1**.
   Right click and select **Edit Family**.

   A new file will open with the column family.

3. Floor Plans
   Lower Ref. Level

   Activate the **Lower Ref. Level** in the Project Browser.

4. Study the parameters assigned to the different dimensions.

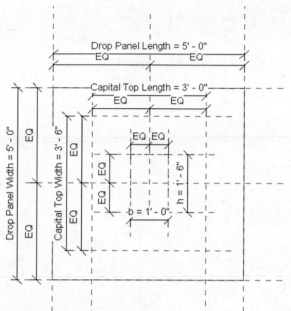

5. Activate the **Front Elevation** in the Project Browser.

Elevations (Elevation 1)
- Back
- **Front**
- Left
- Right

6. Note how the levels control the height of the column.

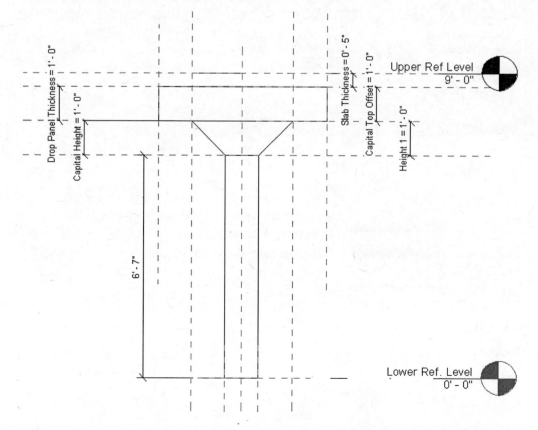

7.  Activate the **Lower Ref. Level** in the Project Browser.

8. Select **Family Types** on the Properties panel.

9. Select **New** under Family Types.

10. Type **12 x 24** for the Name.
Press **OK**.

Name: 12 x 24

11. Change the value of h to **2′ 0″**.

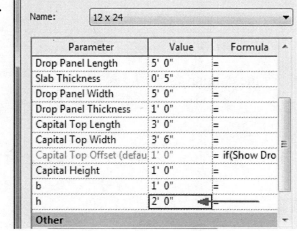

12. Press the **Apply** button.
Observe how the column changes.

Apply

13. 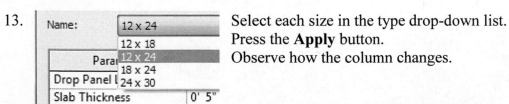 Select each size in the type drop-down list.
Press the **Apply** button.
Observe how the column changes.

14. Press **OK**.

15.

Go to the Applications Menu.
Select **Save As→Family**.

16.

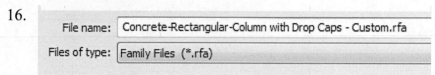

Browse to your exercise folder.
Save the family as a Custom family.

17. Close any open files without saving.

Command Exercise

Exercise 1-3 – Create an Opening in a Structural Column

Drawing Name: **modify_columns.rvt**
Estimated Time to Completion: 10 Minutes

Scope

Modify a Wall Profile

Solution

1. 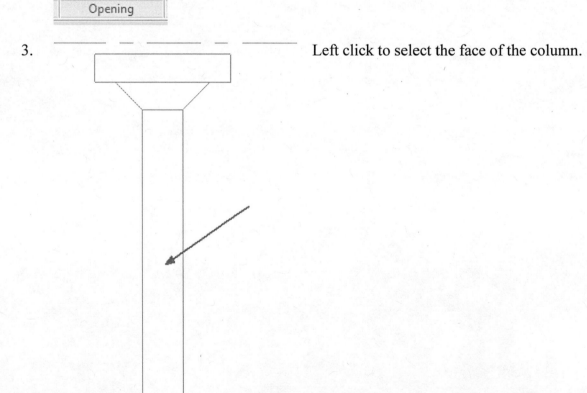 Activate the **West Elevation.**

2. Activate the Structure ribbon.
   Select the **By Face** tool on the Opening panel.

3. Left click to select the face of the column.

4.

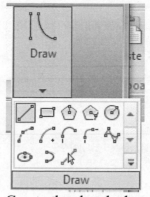

0' - 8"

EEQ

2' - 6"

5' - 6"

Create the sketch shown.

Draw a rectangle.
The rectangle is 2' 6" x 8 ".
Center the rectangle on the column by applying an EQ dimension between the reference plane and two horizontal dimensions.
Position the sketch so it is 5' 6" from the Basement Level.

Add a 1" fillet to each corner using the Fillet Arc tool.

5. Select the Green Check on the Mode panel to finish the opening.

Mode

6.

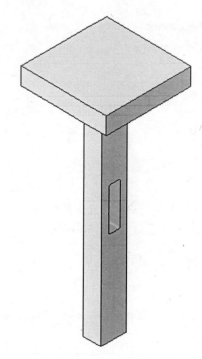

Switch to a 3D view so you can inspect the new opening.

7. Close without saving.

Command Exercise
Exercise 1-4 – Use AutoCAD Profile to Create a Structural Column Family

Drawing Name: **column.dwg**
Estimated Time to Completion: 60 Minutes

Scope

Create a custom column family

Solution

1. 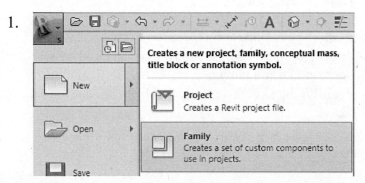 On the Application Menu:
   Go to **New→Family**.

2. 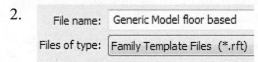 Locate the *Generic Model floor based* template under the *Imperial Templates* folder.
   Press **Open**.

3. Elevations (Elevation 1)   Activate the **Front** elevation.
   Back
   Front
   Left
   Right

4. Activate the **Create** ribbon.
   Select **Revolve** from the Forms panel.
   Revolve

5. Activate the **Insert** ribbon.
   Select the **Import CAD** tool.

6.  Locate the column.dwg file in the exercise folder.

7.

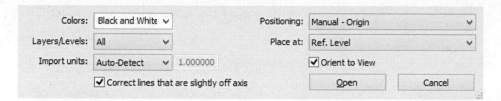

Set Colors to **Black and White**.
Set Layers to **All.**
Set Import Units to **Auto-Detect.**
Set Positioning to **Manual- Origin**.
Press **Open**.

8.

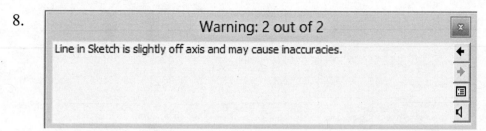

Revit will provide a couple of warnings, which can be ignored.

9. Right click and select Zoom to Fit.

You can also double click the mouse wheel to Zoom to Fit.

10.

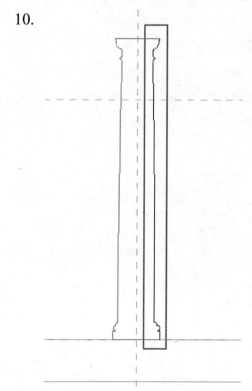

Window around the right side of the column.
Delete the right side by pressing the Delete key on
the keyboard or right click and select **Delete**.

11. 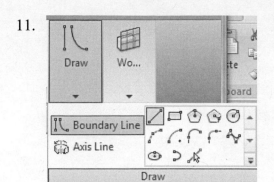 Highlight Boundary Line.
Select the **Line** tool on the Draw panel.

12. 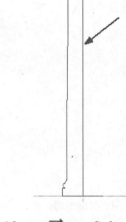 Draw a vertical line to close the profile.

13. Select the **Trim** tool from the Modify panel.

14. Use the Trim tool to clean up the profile.

15. 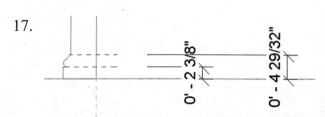   Zoom into the base of the column sketch.
Activate the Create ribbon.
Add two reference planes aligned to the two horizontal lines.

16.   Use the ALIGN tool to lock each horizontal sketch line to the reference plane.

17. 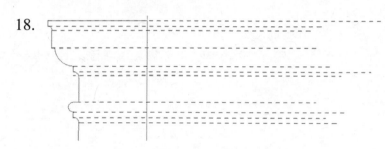   Add an aligned dimension between each new reference plane and the Ref. Level.

Be sure to select the Ref. Level and the reference plane - not the column sketch or floor!

18.   Zoom into the top of the column sketch.
Activate the Create ribbon.
Add eleven reference planes aligned to the each horizontal point that defines the profile.

Reference planes are used to control the geometry.

19.   Use the ALIGN tool to lock each horizontal sketch point/line to the reference plane.

20. 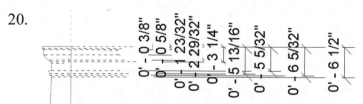   Add an aligned dimension between each new reference plane and the top reference plane.

Be sure to select the reference planes - not the column sketch!

21.

Identity Data	
Name	Column Top

Select the top reference plane so it is highlighted.
In the Properties pane, enter **Column Top** as the name for the reference plane.

Hint: By naming reference planes, they can be selected as work planes and used in formulas.

22.

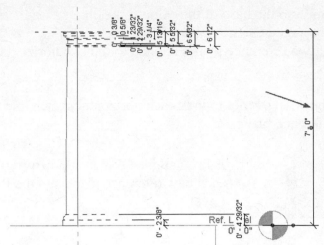

Select the **Aligned Dimension** tool.

Add a dimension between the top reference plane and the Ref. Level at the bottom.

23.

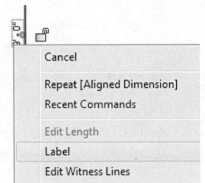

Select the dimension.
Right click and select **Label**.

24.

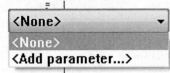

Select the **Add parameter** option from the Label drop-down list.

25.

Set the Name to **Height**.
Enable **Type**.
Press **OK**.

26.

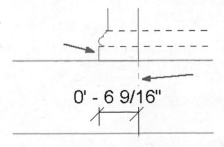

Add an aligned dimension between the base vertical line and the center reference plane.

27.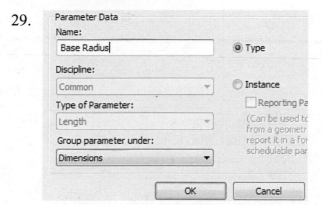
Select the dimension.
Right click and select **Label**.

28. Select the **Add parameter** option from the Label drop-down list.

29.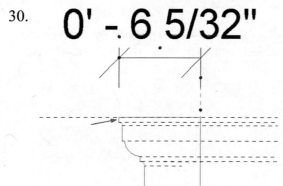
Set the Name to **Base Radius**.
Enable **Type**.
Press **OK**.

30.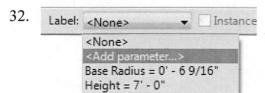
Add an aligned dimension between the top vertical line and the center reference plane.

31.
Select the dimension.
Right click and select **Label**.

32. Select the **Add parameter** option from the Label drop-down list.

33.

Set the Name to **Base Radius**.
Enable **Type**.
Press **OK**.

34.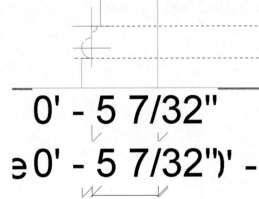

Select each arc in the sketch.

35.

In the Properties pane:
Enable **Center Mark Visible**.
Repeat for each arc.

36.

Add an aligned dimension between the center mark for each arc and the center reference plane.

0' - 5 7/32"

ə0' - 5 7/32")' -

37. Top Radius = 0' - 6"

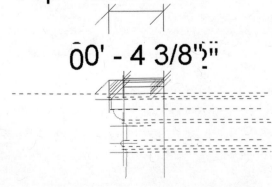

The values of the aligned dimensions don't matter and shouldn't be locked. These dimensions just ensure that the geometry stays in a proper location.

Locate the Concrete
material in the lower
nel.
ect the **Copy to**
ument tool.

`.

0".
...om Radius to **6"**.
.y that the sketch updates.

xis L..e tool.

l ...om the Draw panel.
tical plane.
nto position.

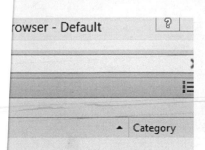

In the Properties pane:
Select the Material column.

ult material.
t the bottom left of the dialog box.

owser - Default

In the Material Browser:
Type **concrete** in the
search field.

Category

48.

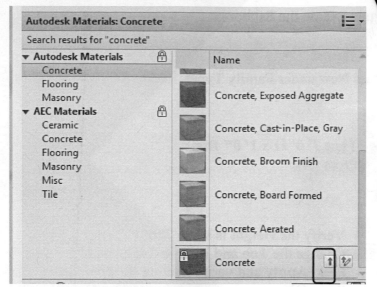

Se...
Doc...

49.

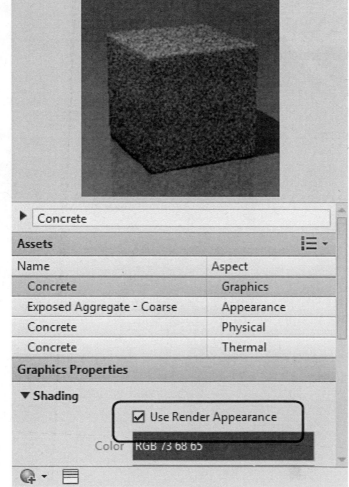

Enable **Use Render Appearance**.

Press **Done**.
Press **OK** to close the Material Browser.

50.

Materials and Finishes	
Material	Concrete
Identity Data	

You should see the material listed in the Properties pane.

51. Switch to a 3D view.

52. Select the **Green Check** to Finish the Revolve.

53. 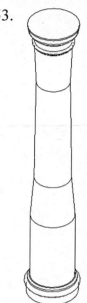 Your column should be formed.

54. Activate the **Create** ribbon.
Select the **Family Categories** tool.

55. Select **Structural Columns**.
Press **OK**.

Family Category

Filter list: Structure

Columns
Generic Models
Mass
Profiles
Split Profile
Structural Columns
Structural Connections
Structural Foundations
Structural Framing
Structural Stiffeners

This adds the properties for Structural Columns to the family.

56. File name: Column - Grecian

Files of type: Family Files (*.rfa)

Save the column in your exercise folder.
Name the file *Column - Grecian*.

Command Exercise

Exercise 1-5 – Add and Modify Structural Columns

Drawing Name: **i_columns.rvt**
Estimated Time to Completion: 30 Minutes

Scope

Add Structural Columns
Modify Structural Columns

Solution

1. 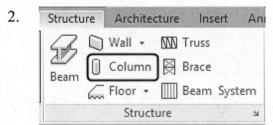 Activate the **First Flr.** under Structural Plans in the Project Browser.

2. Activate the **Structure** ribbon.
   Select **Column**.

3. Use the Type Selector to select **W-Wide Flange Column W10x49**.

4. On the Options bar:
   Set the Height to **ROOF**.

5. 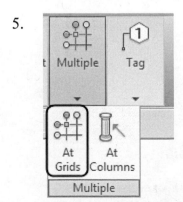 On the ribbon:
   Select **At Grids**.

To place columns at grid intersections, select the vertical and horizontal grid.

6. 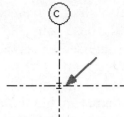 Select the C grid and the 1 grid to place the first column.
Select **Finish** to confirm the placement.
Repeat to place columns at C2, C3, and C4 by performing the following steps:
   1. Select **At Grids**.
   2. Hold down the CTL key.
   3. Select a horizontal and vertical grid to identify the intersection.
   4. Select **Finish** to Place.

7.  To see the At Grids and the Finish buttons you may need to select the ribbon display tools. This is a bug in 2013 and may be fixed in a future service pack/release.

8. Right click and select **Cancel** to finish placing columns.

9.  Select the column at the **C4** intersection.
Press the **SPACEBAR**.
Note that the column rotates.

10. 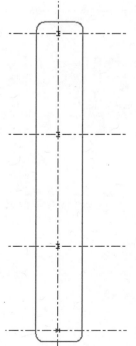 Window around the four columns that have been placed.
You should see the column type in the Properties pane.

11. Select the **Copy** tool from the Modify panel.

12.

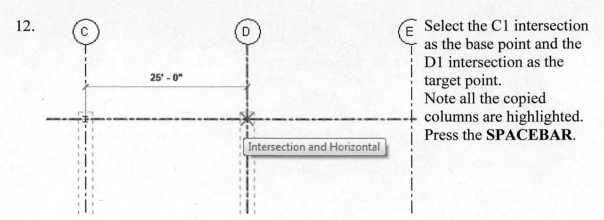

25' - 0"

Intersection and Horizontal

Select the C1 intersection as the base point and the D1 intersection as the target point.
Note all the copied columns are highlighted.
Press the **SPACEBAR**.

13.

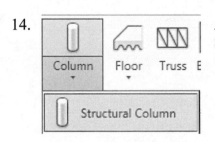

Note that the columns on the D grid have rotated 90 degrees.

Press **ESC** to release the selection.

14.

Column   Floor   Truss   E

Structural Column

Activate the **Structure** ribbon.
Select **Structural Column**.

15.

W-Wide Flange-
Column
W10x33

Use the Type Selector to select **W-Wide Flange Column W10x33**.

16. On the Options bar:

e: ☑ Rotate after placement   Height ▼   ROOF ▼   9' 0"

Enable **Rotate after placement**.
Set the Height to **ROOF**.

17. Select the **At Grids** mode.
    Select the **B** grid.
    Select the **1** grid.
    This sets the intersection to B1. At Grids

18. Press the **SPACEBAR**.
    Note that the column rotates.

19. 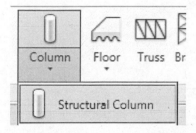 Finish   Select **Finish** from the ribbon to complete the column placement.

    Note: If you press ENTER, you will re-initialize the grid selection and the column is not placed. This is a bug which may be resolved in a later release.

20. Repeat to add columns at E1, F1, B4, E4, and F4.
    Set the columns horizontal at each grid intersection.

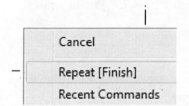

Hint: You can also right click to select Finish once you have placed the column.

21. Right click and select **Cancel** to exit placing columns.

22. 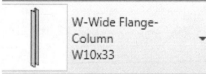   Activate the **Structure** ribbon.
    Select **Structural Column**.

23. W-Wide Flange-Column W10x33   Use the Type Selector to select **W-Wide Flange-Column W10x33**.

24. At Grids   Select the **At Grids** mode.

25. Hold down the **CTRL** key and select A1, A2, G1, and G4 intersections.

26. Select **Finish** from the ribbon.
    Columns are placed at each intersection.

Finish

27. Select **Modify** or **ESC** to exit the column command.

28. Window around the columns so they are all selected.

29.

Constraints	
Column Location ...	
Base Level	BASEMENT
Base Offset	-1' 6"
Top Level	ROOF
Top Offset	-0' 6"
Column Style	Vertical
Moves With Grids	☑
Graphics	

In the Properties pane:
Set the Base Level to **BASEMENT**.
Set the Base Offset to **-1' 6"**.
This places the column's bottom face 1' 6" below the BASEMENT level.
Set the Top Level to **ROOF**.
Set the Top Offset to **-6"**.
This places the column's top face 6" below the ROOF level.

30. Apply   Press the **Apply** button at the bottom of the Properties pane.

31. Select the B grid.
    Change the dimension between A.5 and B to **30' 0"**.

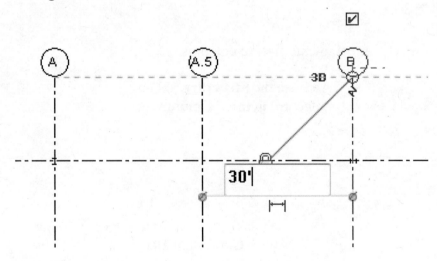

Note that the columns remain aligned to the grid.

32. 3D Views   Activate the 3D view.
    {3D}

33. Close without saving.

Command Exercise

Exercise 1-6 – Edit a Wall Profile

Drawing Name: **wall profile.rvt**
Estimated Time to Completion: 10 Minutes

Scope

Modify a Wall Profile

Solution

1. 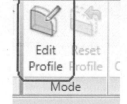 Activate the **West Elevation** in the Project Browser.

2. Select the wall.

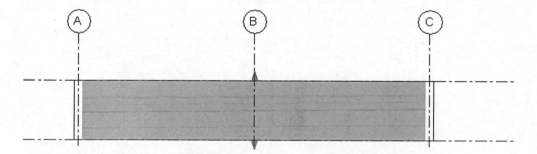

3. Select **Edit Profile** on the Mode panel.

4. Select the **Line** tool from the Draw panel.

You may need to play with the ribbon display tools to see the Draw panel.

5.

Draw a vertical line 5′ 6″ to the right of the A grid and 2′ 6″ high.

6.

Use the TRIM tool to delete the top line for the wall to the right of the short vertical line.
Arrows indicate the selections for the TRIM tool.

7.

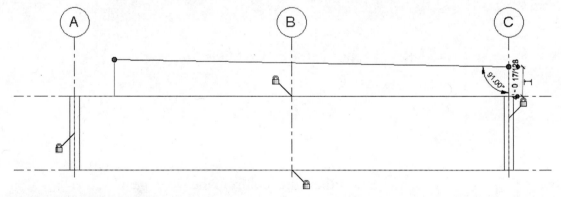

Extend the right vertical line up.
Draw a new slanted line to close the profile.
Set the angle to **91°**.

To set the angle: add a temporary angle dimension using the Angle tool in the Measure panel.

8. Select the **Green Check** on the Mode panel.

9.   Switch to a 3D view.

10. The wall profile has been modified.

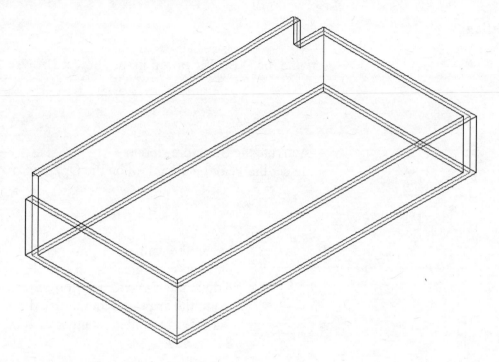

11. Close without saving.

Command Exercise

Exercise 1-7 – Add an Opening in a Wall

Drawing Name: **add_opening.rvt**
Estimated Time to Completion: 10 Minutes

Scope

Add an opening to a wall.

Solution

1.   Elevations (Building Elevation)
       East
       North
       South
       West   Activate the **West Elevation** in the Project Browser.

2.   By Face   Shaft   Wall   Vertical   Dormer   Opening   Activate the Structure ribbon.
Select the **Wall** opening tool on the Opening panel.

3.   Select the wall.
Draw a rectangle.
Adjust the size and position of the rectangle using the grips and temporary dimensions.
Set the size of the rectangle to 4′ 0″ high x 8′ 6″ wide.

4. Position the rectangle 5′ 6″ to the right of the A grid and 3′ 0″ above Level 1.

5.   Switch to a 3D view.

6. 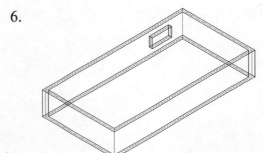   An opening to the wall has been added.

7. Close without saving.

Lesson Two
Placing Framing

Framing is used to support floors. Floor framing is a collection of elements, such as girders and beams that support a floor system. Framing elements are typically added after columns are placed.

Beams are attached to columns and structural walls. Beams are categorized as girders, joists, braces, or purlins, depending on how they are placed. *(Refer to the next page for the definitions for different beam types.)*

Beams can be placed in plan, section or elevation views.

Use the Beam tool instead of the Beam System tool to add beams individually if a structure has irregular bay spacing or shape. Disable the Tag check when placing beams in a framing plan to keep the plan view less cluttered. Duplicate the view and have one view with the tags placed and one view without tags. Use the view without tags while placing elements and modifying the structure.

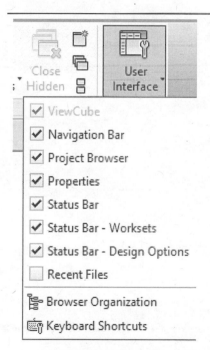

> ➤ If you accidentally turn off the Project Browser or Properties pane, you can bring them back by going to the View ribbon and selecting the User Interface drop-down. Place a check next to the items you wish to be visible in your work area.

Terms to know:

A **purlin** (or **purline**) is a horizontal structural member in a roof. Purlins support the loads from the roof deck or sheathing and are supported by the principal rafters and/or the building walls, steel beams etc. The use of purlins, as opposed to closely spaced rafters, is common in pre-engineered metal building systems and some timber frame construction.

A **girder** is a large main supporting beam, commonly of steel or reinforced concrete, that carries a heavy transverse (crosswise) load. In a floor system, beams and joists transfer their loads to the girders, which in turn frame into the columns.

A **joist** is any wood, steel, or concrete beam set parallel from wall to wall or across abutting girders to support a floor or ceiling.

A **brace** is a structural member used to stiffen framework.

Command Exercise
Exercise 2-1 – Add Structural Framing

Drawing Name: **framing.rvt**
Estimated Time to Completion: 45 Minutes

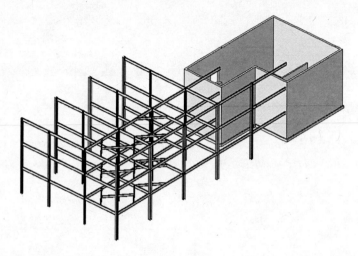

Scope

        Load Beam Family
        Add steel girders
        Add beams between girders
        Tag beams
        Mirror and copy beams

Solution

1.   Structural Plans   Activate the **FIRST FLR.** plan under Structural plans.
              BASEMENT
              FIRST FLR.
              ROOF
              SECOND FLR.

2.   *Home   Insert*   Select the **Beam** tool from the Structure ribbon.

            Beam   Wall

3.   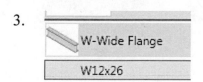   In the Type Selector, only one size is available.

         W-Wide Flange
         W12x26

4. 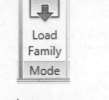 Select **Load Family** on the Mode panel.

5.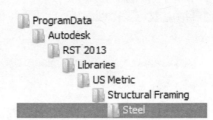

Browse to the Structural/Framing/Steel folder.

Both Imperial and Metric libraries are shown so users can select which units they wish to work in. Metric units and metric files will be referred to in brackets.

6.

| File name: | W-Wide Flange |
| Files of type: | All Supported Files (*.rfa, *.adsk) |

| File name: | M_W-Wide Flange |
| Files of type: | All Supported Files (*.rfa, *.adsk) |

Select the *W-Wide Flange [M_ W-Wide Flange]* family.

Press **Open**.

7.
Types:

Type
W18X40
W18X35
W16X100
W16X89
W16X77
W16X67

Hold down the **CTRL** key. *This allows you to make multiple selections.*

Select **W18x35 [W46x52]** and **W16x26 [W410x38.8]**.

Press **OK**.

In order to keep file size small, only load the beam sizes which are actually used in the project.

8.

→ Overwrite the existing version

→ Overwrite the existing version and its parameter values

Select **Overwrite** the existing version.

This adds the additional family types to the loaded family without modifying any tags or comments placed on any wide flanges which have already been placed.

9. 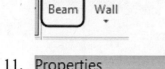 Switch to a Coarse view display.

10. Select the **Beam** tool from the Structure ribbon.

11. Select the **W18x35 W-Wide Flange**.

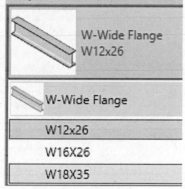

12. On the Options bar:

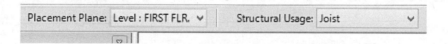

Set the Placement Plane to **FIRST FLR**.
Set the Structural Usage to **Joist**.

13. 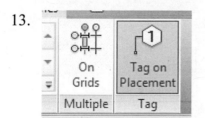 On the ribbon:
Enable **Tag on Placement**.

This will add structural member tags as the members are placed.

14. On the ribbon:
Select **On Grids**.

15. 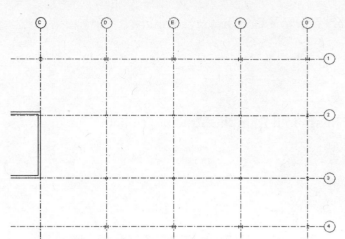 Hold down the CTL key and select Grids D-G and 1-4.

16.  Select **Finish**.

17. 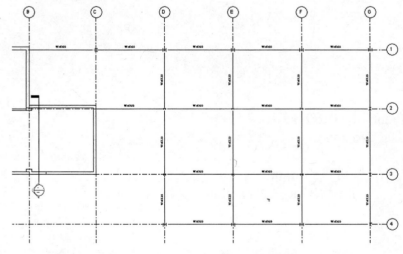 The joists are placed.

Right click and select **CANCEL** to exit the command.

18. 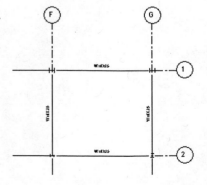 Zoom into the F-G/1-2 bay.

19.

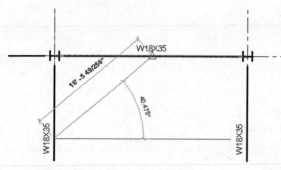

On the Structure ribbon:
Select the **Model Line** tool.

20.

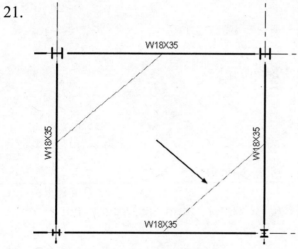

Draw a line from the midpoint of the vertical beam between 1-2 to the midpoint of the horizontal beam between F-G.

Start the line 10′ 8″ below Grid 1.

This is the midpoint of the bay.

21.

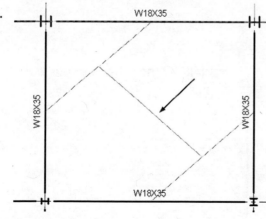

Draw a second line starting from the midpoint of F2 and G2 and parallel to the first line.

22.

Draw a third line using the midpoints of line 1 and line 2.

Cancel/Exit the Model Line tool.

23.

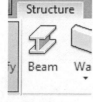

Select the **Beam** tool on the Structure ribbon.

24.  On the Type Selector:
Select the **W12x26 W-Wide Flange**.

25. On the Options bar:

Set the Placement Plane to **FIRST FLR**.
Set the Structural Usage to **Purlin**.

26. 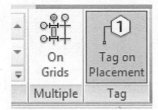 On the ribbon:
Enable **Tag on Placement**.

This will add structural member tags as the members are placed.

27. 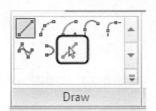 Select the **PICK LINE** tool from the Draw panel.

28. 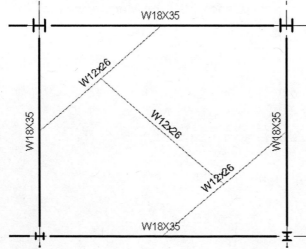 Pick the three lines to place the purlins.

29. 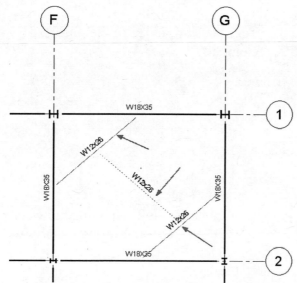 Note how the purlin beam uses a different line type display as the joists.

30. Hold down the CTRL key and select the three W12x26 beams.

31. Select the **Mirror→Pick Axis** tool on the Modify panel.

Select the **F** grid as the mirror axis.

32. 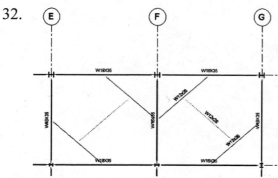 Note the beams are mirrored, but not the tags.

33. Activate the **Annotate** ribbon.

Tag
All

Select the **Tag All** tool from the Tag panel.

34.

Select at least one Category and Tag Family to tag non-tagged objects:

(●) All objects in current view

(○) Only selected objects in current view

☐ Include elements from linked files

Category	Loaded Tags
Structural Column Tags	Structural Column Tag
Structural Foundation Tags	Structural Foundation Tag
Structural Framing Tags	Structural Framing Tag
Structural Framing Tags	Structural Framing Tag : Boxed
Structural Framing Tags	Structural Framing Tag : Standard

Highlight the **Structural Framing Tag**.

Press **OK**.

35.

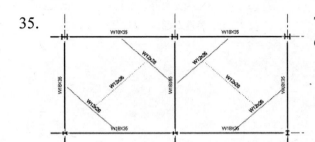

Tags are now added to the mirrored elements.

36. Switch to a 3D view.

37.

Orient the view using the view cube so you can see the framing which was added.

Window around the entire model to select everything.

38. Select the **Filter** tool in the ribbon.

Filter

Filter

39.

☐ Structural Columns	17
☐ Structural Foundations	4
Structural Framing (Girder)	27
☑ Structural Framing (Other)	2
☐ Structural Framing (Purlin)	4
☐ Walls	14

If you have any structural members which are unassigned, they will be listed as **Other.**

Uncheck all the elements listed except for those.

40.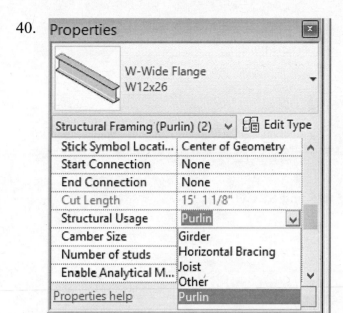

In the Properties pane:

Scroll down until you locate Structural Usage.

Set the Structural Usage to the correct type.

Then reselect the model.

41.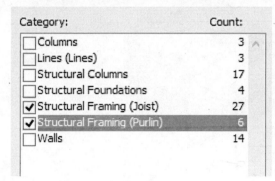

Note that the structural framing has been assigned functions (girder/joist/purlin) based on how it was placed.

Uncheck everything EXCEPT the Girder/Joist/Purlin designated framing.

Press **OK**.

42.

Select the **Copy** tool on the Clipboard panel.

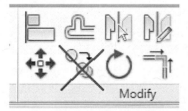

Do not select the COPY tool on the Modify ribbon.

The COPY tool on the Modify ribbon allows you to copy on the SAME work plane/ level. The COPY tool on the Clipboard allows you to copy from one level to another level.

43.  Select **Paste→Aligned to Selected Levels** on the Clipboard panel.

44. 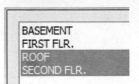 Highlight **ROOF** and **SECOND FLR**.

    Press **OK**.

45. The structural framing is copied to the new levels.

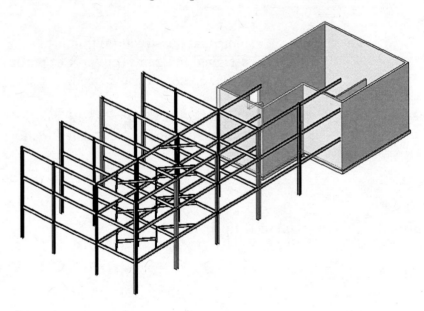

46. Close without saving.

Command Exercise
Exercise 2-2 – Create an Assembly

Drawing Name: **group.rvt**
Estimated Time to Completion: 15 Minutes

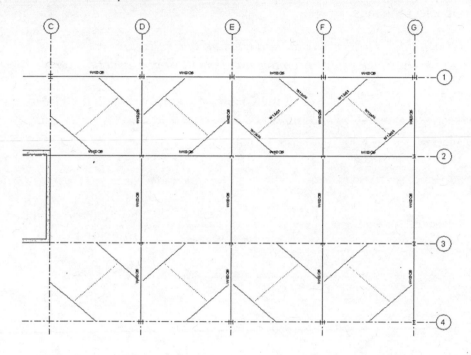

Scope

Create an Assembly
Place an Assembly

Solution

1.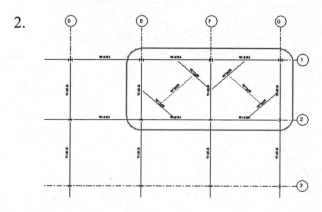

    Structural Plans
        BASEMENT
        FIRST FLR.
        ROOF
        SECOND FLR.

Activate the **FIRST FLR. plan** under Structural plans.

2. Use Zoom Region to zoom to the bay located between grids E1 and G2.

3. 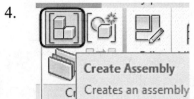 Select the structural beams located inside the bay.

Do not select the tags.

Hold down the CTRL key to add and element to a selection set.
Hold down the SHIFT key to remove an element from a selection set.

4. Select the **Create Assembly** tool on the Create panel.

Create Assembly
Cr Creates an assembly

5.  Name the Assembly: **Interior Purlin**.

Press **OK**.

6. ⊟ 🔲 Assemblies   The Assembly is listed in the Project Browser.
   ┈┈┈ Interior Purlins

7. 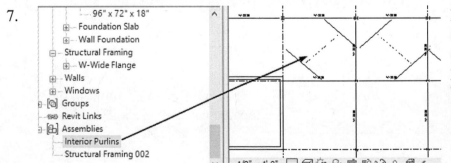 Highlight the assembly and drag a copy so it is placed to the left of the original assembly.

8. Verify that the assembly is still selected.
   Select the Copy tool from the Modify panel.

9. Modify | Model Groups   ☐ Constrain ☐ Disjoin ☑ Multiple   Enable **Multiple** on the Options bar.

10. Select the Grid intersection on Grid E1 as the base/start point.

W18X35

Endpoint

W12X26

W12X26

11. Select the Grid intersection on Grid C3 as the end point.

12. Select the Grid intersection on Grid E3 as the end point.

Right click and select **Cancel** to exit the Copy command.

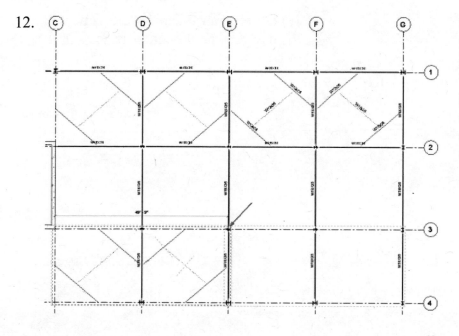

13.

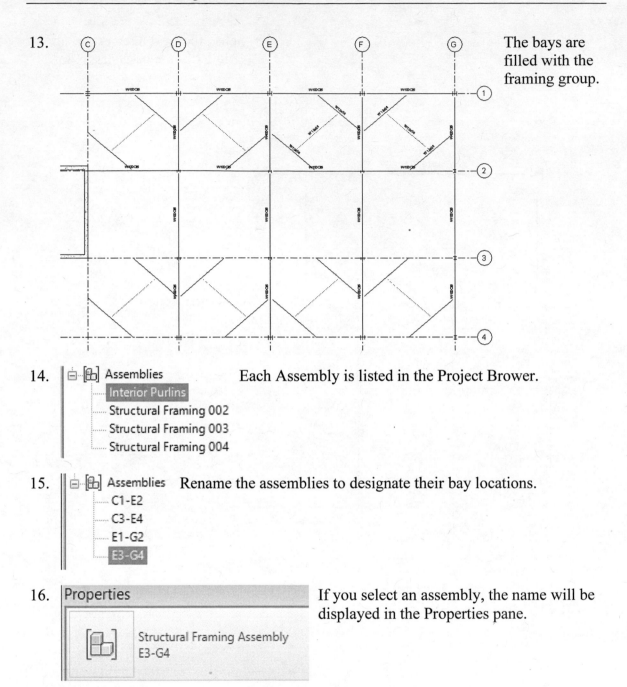

The bays are filled with the framing group.

14.

```
☐ 🔲 Assemblies
    ┈┈ Interior Purlins
    ┈┈ Structural Framing 002
    ┈┈ Structural Framing 003
    ┈┈ Structural Framing 004
```

Each Assembly is listed in the Project Brower.

15.

```
☐ 🔲 Assemblies
    ┈┈ C1-E2
    ┈┈ C3-E4
    ┈┈ E1-G2
    ┈┈ E3-G4
```

Rename the assemblies to designate their bay locations.

16.

Properties

🔲 Structural Framing Assembly
E3-G4

If you select an assembly, the name will be displayed in the Properties pane.

17. Close without saving.

Command Exercise

Exercise 2-3 – Create a Beam System

Drawing Name: **beam system.rvt**
Estimated Time to Completion: 5 Minutes

Scope

Create a Beam System

Solution

1. 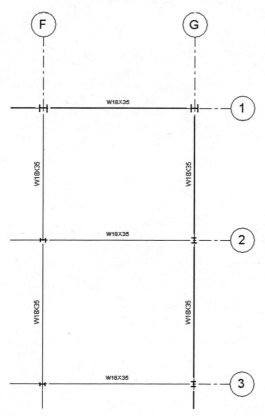 Activate the **FIRST FLR. plan** under Structural plans.

Structural Plans
  BASEMENT
  FIRST FLR.
  ROOF
  SECOND FLR.

2. Zoom into the bay located between F2 and G3.

3. Select the **Beam System** tool on the Structure ribbon.

    Beam
    System

4. Enable the Automatic Beam System mode.

    Automatic | Sketch | Tag on
    Beam System | Beam System | Placement
    Beam System | Tag

5. On the Options bar:

Beam Type: W12x26 ▼ | Justification: Center ▼ | Layout Rule: Fixed Distance ▼ | 6' 9" | ☐3D | ☑Walls Define Slope | Tag Style: System ▼

Set the Beam Type to **W12x26. [W310x38.7]**.
Set Justification to **Center**.
Set the Layout Rule to **Fixed Distance**.
Set the Distance to **6′ 9″[1828.8mm]**.

6. Select the beam located between F2 and
    F3 to place the beam system.

    You should see a preview of the system
    prior to placement.

    Structural Framing : W-Wide Flange : W18X35

The tool tip indicates the beam which is selected NOT the beam which is being placed.

7. Right click and select **Cancel** to exit the command.

8. 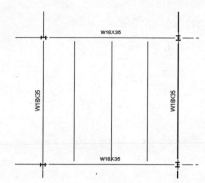 Note that tags were not placed.

9.   Select **Tag All** from the Annotate ribbon.

Tag
All

10.

Category	Loaded Tags
Structural Column Tags	Structural Column Tag
Structural Foundation Tags	Structural Foundation Tag
Structural Framing Tags	Structural Framing Tag
Structural Framing Tags	Structural Framing Tag : Boxed
Structural Framing Tags	Structural Framing Tag : Standard

Highlight the **Structural Framing Tag:Boxed**.

Press **OK**.

11. 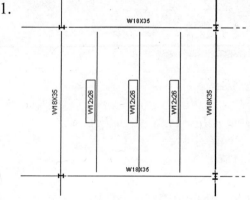 The tags are placed.

12. 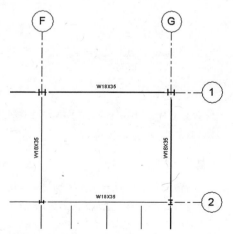 Zoom into the bay between **F1** and **G2**.

13. Select the **Beam System** tool on the Structure ribbon.

14. Enable the **Tag on Placement** tool.

15.
If you need to load the tags:
Select **Yes**.

16.
Browse to the *Structural* folder under *Annotations*.

17.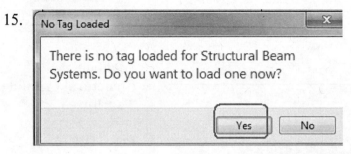
Locate the *Structural Beam System Tag*.
[M_Structural Beam System Tag]
Press **Open**.

18. Select the **Sketch Beam System** tool.

19.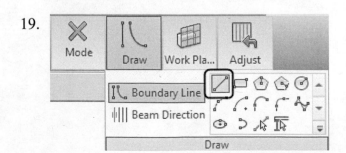
You are automatically placed in Line/ Boundary Line mode.

In order to see this part of the ribbon, I had to collapse and expand the ribbon.

20. Enable **Chain** on the Options bar.

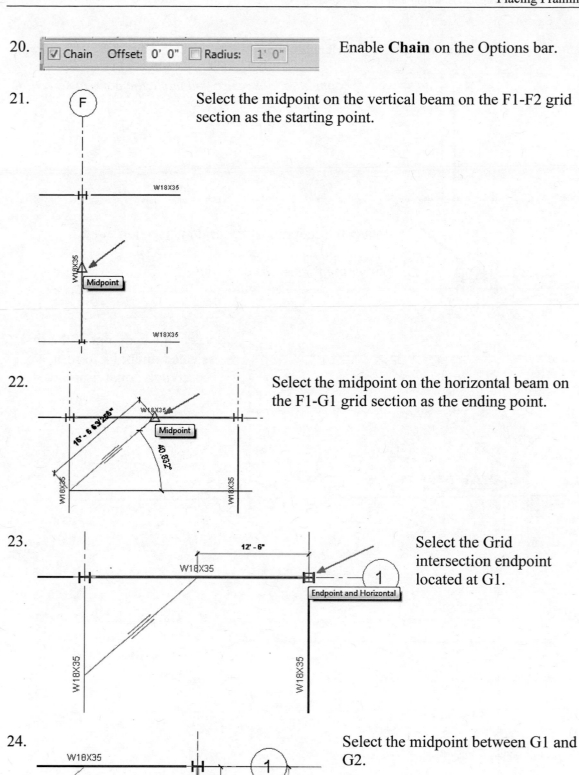

21. Select the midpoint on the vertical beam on the F1-F2 grid section as the starting point.

22. Select the midpoint on the horizontal beam on the F1-G1 grid section as the ending point.

23. Select the Grid intersection endpoint located at G1.

24. Select the midpoint between G1 and G2.

25.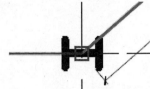

Select the midpoint between F2 and G2.

Zoom in to make sure you make the correct selection.

26.

Select the endpoint at the grid intersection at F2

Zoom in to select the endpoint.

27.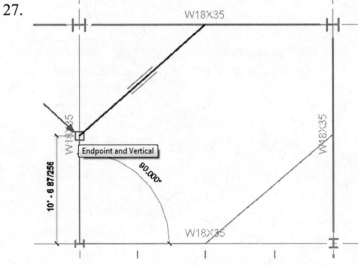

Select the endpoint of the first selected midpoint to form a closed polygonal figure.

28.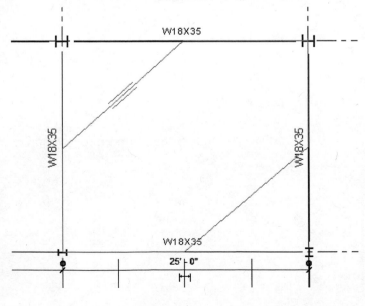

The parallel lines on the first beam line indicate the orientation of the beam system.

29.  Select the Green Check to finish the beam system.

30. Left click in the window to deselect the beam system.

31. Select the **Beam System** tool on the Structure ribbon.

Beam System

32. On the Options bar:

Set the Beam Type to **W12x26. [W310x38.7]**
Set the Layout Rule to **Fixed Number**.
Set the Number to **3**.
Set the Tag Style to **Framing**.

33. 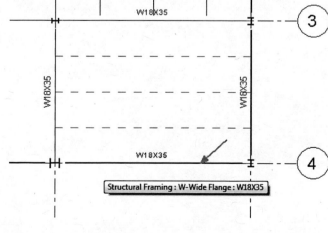 Select the horizontal beam located between F4 and G4 to place the beam system.

You should see a preview of the system prior to placement.

The tool tip indicates the beam which is selected NOT the beam which is being placed.

34. The beam system is placed with tags.

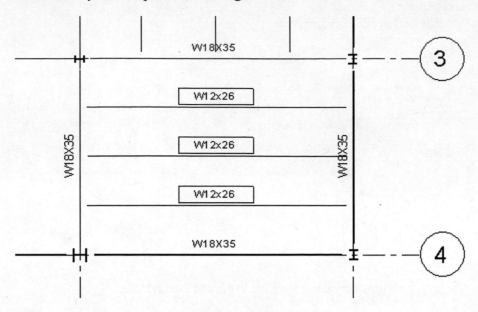

35. Right click and select **Cancel** to exit the command.

36. Close without saving.

Command Exercise

Exercise 2-4 – Create a Moment Frame

Drawing Name: **moment_frame.rvt**
Estimated Time to Completion: 15 Minutes

Scope

Define a moment connection

Beam element properties include moment connection start and end parameters. These parameters can be set to None (the default), Moment Connection, or Cantilever Moment. Moment connections are denoted in the plan view by solid triangle symbols. Cantilever connections are denoted in the plan view by open triangle symbols.

Solution

1.   Views (all)
       Structural Plans
         BASEMENT
         FIRST FLR.
         ROOF
         SECOND FLR.
     Activate the **SECOND FLR. Structural plan** in the Project Browser.

2. 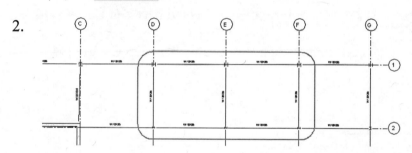 Zoom into the area between grid intersections D1 and F2.

3. Select the beam located between D1 and E1.

4. Hold down the CTRL key and select the beam located between E1 and F1.

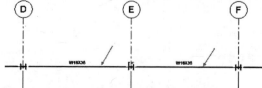

Two beams should be highlighted.

5.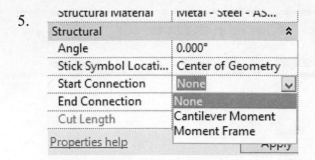

In the Properties pane:
Under the Structural section:
Set the Start Connection to **Moment Frame**.

6.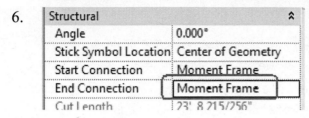

In the Properties pane:
Under the Structural section:
Set the End Connection to **Moment Frame**.

7.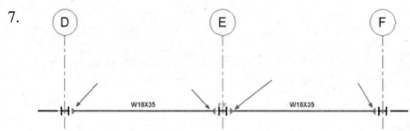

Observe that solid triangles are now displayed to indicate a moment frame.

8.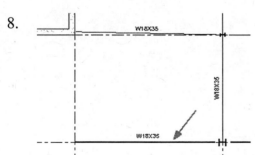

Zoom into the bay located between C3 and D4.

Select the beam located between C4 and D4.

9. In the Properties pane:

Under the Structural section:
Set the Start Connection to **Moment Frame**.
Set the End Connection to **Cantilever Moment**.

10.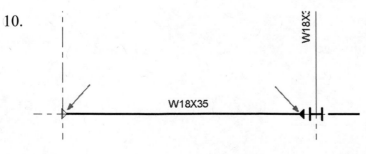

Observe that triangles are now displayed.

11. 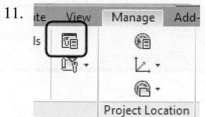 Activate the **Manage** ribbon.

Select the **Structural Settings** tool.

12. 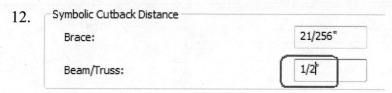 Change the Symbolic Cutback Distance for Beam/Truss to **1/2″**. Press **OK**.

13. 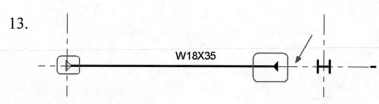 Note that the beam setback adjusts for ends set to None or Moment Frame, but not for Cantilever Moment.

14. Close without saving.

Command Exercise
Exercise 2-5 – Adding Braces

Drawing Name: **braces.rvt**
Estimated Time to Completion: 45 Minutes

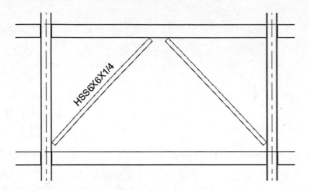

Scope

Create a Framing Elevation
Add braces

Solution

1.  Activate the **FIRST FLR. plan** under Structural plans.

2. 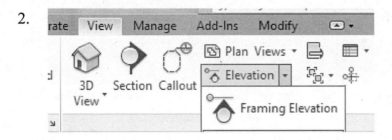 Activate the **View** ribbon.

   Select **Elevation→Framing Elevation**.

3.  On the Options bar: Enable **Attach to Grid**.

4. On the Properties pane: Use the Type Selector to set the view type to **Building Elevation**.

5. 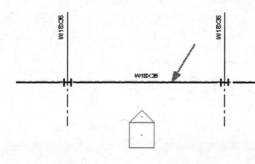 Move the cursor to the middle of the beam located between E4 and F4.

Orient the marker so it is below the beam.

Left click to place.

Right click to CANCEL out of the command or press ESC.

6. Double left click on the triangle on the elevation marker to open the elevation view.

7. 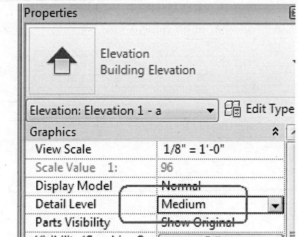 In the Properties pane:

Set the Detail Level for the view to **Medium**.

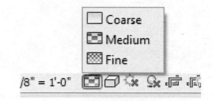

This can also be controlled using the View Display bar.

If the Detail Level is set to Coarse, structural members are displayed as stick symbols.

8. 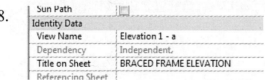 In the Properties pane:

Type **BRACED FRAME ELEVATION** for the Title on Sheet.

9. 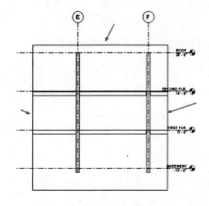 Adjust the crop region so that the columns are displayed.

10. On the View Control bar:

Toggle **Hide Crop Region** so that region rectangle is not displayed.

11. 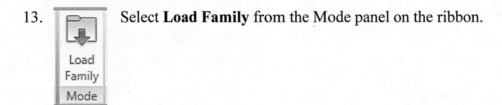 Activate the **Structure** ribbon.

Brace Select the **Brace** tool on the Structure panel.

12. Toggle the Tag on Placement so it is shaded/ON.

13. Select **Load Family** from the Mode panel on the ribbon.

14.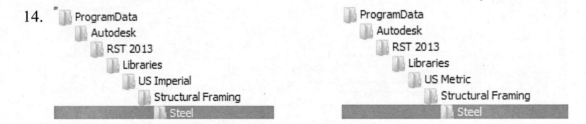

Browse to the *Structural/Framing/Steel* folder.

If you are using metric, use the same folder path, except under the Metric library.

15. 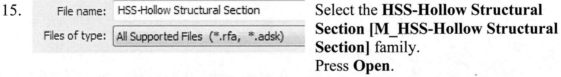 Select the **HSS-Hollow Structural Section [M_HSS-Hollow Structural Section]** family.
Press **Open**.

16. 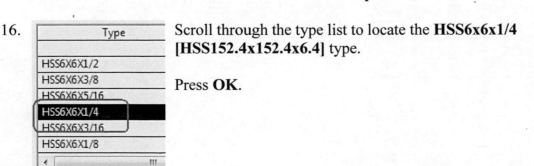 Scroll through the type list to locate the **HSS6x6x1/4 [HSS152.4x152.4x6.4]** type.

Press **OK**.

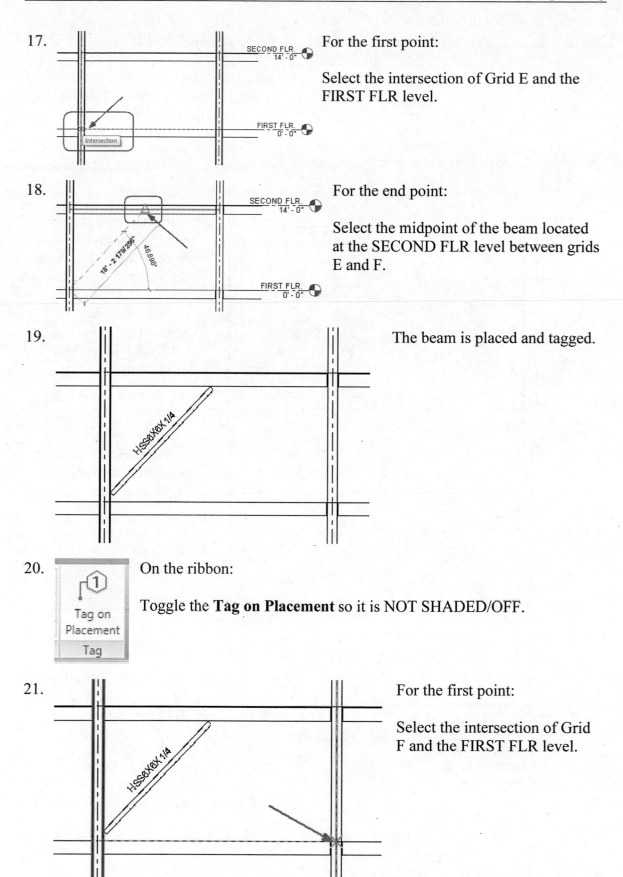

17. For the first point:

Select the intersection of Grid E and the FIRST FLR level.

18. For the end point:

Select the midpoint of the beam located at the SECOND FLR level between grids E and F.

19. The beam is placed and tagged.

20. On the ribbon:

Toggle the **Tag on Placement** so it is NOT SHADED/OFF.

21. For the first point:

Select the intersection of Grid F and the FIRST FLR level.

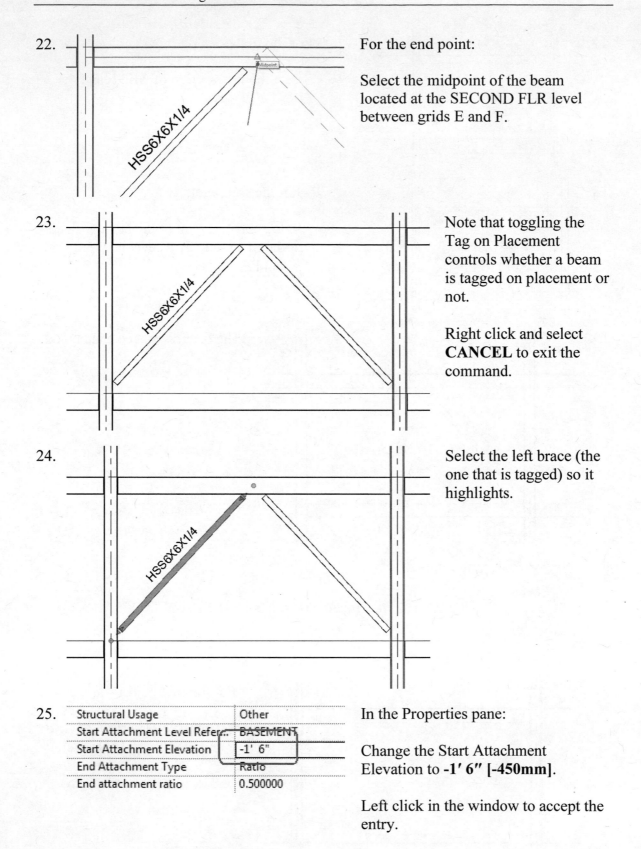

22. For the end point:

    Select the midpoint of the beam located at the SECOND FLR level between grids E and F.

23. Note that toggling the Tag on Placement controls whether a beam is tagged on placement or not.

    Right click and select **CANCEL** to exit the command.

24. Select the left brace (the one that is tagged) so it highlights.

25.

Structural Usage	Other
Start Attachment Level Refer...	BASEMENT
Start Attachment Elevation	-1' 6"
End Attachment Type	Ratio
End attachment ratio	0.500000

In the Properties pane:

Change the Start Attachment Elevation to **-1' 6" [-450mm]**.

Left click in the window to accept the entry.

26.

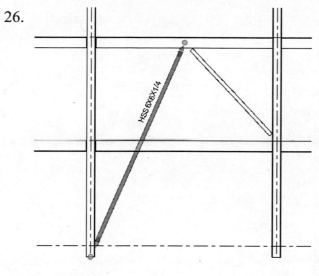

The brace will adjust the position.

27.

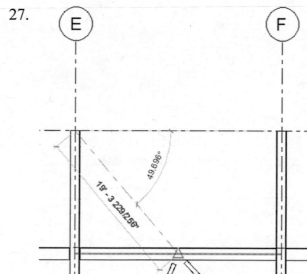

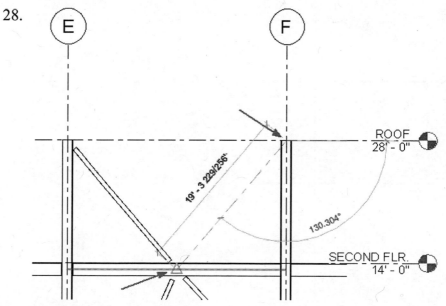

Brace Select the Brace tool from the Structure ribbon.

Place a brace from the intersection of Grid E and the Roof level to the midpoint of the beam located on the SECOND FLR.

28.

Place a brace from the intersection of Grid F and the Roof level to the midpoint of the beam located on the SECOND FLR.

29.

Right click and select **CANCEL** to exit the Beam command.

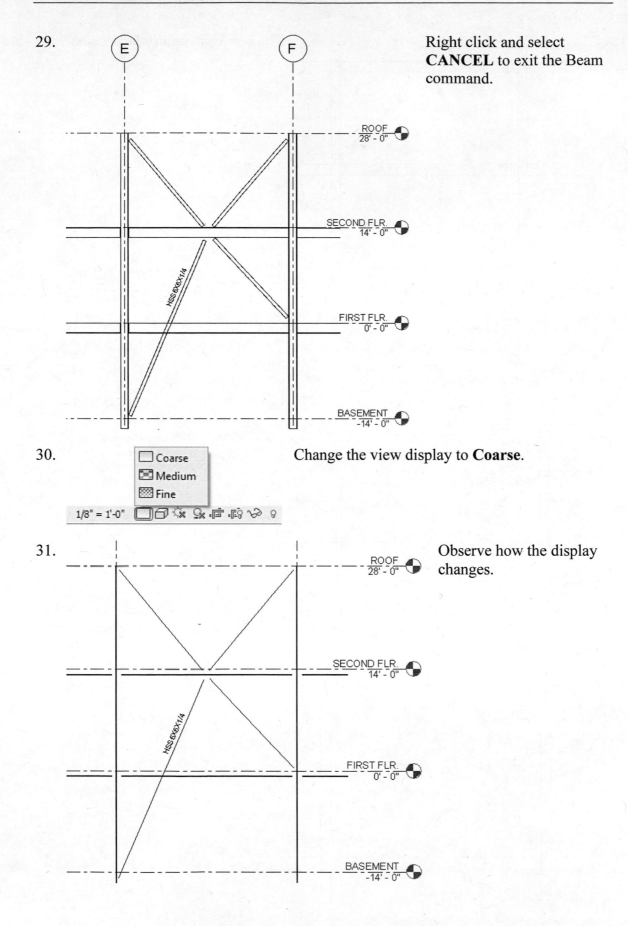

30.

Change the view display to **Coarse**.

31.

Observe how the display changes.

32.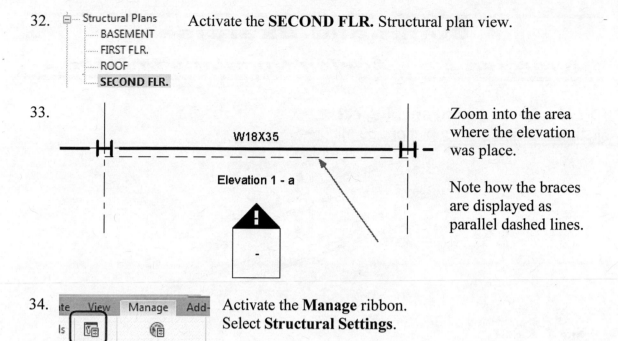

Structural Plans
— BASEMENT
— FIRST FLR.
— ROOF
— **SECOND FLR.**

Activate the **SECOND FLR.** Structural plan view.

33.

W18X35

Elevation 1 - a

Zoom into the area where the elevation was place.

Note how the braces are displayed as parallel dashed lines.

34.

te   View   Manage   Add-

ls

Project Location

Activate the **Manage** ribbon.
Select **Structural Settings**.

35.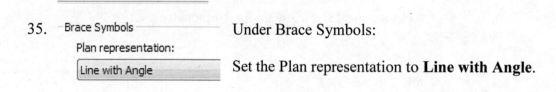

Brace Symbols

Plan representation:

Line with Angle

Under Brace Symbols:

Set the Plan representation to **Line with Angle**.

Press **OK**.

36.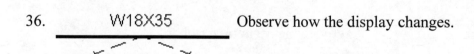

W18X35

Observe how the display changes.

37.   Switch to a 3D view.

38. Close without saving.

Command Exercise

Exercise 2-6 – Adding Openings in Beams

Drawing Name: **beam_opening.rvt**
Estimated Time to Completion: 30 Minutes

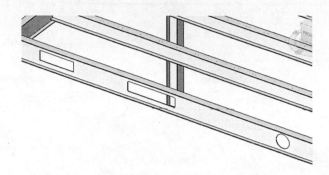

Scope

Add an opening to a beam

Solution

1.   3D Views
           Canopy Systems
           {3D}
                              Activate the **{3D} view** in the Project Browser.

2.   FRONT   Switch to a **FRONT** view.

3.   By Face Shaft Wall Vertical Dormer   Activate the **Structure** ribbon.

   Opening   Select the **By Face** tool on the Opening panel.

4.   Select the face of the beam indicated.

5.   Draw   Select the Rectangle tool from the Draw ribbon.

6. On the Options bar:

Enable **Radius**. Set the Radius value to **2″**.

7.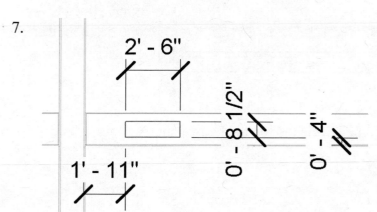

Place a rectangle as shown.

The rectangle should be located 1′ 11″ to the left of the column.

The rectangle should be 4″ above the bottom of the beam.

The rectangle should be 2′ 6″ long by 8 ½″ high.

8.  Press the **Green Check** to finish defining the opening.

9. Switch back to the default 3D view to inspect the hole.

10.  Inspect the opening that was made.

11. Switch to a **FRONT** view.

12.  Activate the **Structure** ribbon.

Select the **By Face** tool on the Opening panel.

13. 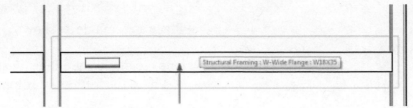 Select the face of the beam indicated.

14. 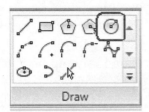 Select the **Circle** tool on the Draw panel.

15. Place a circle that is **6″** in radius **15′ 6″** to the right of the rectangle and **4″** from the center of the circle to the bottom of the rectangle.

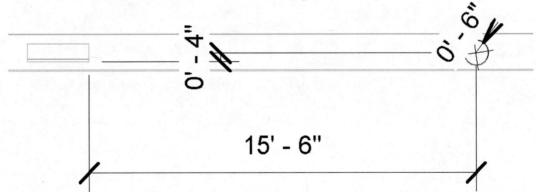

16.  Press the **Green Check** to finish defining the opening.

17. ⇐ Switch back to the default 3D view to inspect the hole.

18. 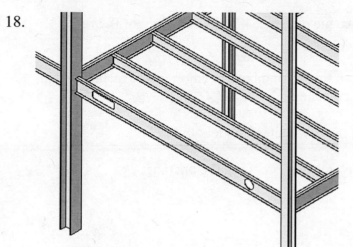 Inspect the new opening.

19. 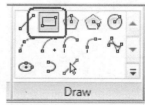 Switch to a **FRONT** view.

20.  Activate the **Structure** ribbon.

    Select the **By Face** tool on the Opening panel.

21. Select the face of the beam indicated.

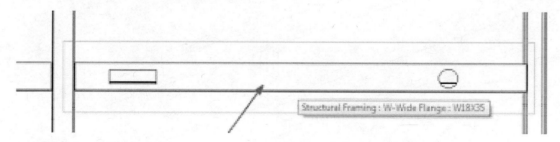

22. Select the Rectangle tool from the Draw ribbon.

23. On the Options bar:

    Enable **Radius**. Set the Radius value to **1″**.

24.  Place the rectangle **4′ 0″** to the right of the first rectangle.

Align the top and bottom edges of the rectangle with the first rectangle.

Set the new rectangle's length to **3′ 6″**.

25.  Press the **Green Check** to finish defining the opening.

26. 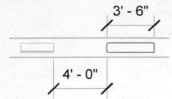 Switch back to the default 3D view to inspect the hole.

27. Inspect the openings.

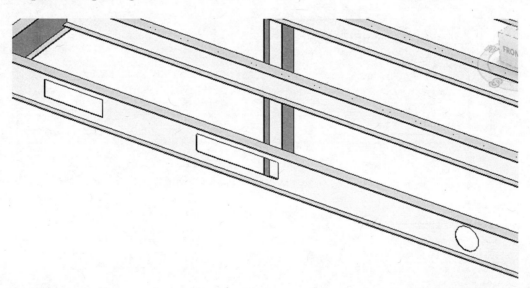

Close without saving.

Command Exercise

Exercise 2-7 – Sloped Beams

Drawing Name: **sloped_beam.rvt**
Estimated Time to Completion: 5 Minutes

Scope

Add a sloped beam

Solution

1.  Activate the **Elevation 3** in the Project Browser.

2.  Activate the **Structure** ribbon.
    Select the **Beam** tool.

3. Enable **Name**.
    From the drop-down list, select **Grid .5**.

    Press OK.

4. Select **W18x35 [W460x52]** from the Type Selector on the Properties pane.

    W-Wide Flange W18X35

5. On the Options bar:

    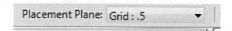

    Note that the Placement Plane has been set to your selection: **Grid .5**.

    You can modify it using the drop-down list if you don't see Grid .5.

6.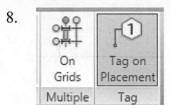

You can assign a structural usage to the beam from the drop-down list next to Structural Usage.

If you select Automatic, Revit will assign usage based on the placement of the beam.

Set the Usage to **Automatic**.

7.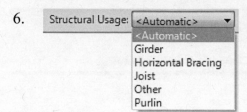

Disable **3D Snapping** and **Chain**.

8.

On the ribbon:
Toggle the **Tag on Placement** on so the button is shaded.

9.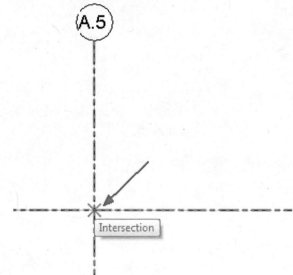

Locate the intersection of Grid A.5 and the FIRST FLR.

DO NOT SELECT.

10.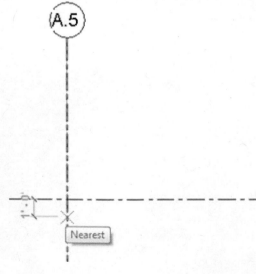

Drag the mouse down 1′ 0″. Watch the *listening dimension* and click to place.

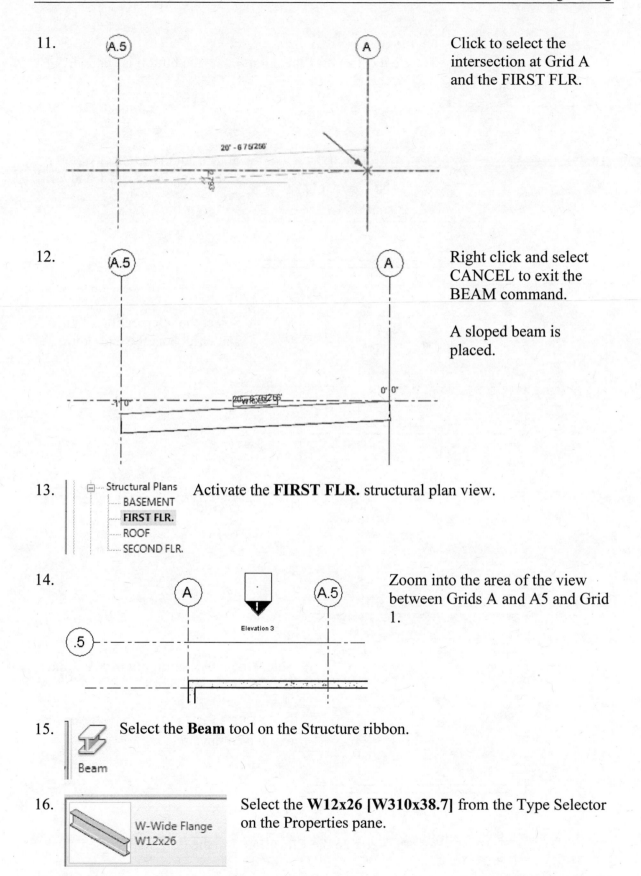

11. Click to select the intersection at Grid A and the FIRST FLR.

12. Right click and select CANCEL to exit the BEAM command.

    A sloped beam is placed.

13. Activate the **FIRST FLR.** structural plan view.

14. Zoom into the area of the view between Grids A and A5 and Grid 1.

15. Select the **Beam** tool on the Structure ribbon.

16. Select the **W12x26 [W310x38.7]** from the Type Selector on the Properties pane.

17. 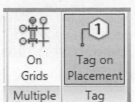 On the ribbon:
Toggle the **Tag on Placement** on so the button is shaded.

18. 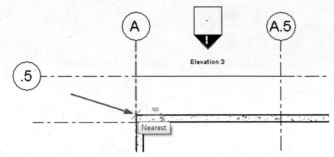 Start from the exterior of the wall located on Grid 1 and Grid A.

19. 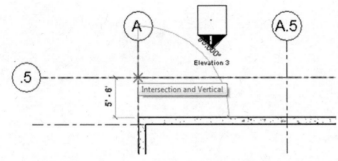 Select the intersection of Grid A and Grid .5 as the end point.

20. 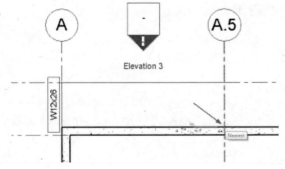 Start from the exterior of the wall located on Grid 1 and Grid A.5.

21. 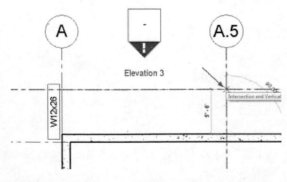 Select the intersection of Grid A.5 and Grid .5 as the end point.

Press ESC or right click Cancel twice to exit the command.

22. Elevations (Building Elevation)
    Elevation 1
    Elevation 2
    Elevation 3

Activate the **Elevation 3** in the Project Browser.

23. 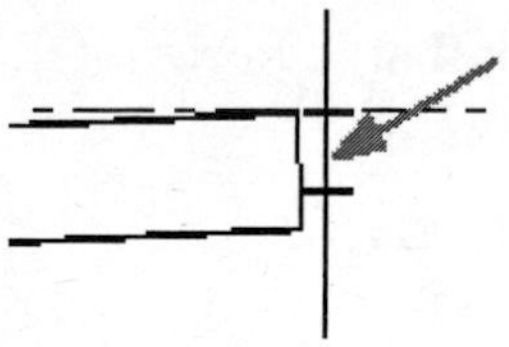

Zoom in to see the beams just placed.

Note that they are oriented horizontally.

24. 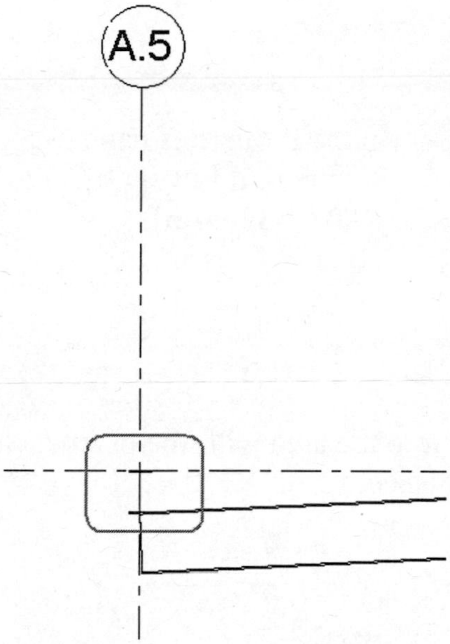
A.5

Select the horizontal beam placed at A.5.

25. 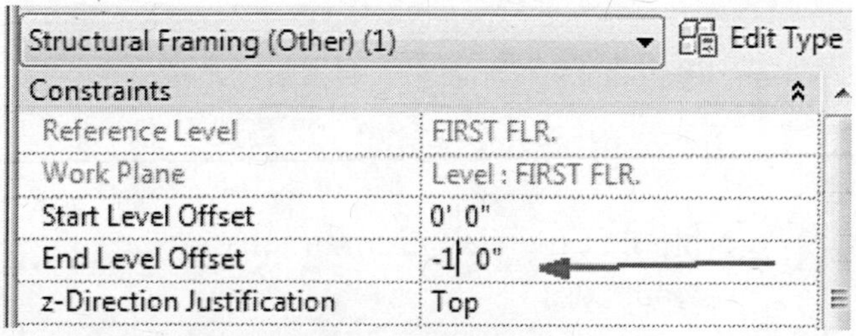
Structural Framing (Other) (1)
Edit Type
Constraints
Reference Level
FIRST FLR.
Work Plane
Level : FIRST FLR.
Start Level Offset
0' 0"
End Level Offset
-1' 0"
z-Direction Justification
Top

In the Properties pane:
Set the End Level Offset to **-1′ 0″ [-300mm]**.

26. 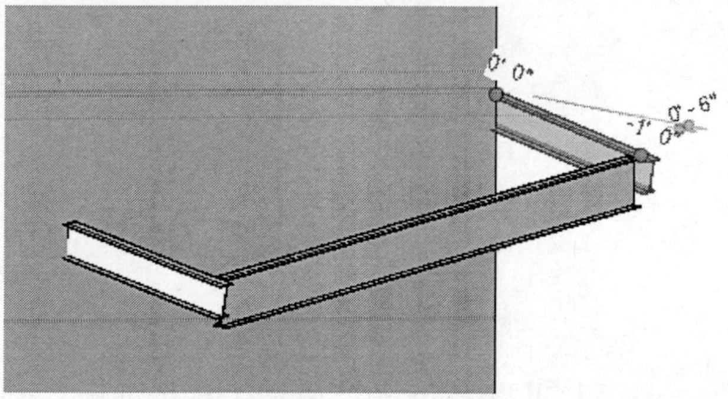

Repeat for the horizontal beam placed at A.
In the Properties pane:
Set the End Level Offset to **-1′ 0″ [-300mm]**.

27. 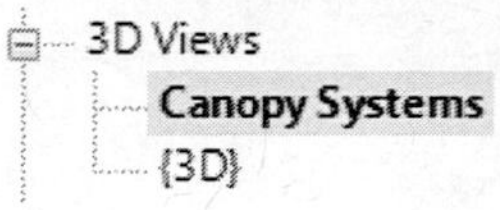
3D Views
Canopy Systems
{3D}

Activate the **Canopy Systems** view under 3D Views.

28.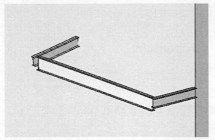

Select the beam on the right that is horizontal.

29.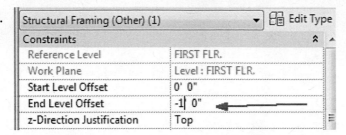

In the Properties pane:
Set the End Level Offset to **-1′ 0″ [-300mm]**.

30.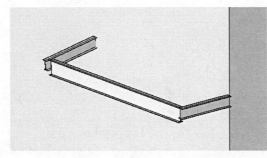

Zoom into the area with the beams which were placed.

31.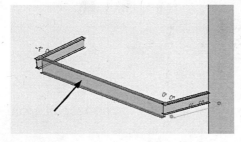

Select the cross beam.

Note that the elevation dimensions are displayed.

32.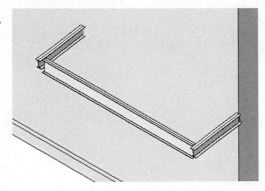

In the Properties pane:
Set the End Level Offset to **-1′ 0″ [-300mm]**.

33.

Orbit around the view to inspect the sloped beams.

Close without saving.

Command Exercise
Exercise 2-8 – Curved Beams

Drawing Name: **curved_beams.rvt**
Estimated Time to Completion: 45 Minutes

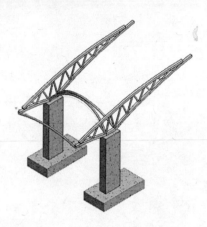

Scope

Add a curved beam

Solution

1. 3D Views
    3D Analytical
    {3D}

    Activate the **3D view** in the Project Browser.

2.

    Set   Show   Ref
                 Plane

    Work Plane

    Activate the **Structure** ribbon.

    Select the **Set** tool on the Work Plane panel.

3.

    Specify a new Work Plane

    ⦿ Name   Reference Plane : Right Curved Beam ▾

    ⚬ Pick a plane

    ⚬ Pick a line and use the work plane it was sketched in

    Select the **Right Curved Beam** plane from the Name drop-down list.
    Press **OK**.

4.

    Beam

    Select the **Beam** tool from the Structure ribbon.

5.

    HSS-Round Structural Tubing
    HSS5X0.250

    Verify that the **HSS5x0.250 [HSS127x6.4]** round tubing is selected on the Properties pane.

6. 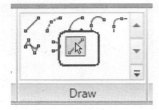 Verify that the z-direction Justification is set to **Center**.
Verify that the Lateral Justification is set to **Center**.

7. 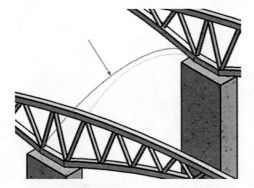 Select the **Pick Line** tool from the Draw panel.

8. Select the orange model arc-line.

9. Note the beam has been placed.

10.  Activate the **Structure** ribbon.

Select the **Set** tool on the Work Plane panel.

11. 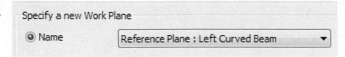 Select the **Left Curved Beam** plane from the Name drop-down list.
Press **OK**.

12. Select the **Beam** tool from the Structure ribbon.

13. 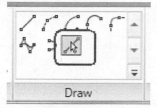 Verify that the **HSS5x0.250 [HSS127x6.4]** round tubing is selected on the Properties pane.

14.

Constraints	
Reference Level	
z-Direction Justification	Center
z-Direction Offset Value	0' 0"
Lateral Justification	Center

Verify that the z-direction Justification is set to **Center**.
Verify that the Lateral Justification is set to **Center**.

15. Select the **Pick Line** tool from the Draw panel.

16. 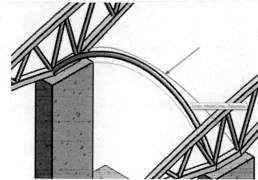 Select the orange model arc -line.

Cancel the BEAM command.

17.  Inspect the beams that were placed.

18. Structural Plans — Level 1, Level 2, Level 3   Activate **Level 3** Structural Plan.

19. 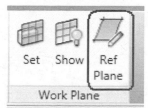 Activate the Structure ribbon.

Select the **Ref Plane** tool on the Work Plane panel.

20. 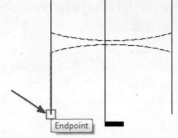   Select the end point of the left beam as the start point.

21. 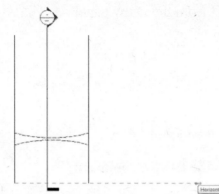   Place a horizontal plane.

22.

Reference Planes (1)	
Identity Data	
Name	Front Curved Beam
Extents	
Scope Box	None

Select the plane that was just placed.

Type **Front Curved Beam** as the Name in the Properties pane.

Press **Apply**.

23.   **3D**

When the plane is selected, the name should display.

Front Curved Beam

Left click anywhere in the display window to de-select.

24. Elevations (Building Elevation)   Activate the **South** Elevation.
     East
     North
     South
     West

25.   Activate the Structure ribbon.

   Model   Select the **Model Line** tool from the Model panel.
   Line

26.    Select the **Start-End-Radius** arc tool from the Draw menu.

Draw

27.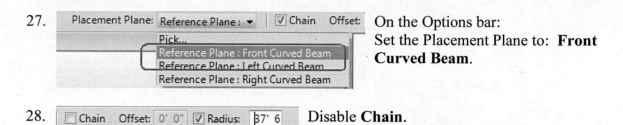

On the Options bar:
Set the Placement Plane to: **Front Curved Beam**.

28.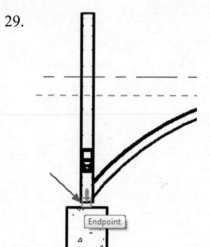

Disable **Chain**.
Enable **Radius**.
Set the Radius to **37' 6"**.

29.

Select the midpoint at the bottom of the left beam as the start point.

30.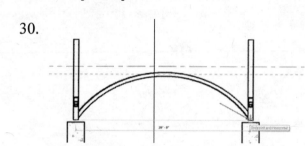

Select the midpoint at the bottom of the right beam as the end point.

31.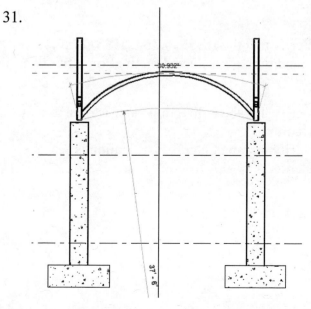

The arc will be previewed.
Pull the arc in the up direction.

Left click to place.

Press ESC or right click CANCEL to end the arc command.

32. 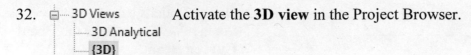 Activate the **3D view** in the Project Browser.

33. 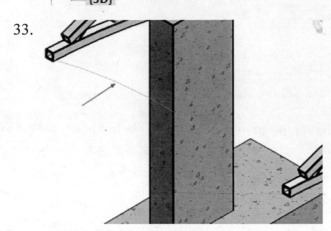 Adjust the position of the model line using the MOVE tool if necessary.

34. 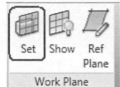 Activate the **Structure** ribbon.

Select the **Set** tool on the Work Plane panel.

35.

Specify a new Work Plane	
⦿ Name	Reference Plane : Front Curved Beam ▼
○ Pick a plane	
○ Pick a line and use the work plane it was sketched in	

Select the **Front Curved Beam** plane from the Name drop-down list.
Press **OK**.

36.   Select the **Beam** tool from the Structure ribbon.

Beam

37. 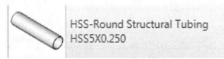 Verify that the **HSS5x0.250 [HSS127x6.4]** round tubing is selected on the Properties pane.

HSS-Round Structural Tubing
HSS5X0.250

38.

Constraints	
Reference Level	
z-Direction Justification	Center
z-Direction Offset Value	0' 0"
Lateral Justification	Center

Verify that the z-direction Justification is set to **Center**.
Verify that the Lateral Justification is set to **Center**.

39. 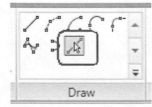 Select the **Pick Line** tool from the Draw panel.

Draw

40.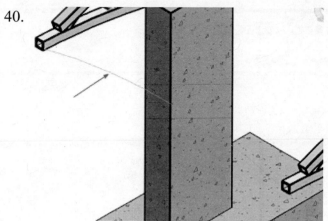
Select the orange model arc-line.

41.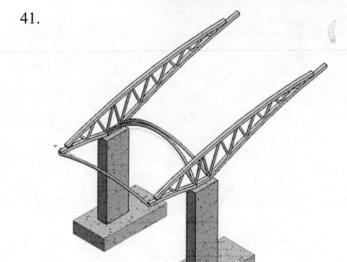
Inspect the placed curved beams.

42.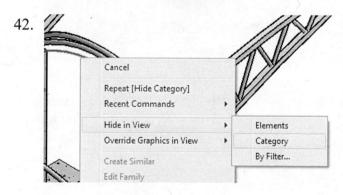
To turn off the visibility of the model lines:
Select a model line.
Right click and select **Hide in View→Category**.

43. Close without saving.

Command Exercise
Exercise 2-9 – Truss

Drawing Name: **truss.rvt**
Estimated Time to Completion: 20 Minutes

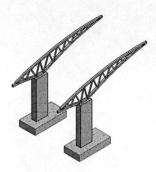

Scope

Add a truss

Solution

1. Elevations (Building Elevation)   Activate the **West Elevation** in the Project Browser.
     East
     North
     South
     West

2.    Activate the **Structure** ribbon.

    Set Show Ref
               Plane

    Work Plane   Select the **Set** tool on the Work Plane panel.

3. Specify a new Work Plane   Select the **Left Truss** plane
    ⦿ Name   Reference Plane : Left Truss   ▾   from the Name drop-down list.
    ○ Pick a plane   Press **OK**.
    ○ Pick a line and use the work plane it was sketched in

4. 〥〥〥   Select the **Truss** tool on the Structure ribbon.

    Truss

5.   Select the **Short Truss 1** from the Type Selector on the
        Short Truss 1   Properties pane.
        Truss Type 1

6.

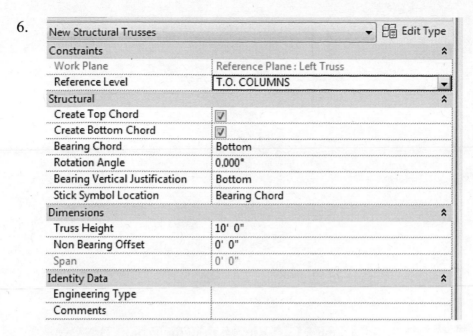

Set the Reference Level to **T.O. COLUMNS**.

Set the Bearing Chord to **Bottom**.
Set the Bearing Vertical Justification to **Bottom**.
Set Truss Height to **10′ 0″**.

7.

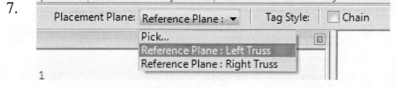

On the Options bar:
Verify that the placement
plane is set to **Left Truss**.

8.

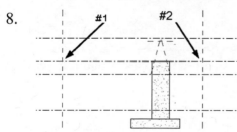

Select the intersection of the left/rear reference
plane and the **T.O. COLUMNS** level as the
starting point.

9.

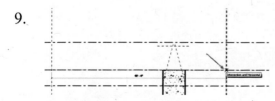

Select the intersection of the right/front curved
beam reference plane and the **T.O. COLUMNS**
level as the end point.

10.

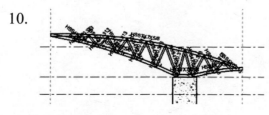

The truss is placed.

Right click and select **Cancel** to exit the Truss
command.

11. 3D Views
    3D Analytical
    {3D}

Activate the **3D view** in the Project Browser.

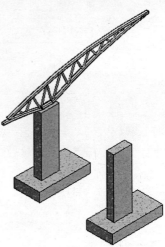

12. Elevations (Building Elevation)
    East
    North
    South
    West

Activate the **East Elevation** in the Project Browser.

13. Select the **Truss** tool on the Structure ribbon.

Truss

14. Short Truss 1
Truss Type 1

Select the **Short Truss 1** from the Type Selector on the Properties pane.

15.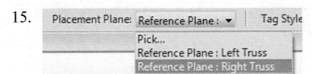
Placement Plane: Reference Plane : ▼   Tag Style
Pick...
Reference Plane : Left Truss
Reference Plane : Right Truss

On the Options bar:
Verify that the placement plane is set to **Right Truss**.

16.

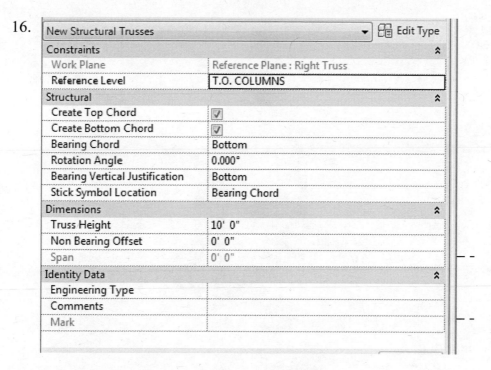

New Structural Trusses	▼ 🔡 Edit Type
Constraints	⚷
Work Plane	Reference Plane : Right Truss
Reference Level	T.O. COLUMNS
Structural	⚷
Create Top Chord	☑
Create Bottom Chord	☑
Bearing Chord	Bottom
Rotation Angle	0.000°
Bearing Vertical Justification	Bottom
Stick Symbol Location	Bearing Chord
Dimensions	⚷
Truss Height	10' 0"
Non Bearing Offset	0' 0"
Span	0' 0"
Identity Data	⚷
Engineering Type	
Comments	
Mark	

Set the Reference Level to **T.O. COLUMNS**.

Set the Bearing Chord to **Bottom**.
Set the Bearing Vertical Justification to **Bottom**.
Set Truss Height to **10′ 0″**.

17.

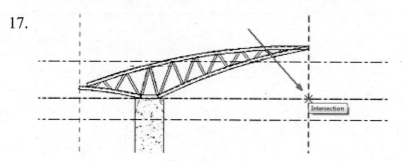

Select the intersection of the right reference plane and the **T.O. COLUMNS** level as the starting point.

18. Select the intersection of the left reference plane and the **T.O. COLUMNS** level as the end point.

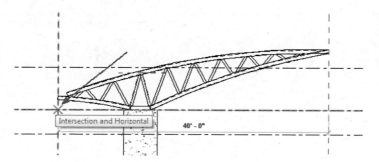

The truss is placed.

Right click and select **Cancel** to exit the Truss command.

19.    3D Views
         3D Analytical
         {3D}

Activate the **3D view** in the Project Browser.

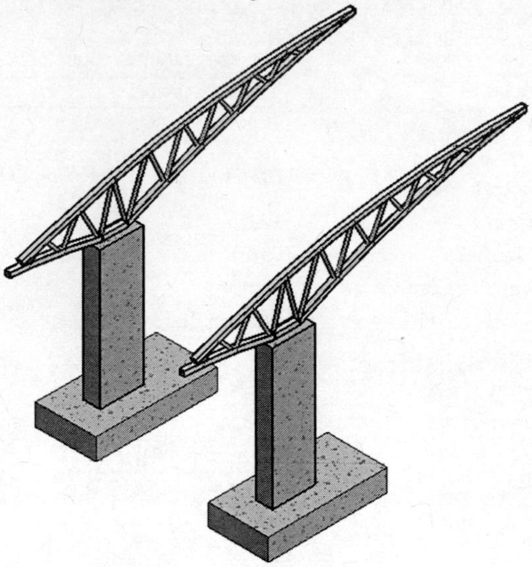

20.   Close without saving.

Lesson Three
Boosting Productivity – Setting up Your Project

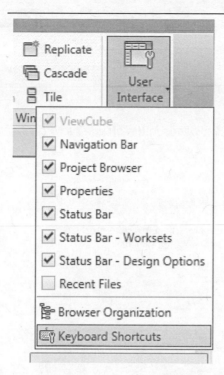

> ➢ You can define or modify Keyboard Shortcuts from the User Interface drop-down located on the View ribbon.

Command Exercise

Exercise 3-1 – Browser Organization

Drawing Name: **new file**
Estimated Time to Completion: 5 Minutes

Scope

Creating types and disciplines in the browser to organize views

Solution

1.

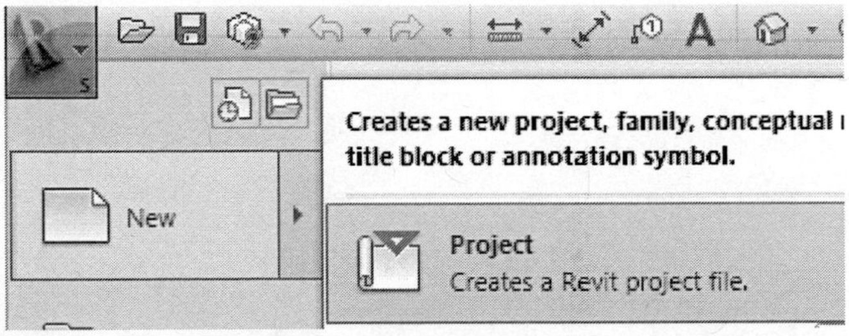

Start a new Project.

2.

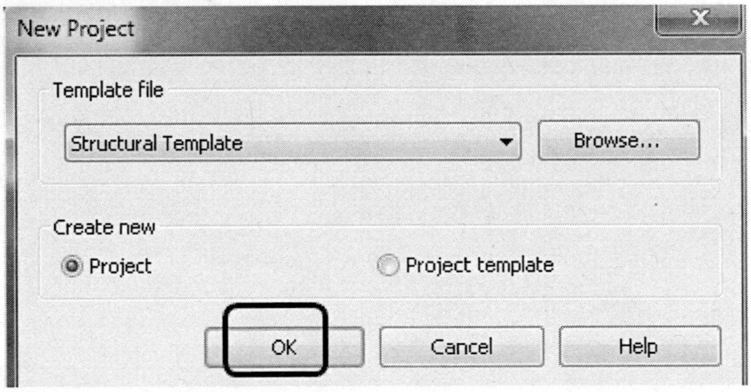

Press **OK**.

3.

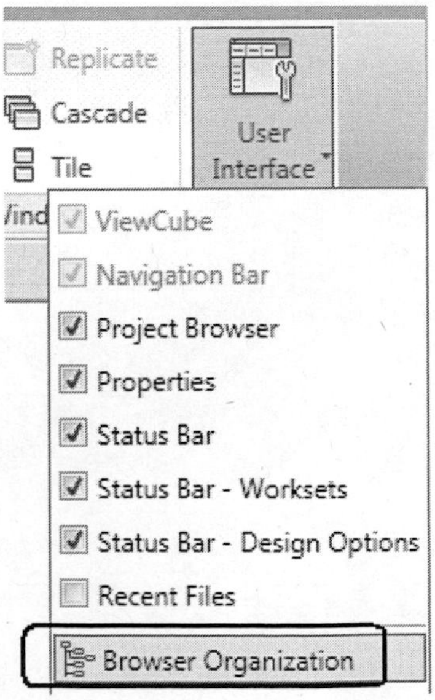

Activate the **View** ribbon.

Go to **User Interface→Browser Organization**.

4. 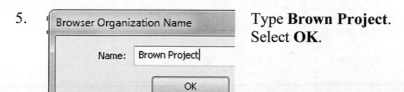 Select the **Views** tab.
Select **New**.

5.  Type **Brown Project**.
Select **OK**.

6. 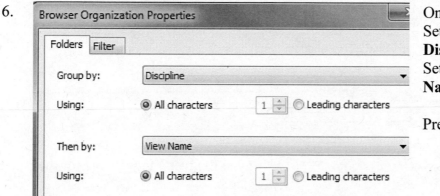 On the **Folders** tab:
Set the Group by: to **Discipline**.
Set the Sort by: to **View Name**.

Press **OK**.

7. 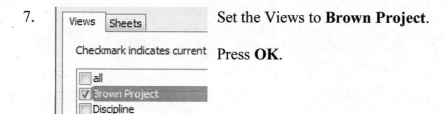 Set the Views to **Brown Project**.

Press **OK**.

8. 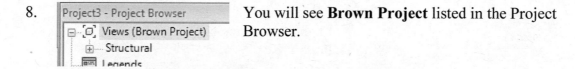 You will see **Brown Project** listed in the Project Browser.

9. 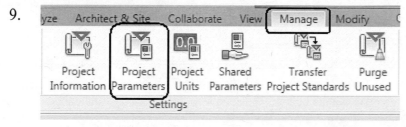 Activate the **Manage** ribbon.
Select **Project Parameters** on the Settings panel.

10. 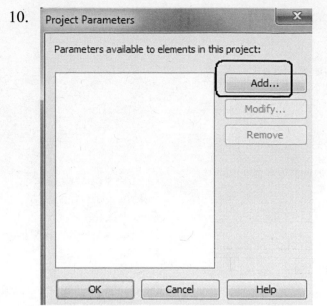   Select **Add**.

11. 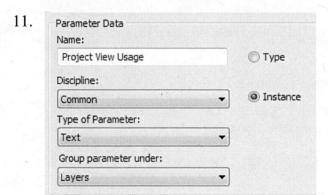   Type **Project View Usage** for the Name.
Set Discipline to **Common**.
Set Type of Parameter to **Text**.
Set Group parameter under: **Layers**.
Enable **Instance**.

12. 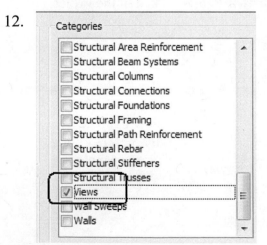   Enable **Views** under Categories.
Press **OK**.

13.

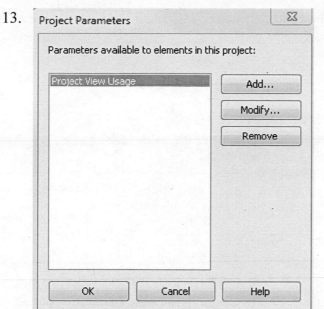

You should see the parameter listed.

Press **OK**.

14.

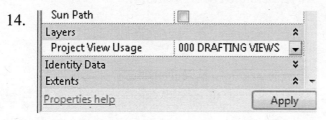

In the Properties panel:
Scroll down until you see the Layers category.

The new parameter has been added.
Type **000 DRAFTING VIEWS**.

Press **Apply**.

15.

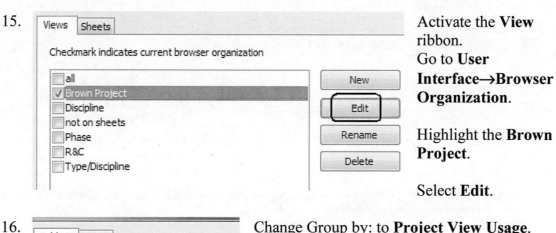

Activate the **View** ribbon.
Go to **User Interface→Browser Organization**.

Highlight the **Brown Project**.

Select **Edit**.

16.

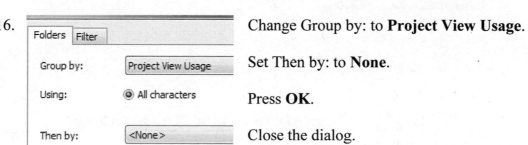

Change Group by: to **Project View Usage**.

Set Then by: to **None**.

Press **OK**.

Close the dialog.

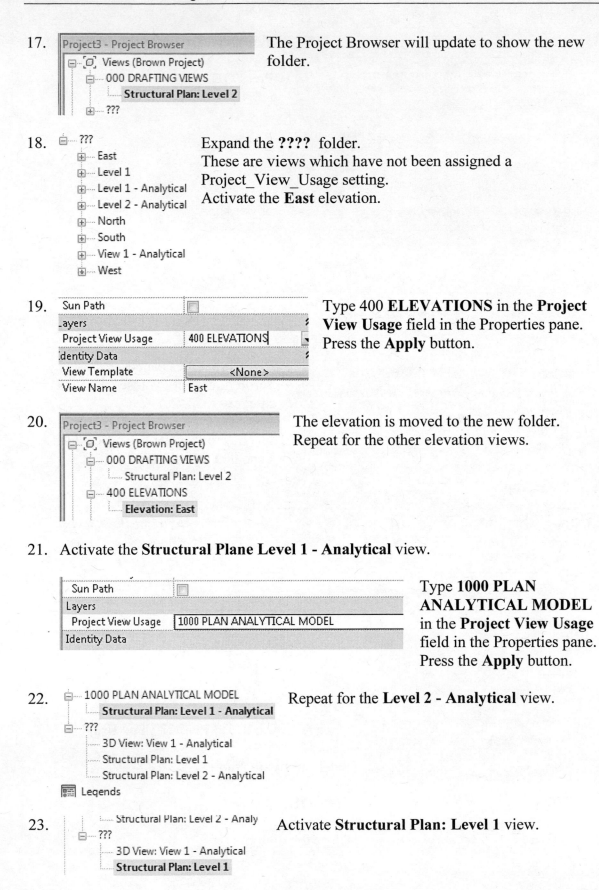

17. The Project Browser will update to show the new folder.

18. Expand the **????** folder.
These are views which have not been assigned a Project_View_Usage setting.
Activate the **East** elevation.

19. Type 400 **ELEVATIONS** in the **Project View Usage** field in the Properties pane.
Press the **Apply** button.

20. The elevation is moved to the new folder.
Repeat for the other elevation views.

21. Activate the **Structural Plane Level 1 - Analytical** view.

Type **1000 PLAN ANALYTICAL MODEL** in the **Project View Usage** field in the Properties pane.
Press the **Apply** button.

22. Repeat for the **Level 2 - Analytical** view.

23. Activate **Structural Plan: Level 1** view.

24. | Default Analysis Display Style | None |
       | Layers | |
       | Project View Usage | 000 PLANS |

Type **000 PLANS** in the **Project View Usage** field in the Properties pane.
Press the **Apply** button.

25.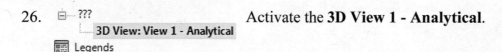

       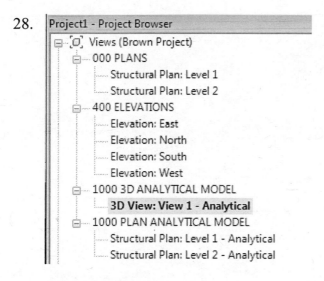

Move the Structural Plan: Level 2 to the 000 PLANS folder in the browser.
Select the view.
Then change the **Project_View_Usage** to **000 PLANS.**

26.   ⊟ ???
       └─ **3D View: View 1 - Analytical**
       ▦ Legends

Activate the **3D View 1 - Analytical**.

27. | Layers | |
       | Project View Usage | 1000 3D ANALYTICAL MODEL |

Type **1000 3D ANALYTICAL MODEL** in the **Project View Usage** field in the Properties pane.
Press the **Apply** button.

28.   Project1 - Project Browser
       ⊟ [O] Views (Brown Project)
          ⊟ 000 PLANS
            ├─ Structural Plan: Level 1
            └─ Structural Plan: Level 2
          ⊟ 400 ELEVATIONS
            ├─ Elevation: East
            ├─ Elevation: North
            ├─ Elevation: South
            └─ Elevation: West
          ⊟ 1000 3D ANALYTICAL MODEL
            └─ **3D View: View 1 - Analytical**
          ⊟ 1000 PLAN ANALYTICAL MODEL
            ├─ Structural Plan: Level 1 - Analytical
            └─ Structural Plan: Level 2 - Analytical

The project browser should look like the image.

29.   Close without saving.

Command Exercise

Exercise 3-2 – Recover and Use Backup Files

Drawing Name: **new**
Estimated Time to Completion: 5 Minutes

Scope

Recover and Use Backup Files

Solution

1. 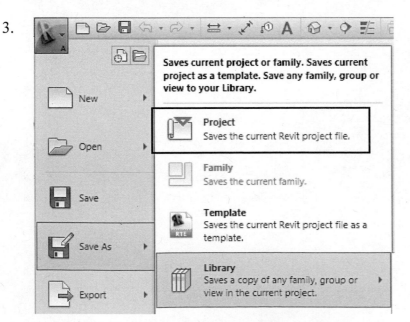   Close any open projects.
    Press **New** under Projects.

2. 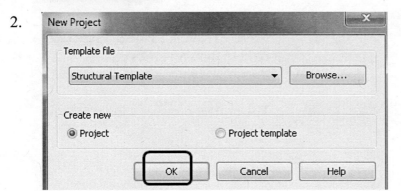   Press **OK**.

3. 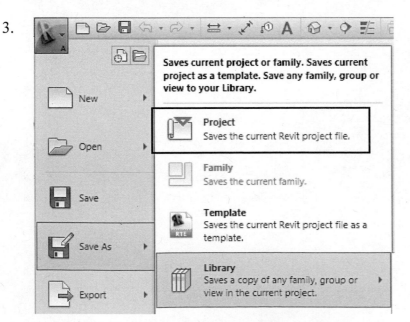   Go to **File→Save As→ Project**.

4.   [Options...]   Select the Options button next to the file name.

5.  Set the Maximum backups: to **5**.

Some students prefer not to save any backups so that their flash drive doesn't fill up. Those students set the number of backups to 0.

Press **OK**.

6.   File name: backup-example   Save as *backup-example.rvt*.
Files of type: Project Files (*.rvt)

7. Views (all)   Activate **Level 1**.
     Structural Plans
       Level 1
       Level 1 - Analytical
       Level 2
       Level 2 - Analytical

8. Activate the **Home** ribbon.

Grid   Select the **Grid** tool on the Datum Panel.

9. 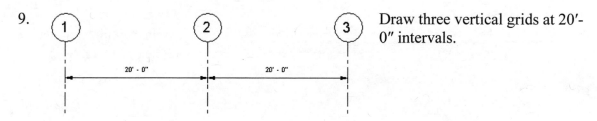 Draw three vertical grids at 20'-0" intervals.

10. Draw three horizontal grids at 16'-0" intervals.

11. Press **Save**.

12. Select the **Column** tool on the Structure panel.

13.

Select **Wide Flange Column W10 x 49** from the Type Selector list on the Properties pane.

14. On the Options bar set the height to **Level 2**.

15.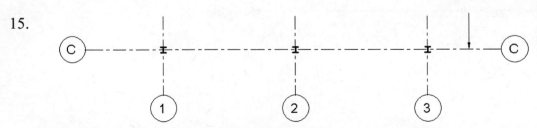

Place the column at C1, C2, and C3 intersections.

Hold down the CTL key then select the C grid and 1, 2, 3 grids.
Press Finish.

16.   Press **Save**.

17.

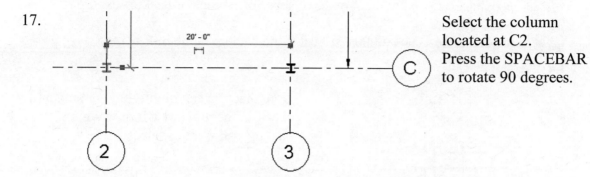

Select the column
located at C2.
Press the SPACEBAR
to rotate 90 degrees.

18.   Press **Save**.

19.

Window around the three columns
to select them.

20.   Use the COPY tool to copy the three columns to the A and B grids.

☐ Constrain ☐ Disjoin ☑ Multiple

*Enable **Multiple** on the Options bar to place more than one copy.*

21. There should be a column at each grid intersection.

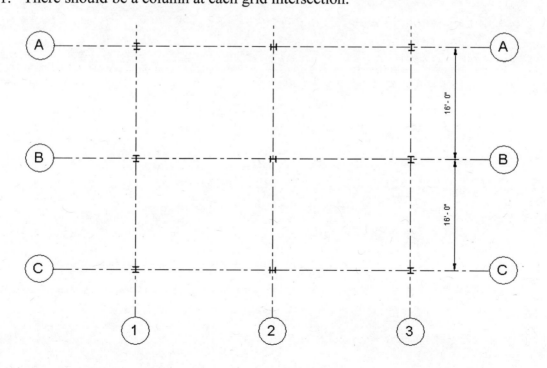

22.   🖫   Press **Save**.

23.   📂   Select **Open**.

24.   📄 backup-example.0001 Note that you have several versions of backup-example.
      📄 backup-example.0002
      📄 backup-example.0003 The .0000x indicates the backup number.
      📄 backup-example

25. 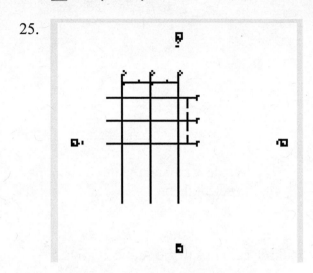   Note that you can highlight a version and check in the preview window which backup you want to select.

26. Open *backup-example.0001.rvt*.
This is the first save you did.

27.   [backup-example.0001 - Structural Plan: Level 2] Note the file name at the top of the screen.

28. Close all files without saving.

Command Exercise

Exercise 3-3 – Create a View Template

Drawing Name: **view_template.rvt**
Estimated Time to Completion: 20 Minutes

Scope

Create a view template
Apply view settings to a view

Solution

1. ⊟ Elevations (Interior Elevation)   Activate **Elevation 2-a** in the Project browser.
       Elevation 2 - a

2.

Identity Data	
View Template	Structural Framing Elevation
View Name	Elevation 2 - a
Dependency	Independent
Title on Sheet	
Referencing Sheet	
Referencing Detail	

On the Properties pane:
Set the Default View template to: **Structural Framing Elevation**.

3.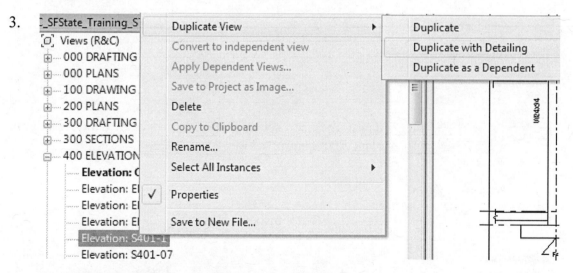

Highlight **Elevation 2-a** in the Project browser.
Right click and select **Duplicate View→Duplicate with Detailing**.

4. 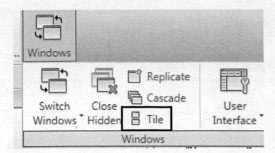 Use the Tile tool on the View window to display a window with the **Elevation 2-a** view and a window with the **Copy of Elevation 2-a** view.

This way you can compare the two views side by side.

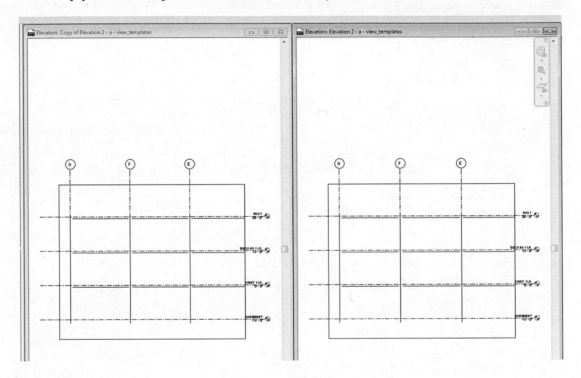

5. Zoom In Region
Zoom Out (2x)
Zoom To Fit
Previous Pan/Zoom

Right click and select Zoom to Fit in each window so you can see the entire view.

6. Click inside the **Copy of Elevation 2-a** view so it is active.

Identity Data		
View Template	Structural Framing Elevation	
View Name	Copy of Elevation 2 - a	
Dependency	Independent	
Title on Sheet		
Referencing Sheet		

In the Properties pane: Select the View template.

7.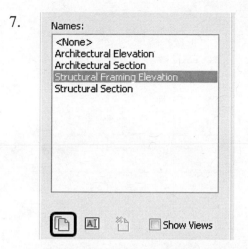

Highlight **Structural Framing Elevation**.

At the bottom of the dialog, select **Duplicate**.

8.

Name the new template:
Brown Structural Framing Elevation.
Press **OK**.

9.

Display Model	Normal
Detail Level	Medium
V/G Overrides Model	Edit...
V/G Overrides Annotation	Edit...
V/G Overrides Import	Edit...
V/G Overrides Filters	Edit...
Visual Style	Hidden Line

Select **Edit** in the V/G Overrides Annotation field.

10.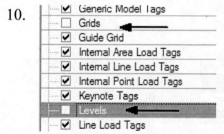

On the Annotation Categories tab:
Disable Grids.
Disable Levels.

11.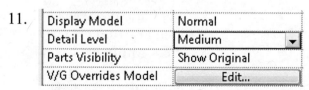

Set the Detail Level to **Medium**.

Press **OK** to close the dialog.

12.

Compare the two views.

13. Click inside the **Copy of Elevation 2-a** view so it is active.

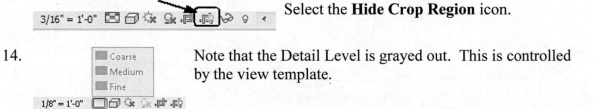

Select the **Hide Crop Region** icon.

14. Note that the Detail Level is grayed out. This is controlled by the view template.

15. Activate the Annotate ribbon.
Select the **Tag All** tool.

Tag
All

16.

Category	Loaded Tags
Structural Column Tags	Structural Column Tag
Structural Foundation Tags	Structural Foundation Tag
Structural Framing Tags	Structural Framing Tag
Structural Framing Tags	Structural Framing Tag : Boxed
Structural Framing Tags	Structural Framing Tag : Standard

Leader
☐ Create   Length: 1/2"

Orientation:
Horizontal

| OK | Cancel | Apply | Help |

Hold down the CTRL key so you can select more than one item.
Highlight the Structural Column Tags.
Highlight the Structural Framing Tags.
Press **Apply**.

Press OK to close the dialog.

17. You should see the tags on the structural members.

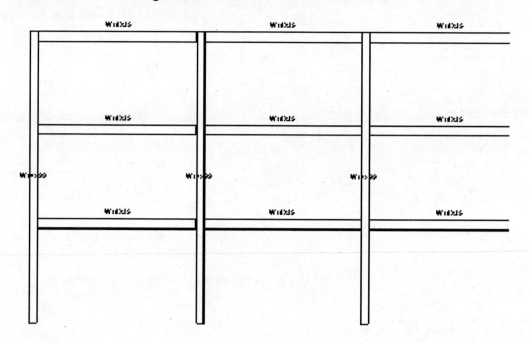

Press **OK**.

18. 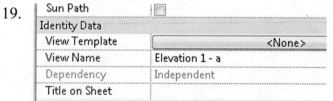 Activate **Elevation 1-a**.

19.  In the Properties pane: Note that no view template is applied.

20. Activate the **View** ribbon.
Select **View Templates→Apply Template Properties to Current View**.

21.  Highlight the **Brown Structural Framing Elevation** template just created.

Press **OK**.

22. Tile the views so you can compare them.

23. Compare the two views.

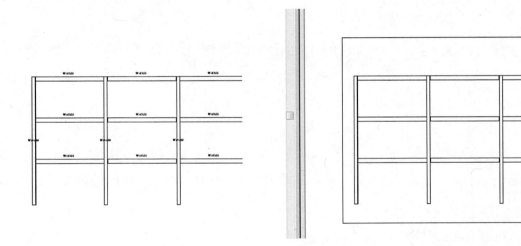

Note that hiding the crop region is not part of the view template settings.

Annotations, like dimensions and tags, are view specific. If the tags had been placed BEFORE the view was duplicated, they would be visible in both views.

Command Exercise

Exercise 3-4 – Transfer Project Standards

Drawing Name: **standards.rvt**
Estimated Time to Completion: 20 Minutes

View templates are stored internally in the project (RVT) file. If you need view templates available in all new projects, create or transfer the view templates to a default template project or any project template file used to create new project models.

Scope

Copy view templates, custom parameters and project browser settings from one project to another.

Solution

1. Open the standards.rvt file.
    Then open a NEW blank project file.

2.

    Transfer
    Project Standards

    In the new project file:

    Activate the **Manage** ribbon.

    Select the **Transfer Project Standards** tool.

3. | Select Items To Copy | | X |
    | --- | --- | --- |
    | Copy from: | standards ▼ | |
    | ☑ Annotation Family Label Types | | Check All |
    | ☑ Area and Volume Computations | | Check None |
    | ☑ Arrowhead Styles | | |
    | ☑ Browser Organization | | |
    | ☑ Building Type Settings | | |
    | ☑ Cable Tray Settings | | |
    | ☑ Cable Tray Sizes | | |
    | ☑ Callout Tags | | |
    | ☑ Ceiling Types | | |
    | ☑ Color Fill Schemes | | |
    | ☑ Conduit Settings | | |
    | ☑ Conduit Sizes | | |
    | ☑ Conduit Standard Types | | |
    | ☑ Curtain System Types | | |
    | ☑ Curtain Wall Types | | |

    Note that you can select which project to copy from.

    Verify that **standards** is selected.

    Select **Check None** to clear the selections.

4. Place a check next to **Browser Organization**.

5. Scroll down the list.
    Place a check next to **Project Parameters**.

6. Place a check next to **View Templates**.

    Press **OK**.

7. Select **Overwrite** since this is a new project with no content.

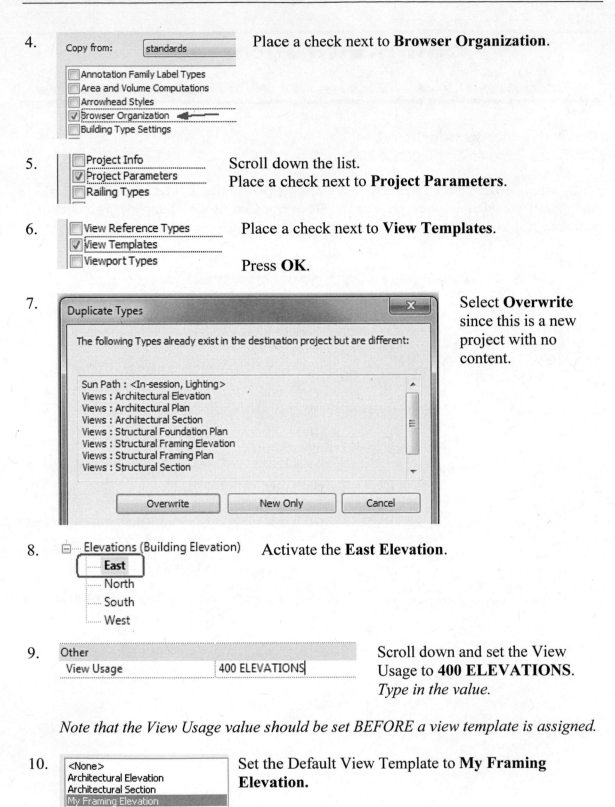

8. Activate the **East Elevation**.

9. Scroll down and set the View Usage to **400 ELEVATIONS**.
    Type in the value.

Note that the View Usage value should be set BEFORE a view template is assigned.

10. Set the Default View Template to **My Framing Elevation**.

11.  Activate the **View** ribbon.

Select **User Interface→Browser Organization**.

12. Enable **Company Standard**.

Press **OK**.

13. Note that the Project Browser upates.

14. Close without saving.

Notes:

Lesson Four
Foundations and Slabs

The Structural Usage parameter of a Foundation slab can be set to either Foundation or Slab on Grade. If set to Foundation, the slab will provide support for other elements connected to it. If set to Slab on Grade, the slab will only support itself.

Foundation slabs are constrained so that the top is aligned to the assigned level and thickness is added below the level in which they are drawn. Therefore, foundation slabs are not visible in a plan view except as an underlay (displayed in halftone). In order to display as an underlay, you must have a level defined below the active plan view. For example, if you are looking at Level 1 plan, in order to see the foundation slab below Level 1, there must be a level below Level 1; i.e. Foundation or Slab, which can be utilized for the underlay.

The Foundation Slab type has 3 more foundation-specific values than a regular structural floor has. These additional values, which are instance parameters displayed in the Properties palette, are: Width, Length, and Elevation at Bottom (a read-only parameter). Using these values, an analysis tool can distinguish between a standard structural floor and a foundation slab.

The Elevation at Bottom parameter is used for tagging the Bottom of the Foundation elevation. You can modify parameter names, values, and descriptions for Foundation Slabs.

Foundation slabs may be used to model structural floors on a grade, which do not require support from other structural elements. Foundation slabs may also be used to model complex foundation shapes that cannot be created using Isolated or Wall Foundation tools.

Command Exercise

Exercise 4-1 – Creating a Sloped Floor Slab

Drawing Name: **i_floor.rvt**
Estimated Time to Completion: 30 Minutes

Scope

Create a sloped floor slab
Change span direction
Attach beams to sloped floor

Solution

1. Structural Plans
    BASEMENT
    FIRST FLR.
    ROOF
    SECOND FLR.

    Activate the SECOND FLR Structural plan.

2.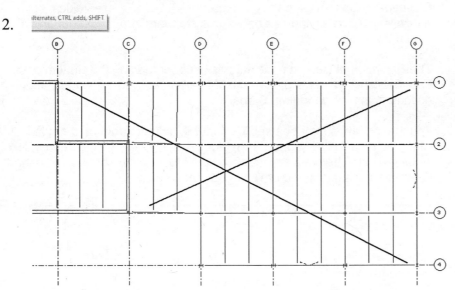

    We will be focusing on the area between the B1 and G4 grid intersections.

3.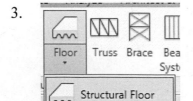

    Activate the Structure ribbon.

    Select **Floor→Structural Floor**

4. ⊞ Edit Type

    In the Properties pane:
    Select **Edit Type**.

5. Duplicate...

    Select **Duplicate**.

6.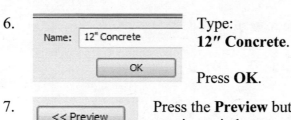

Type:
12" Concrete.

Press **OK**.

7.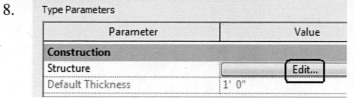

Press the **Preview** button to expand the dialog so you can see the preview window.

8.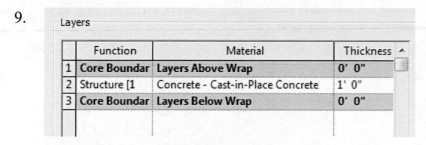

Press the **Edit** button in the Structure field.

9.

Set the Structure to **Concrete - Cast-In-Place Concrete**.

10.

If you left click in the Material column, the Material Editor should appear.

Left click on the Concrete - Cast-In-Place Concrete material and press OK.

Close the Material dialogs.

Set the Thickness to **1'-0" [304.8]**.

Press **OK**.

11. Press **OK** to close the Edit Assembly dialog and Type Properties dialog.

12.

Select the **Line** tool in the Draw panel.

13.

Enable **Chain** on the Options bar.

14.

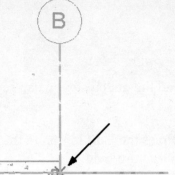

Select the intersection at **B1**.

The first line placed controls span direction.
You can change this by using the Span direction tool and then selecting a different
boundary line. The span direction dictates the direction the floor joists are laid.

15.

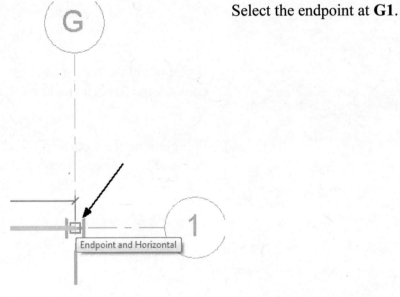

Select the endpoint at **G1**.

16.

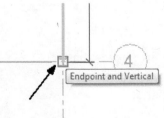

Select the endpoint at **G4**.

17. Select the endpoint at D4.

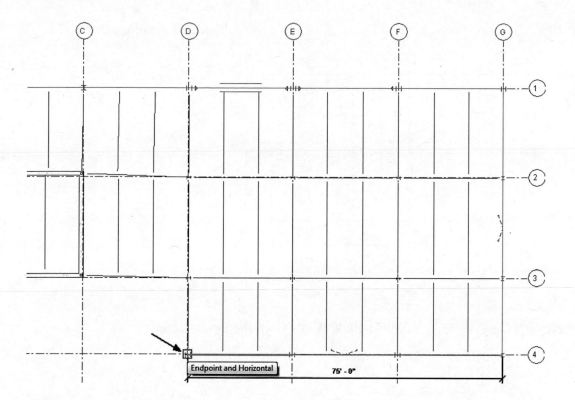

18. Select the endpoint at D3.

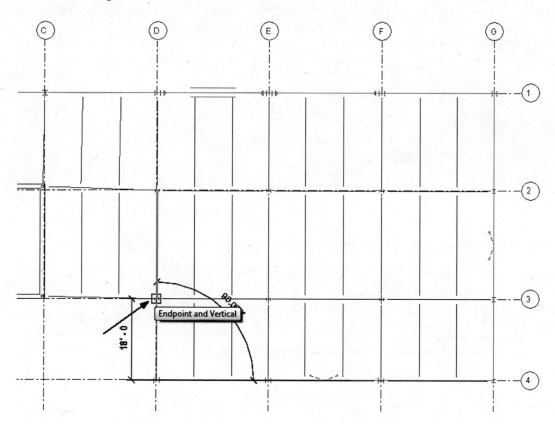

19. 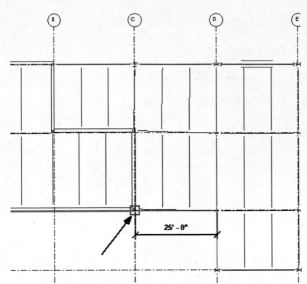 Select the endpoint at C3.

20.  Select **Pick Walls** from the Draw panel.

21. 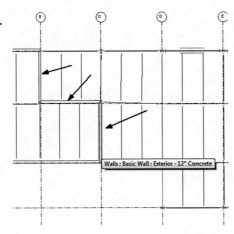 Pick the three walls indicated to close the boundary for the floor.

22. Select the **Trim** tool from the Modify panel.

23. 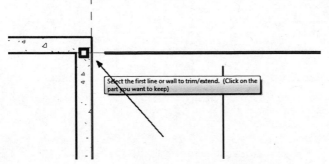 Use the Trim tool to clean up the corner of the boundary at B1.

24.  Use the Trim tool to clean up the corner of the boundary at C3.

25.  Set the Detail Level for the view to **Medium**.

26. Select the **Pick Lines** tool on the Draw panel.

27.  Set the Offset to **3″ [76.2]** in the Options bar.

28. 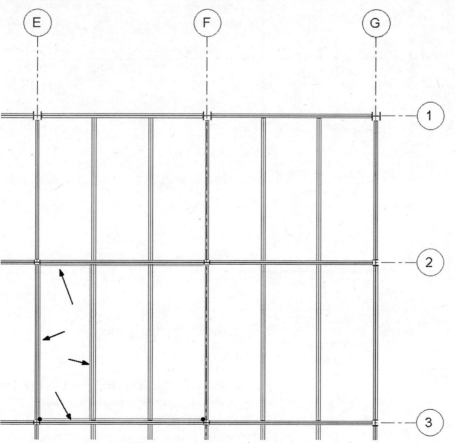 Select inside the supports for the bay located to the right of E2 and above E3.

29. Use the TRIM tool to create a clean rectangle.

This creates an opening in the floor.

30. Slope Arrow   Select the **Slope Arrow** tool.

31. Select the **Line** tool on the Draw panel.

Draw

32. 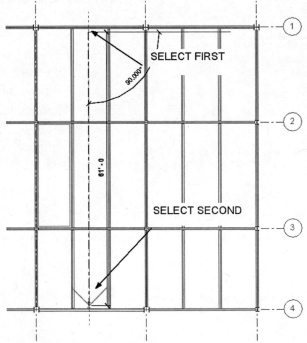 Place the slope arrow by picking two points.

Pick a point between E1 and F1.

Pick a second point between E4 and F4.

33.

Constraints	
Specify	Slope
Level at Tail	SECOND FLR.
Height Offset at Tail	-2' 2"
Level at Head	Default
Height Offset at Head	0' 0"
Dimensions	
Slope	2.00°

On the Properties pane:

Specify **Slope**.
Set the Level at Tail to **SECOND FLR**.
Set the Height Offset at Tail **to -2' 2"**.
Set the Slope to **2°**.
(This is approximately 1/4":1').

34.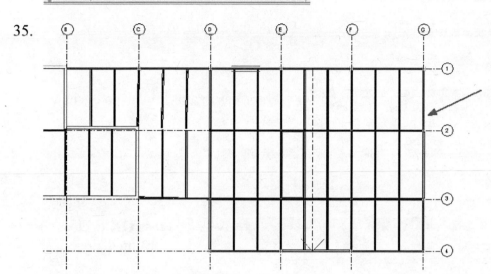

Select the **Span Direction** tool on the ribbon to change the span direction.

35.

Select the line indicated on the right side.

Note that the parallel lines shift to the newly designated line.

36.   Select the Green Check on the Mode panel to finish the floor.

Error - cannot be ignored

Lines cannot intersect each other. The highlighted lines currently intersect.

[Show]   [More Info]   [Expand >>]

If you get this error, it means that you need to trim one of the corners. If you press SHOW, the corner that needs trimming will highlight in the display window. Then, press **Continue**.

Correct the error and press the Green Check.

37. Revit

No Span Direction Symbol family is loaded in the project. Would you like to load one now?

[Yes]   [No]

If you see this dialog, press **Yes**.

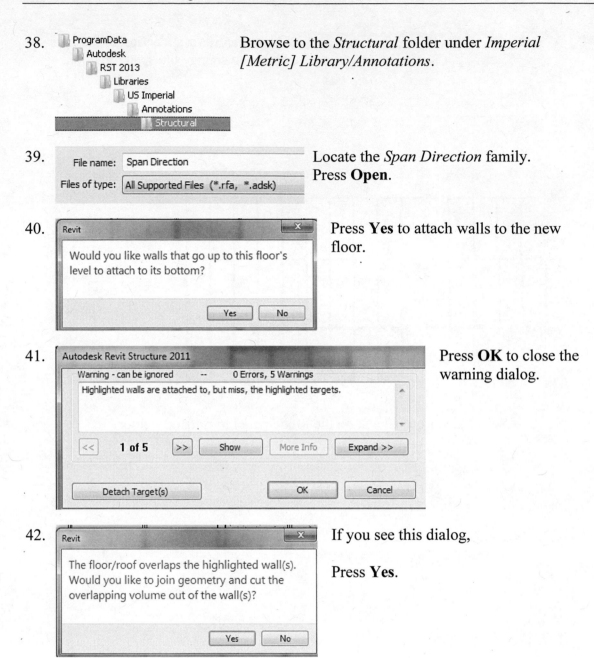

38. Browse to the *Structural* folder under *Imperial [Metric] Library/Annotations*.

ProgramData
Autodesk
RST 2013
Libraries
US Imperial
Annotations
Structural

39. File name: Span Direction

Files of type: All Supported Files (*.rfa, *.adsk)

Locate the *Span Direction* family. Press **Open**.

40. Revit

Would you like walls that go up to this floor's level to attach to its bottom?

Yes   No

Press **Yes** to attach walls to the new floor.

41. Autodesk Revit Structure 2011

Warning - can be ignored   --   0 Errors, 5 Warnings

Highlighted walls are attached to, but miss, the highlighted targets.

<<   1 of 5   >>   Show   More Info   Expand >>

Detach Target(s)   OK   Cancel

Press **OK** to close the warning dialog.

42. Revit

The floor/roof overlaps the highlighted wall(s). Would you like to join geometry and cut the overlapping volume out of the wall(s)?

Yes   No

If you see this dialog,

Press **Yes**.

43. Note that the span direction annotation is placed to indicate the span direction.

44. Annotate   Analyze   Architect & Site   Collabo

Angular Radial Arc   Spot   Spot   Spot
             Length Elevation Coordinate Slope

Dimension ▼

Activate the **Annotate** ribbon.

45. Detail Line

Select the **Detail Line** tool from the Detail panel.

46.  Disable **Chain** on the Options bar.

47. 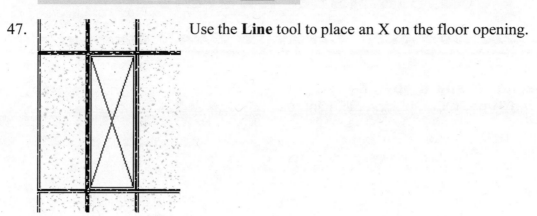 Use the **Line** tool to place an X on the floor opening.

48. 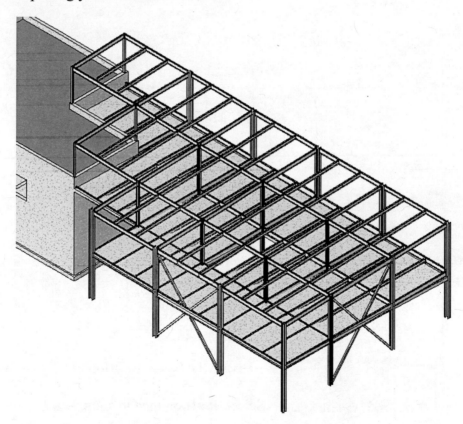 Switch to a **3D** view.

49. Note the opening you created in the floor.

50. Close without saving.

Command Exercise

Exercise 4-2– Create a Shaft Opening

Drawing Name: **shaft_opening.rvt**
Estimated Time to Completion: 15 Minutes

Scope

Create a Shaft Opening

Solution

1.
   Structural Plans
   — BASEMENT
   — FIRST FLR.
   — ROOF
   — **SECOND FLR.**

   Activate the **SECOND FLR** under Structural Plans in the Project Browser.

2. 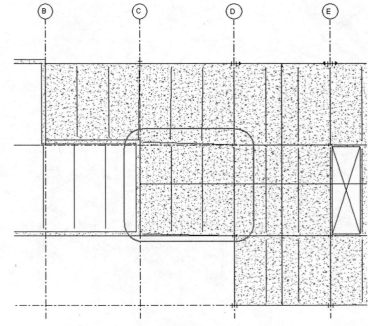 Zoom into the bay located between Grids C and D and Grids 2 and 3.

3. 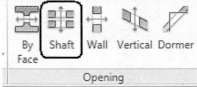 Activate the **Structure** ribbon.

   Select **Shaft** on the Opening panel.

4. 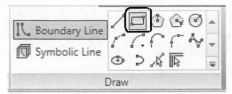 Select the **Rectangle** tool in the Draw panel.

5.

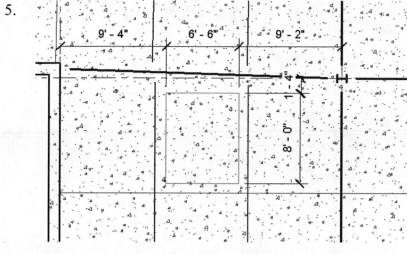

In the x-direction (horizontal), set the dimensions so that the opening is located **9' 4" [2844.7]** from Grid C. Pin the left vertical side of the rectangle in position so it doesn't shift.

Set the width of the rectangle to **6' 6" [1981.2]**.

6.

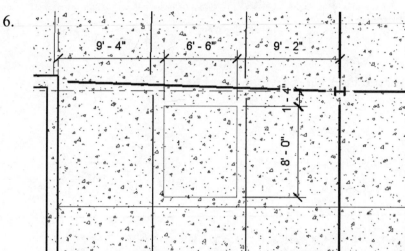

In the y-direction (vertical), set the dimensions so that the opening is located **1' 4" [406.4]** below Grid 2.

Set the height of the rectangle to **8' 0" [2438.4]**.

Do not add dimensions. They are shown to help you place the opening.

7.

Shaft Openings (1)	▾ Edi
Constraints	
Top Offset	1' 0"
Base Offset	-2' 0"
Unconnected Height	17' 0"
Base Constraint	SECOND FLR.
Top Constraint	Up to level: ROOF
Phasing	
Phase Created	New Construction
Phase Demolished	None

In the Properties pane:

Set the Base Constraint to **SECOND FLR**.
Set the Top Constraint **Up to level: Roof**.

Set the Top Offset to **1' 0"**.
Set the Base Offset to **-2' 0"**.

8.

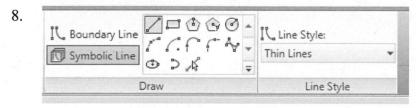

On the Draw panel:
Enable **Symbolic Line**.
Set the Line Style to **Thin Lines**.

9. 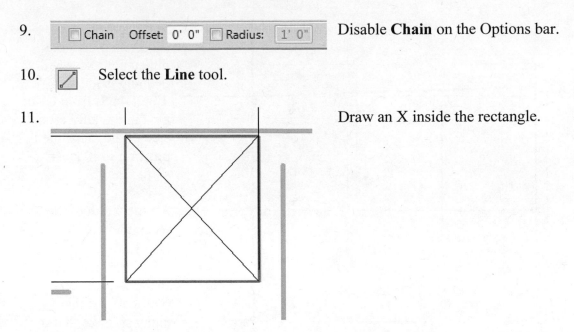 Disable **Chain** on the Options bar.

10. 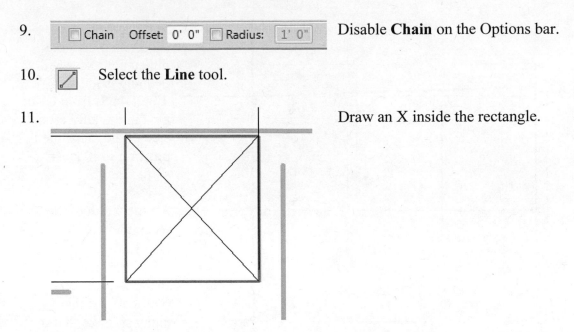 Select the **Line** tool.

11. 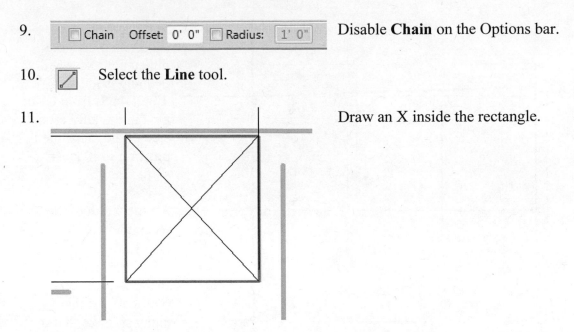 Draw an X inside the rectangle.

12. 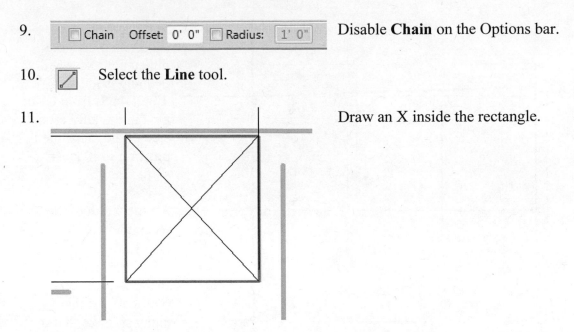 Select the **Green Check** on the Mode panel to finish the shaft opening.

13. Switch to a 3D view.

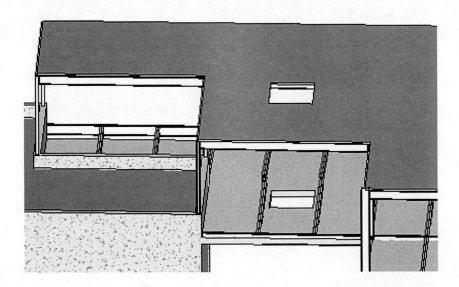

Note how the shaft opening cuts through the floor and the roof above it.

Close without saving.

Command Exercise

Exercise 4-3– Attach Columns to a Floor

Drawing Name: **attach_columns.rvt**
Estimated Time to Completion: 10 Minutes

Scope

> *Attach Columns to Floor*

Solution

1. 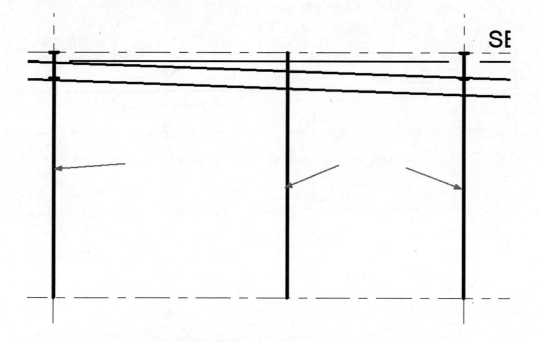 Activate the **Attach Columns view** under Elevations (Building Elevation) in the Project Browser.

2. Note the three columns indicated.

Select the column on the far left.

3.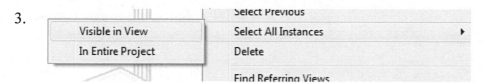

Right click and select **Select All Instances→Visible in View**.

4.

Note that all three columns highlight.

5. 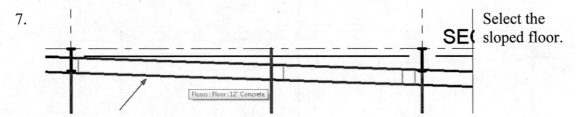 Select **Attach Top/Base** from the Modify Column panel.

6. Enable **Top**.

Set the Attachment Style to **Cut Column**.

7.  Select the sloped floor.

Repeat and attach the selected columns again if additional trimming is needed.

8. 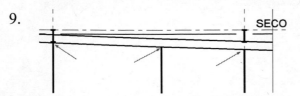 Select **Unjoin Elements**.

9. Note how the columns are trimmed to meet the floor.

10. Close without saving.

Command Exercise

Exercise 4-4 – Add Slab Edges

Drawing Name: **slab_edge.rvt**
Estimated Time to Completion: 5 Minutes

Slab edges are located on the boundaries of floors. Slab edges are placed using an assigned profile and then sweeping around the defined boundary.

Scope

> *Add slab edges.*

Solution

1. Activate the **Ground floor plan** under Floor Plans in the Project Browser.

2. Select the **Slab Edge** tool on the Structure ribbon.

3. 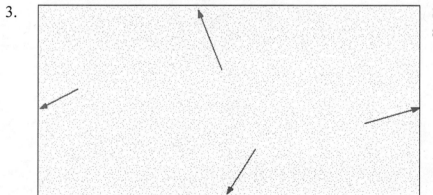 Select each of the sides of the floor.

4. ⇆ When you select an edge, you will see an orientation icon indicating the exterior side of the edge.

5.  Activate the 3D view called **Floors Only**.

6. 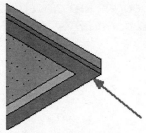 Select a bottom corner of the view cube to re-orient the view.

7. Inspect the slab edges which were placed.

8. Close without saving.

Command Exercise
Exercise 4-5 – Define Slab Edge

Drawing Name: **define_slab_edge.rvt**
Estimated Time to Completion: 10 Minutes

Scope

Create a new slab edge family

Solution

1. **3D Views**
    Floors Only
    {3D}
    Activate the 3D view called **Floors Only**.

2. Select a bottom corner of the view cube to re-orient the view.

3. Select the slab edge which was placed.

4. ▼ ⊞ Edit Type   Select **Edit Type** in the Project Browser.

5. Duplicate...   Press **Duplicate**.

6. Name: Thickened 36" x 12"   Change the name to **Thickened 36″ x 12″**.

    OK   Press **OK**.

7. 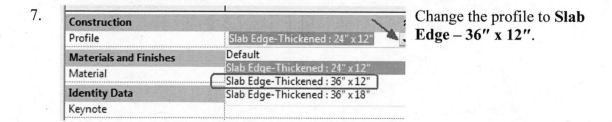   Change the profile to **Slab Edge – 36″ x 12″**.

8. Set the Material to **Concrete - Cast-in-Place Concrete**.

Materials and Finishes	
Material	Concrete - Cast-in-Place Concrete

Press **OK**.

9. 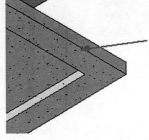 Note how the slab edge updates.

10. Close without saving.

Command Exercise
Exercise 4-6– Add Footings

Drawing Name: **foundations.rvt**
Estimated Time to Completion: 20 Minutes

Scope

Create a new foundation type
Add foundations

Solution

1. Activate the **FIRST FLR structural plan** under Structural Plans in the Project Browser.

2. In the Project Browser, under Families:
Locate the Footing - Rectangular.
Note the two types that are already available.

3. Highlight the **Footing - Rectangular** family.
Right click and select **New Type**.

4. Rename the new type: **60″ x 60″ x 24″ (1500 x 1500 x 600)**.

   To rename, left click or press F2.

5. Right click on the new type.
Select **Type Properties**.

6. Set the Width to **5′ 0″ (1500)**.
Set the Length to **5′ 0″ (1500)**.
Set the Thickness to **2′ 0″ (600)**.

   Press **OK**.

7. 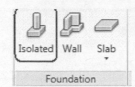 Activate the **Structure** ribbon.

Select the **Isolated** tool on the Foundation panel.

8.  Set the Type Selector to use the **60″ x 60″ x 24″ (1500 x 1500 x 600) footing**.

9. Enable **At Grids** on the ribbon.

10. 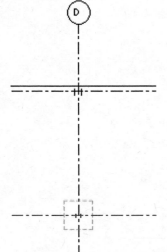 Select Grid D and Grid 2.

You will see a preview of the footing.

11. Click **Finish**.

12. 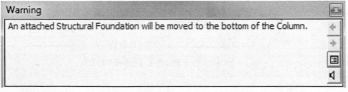 A warning will appear.

Footings are automatically attached to the bottom of the column indicated regardless of what level they are placed in.
Click the x to close the window.

13.  Select the **Isolated** tool on the Foundation panel.

14. 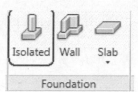 Set the Type Selector to use the **60″ x 60″ x 24″ (1500 x 1500 x 600) footing.**

Footing-Rectangular
60" x 60" x 24"

15. 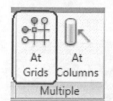 Enable **At Grids** on the ribbon.

16. 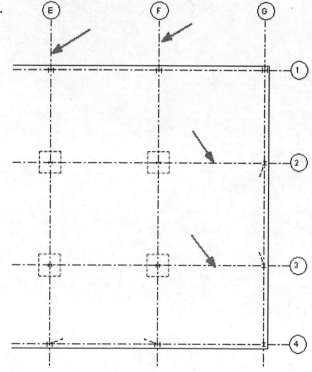 Hold down the CTRL button and select Grids 2, 3, E, and F.

The footings will preview.

17. Click **Finish**.

18.

Warning	
An attached Structural Foundation will be moved to the bottom of the Column.	

A warning will appear.

Click the x to close the window.

19.   3D Views
        Footings
        {3D}

Activate the **Footings** view under 3D Views in the Project Browser.

20. The footings are visible.

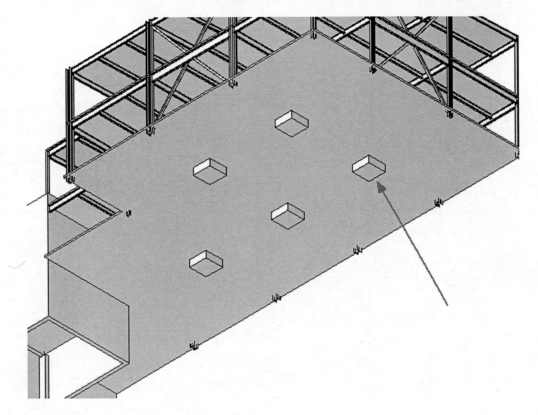

21. Close without saving.

Command Exercise

Exercise 4-7– Add Wall Foundations

Drawing Name: **wall_foundations.rvt**
Estimated Time to Completion: 10 Minutes

Scope

Add foundations to walls

Solution

1. Structural Plans
   - **BASEMENT**
   - FIRST FLR.
   - ROOF
   - SECOND FLR.

   Activate the **BASEMENT structural plan** under Structural Plans in the Project Browser.

2. Isolated Wall Slab

   Foundation

   Activate the **Structure** ribbon.

   Select the **Wall** tool on the Foundation panel.

3. Wall Foundation
   - Continuous Footing
   - Continuous Footing 14"x12"
   - Continuous Footing 24"x16"

   Select the **Continuous Footing 24″ x 16″ [Continuous Footing 600 x 400]** from the Type Selector drop-down list.

4. Select Multiple Finish Cancel

   Select Multiple

   Enable **Select Multiple** on the ribbon.

5.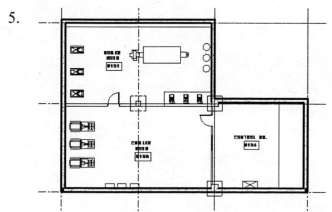

   Hover your mouse over one wall. Press the TAB key so that all the walls highlight.
   Left click to select all the walls at once.

6.  Select the **Finish** tool on the ribbon.

7. 3D Views
    Wall Foundation
    {3D}

    Activate the **Wall Foundation** view under 3D Views in the Project Browser.

8. Inspect the wall foundation that was placed.

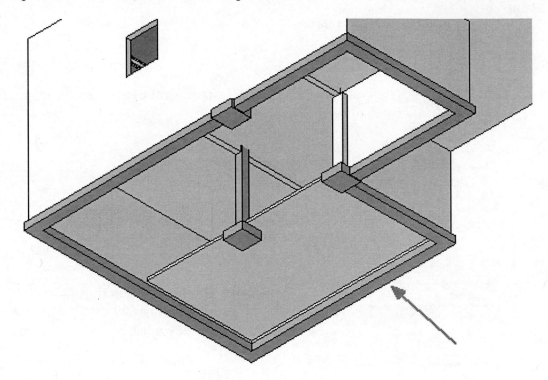

9. Close without saving.

Command Exercise

Exercise 4-8 – Add Ramp

Drawing Name: ramp.rvt
Estimated Time to Completion: 10 Minutes

When sketching a ramp, keep track of the different colors. Green represents the boundary lines. Blue represents rise and run. Black represents rise and run limits.

Ramps can be created in plan or 3D views. Railings are automatically added to ramps. You can reset the railing type either before or after the ramp has been placed.

Pedestrian ramps have strict controls on the slope and run length between landings. As a default, Revit will draw a handicapped-accessible ramp with a 1-inch-rise-to-12-inch-run slope with a landing after every 30 inches of rise (30 feet of run). Ramps are system families, so they are unique to each project.

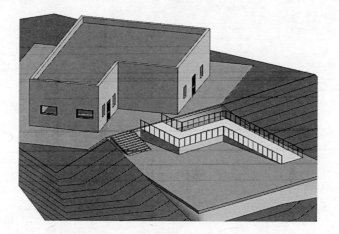

Scope

Add a sloped ramp

Solution

1.    Activate the **T.O. PAD structural plan** under Structural Plans in the Project Browser.

2.   Activate the **Architecture** ribbon.

     Select the **Ramp** tool on the Circulation panel.

3. ▼ 🔲 Edit Type   Select **Edit Type** in the Properties pane.

4.  **Duplicate...**   Select **Duplicate**.

5.  Name: Wheelchair Access   Rename **Wheelchair Access**.

   OK   Press **OK**.

6. 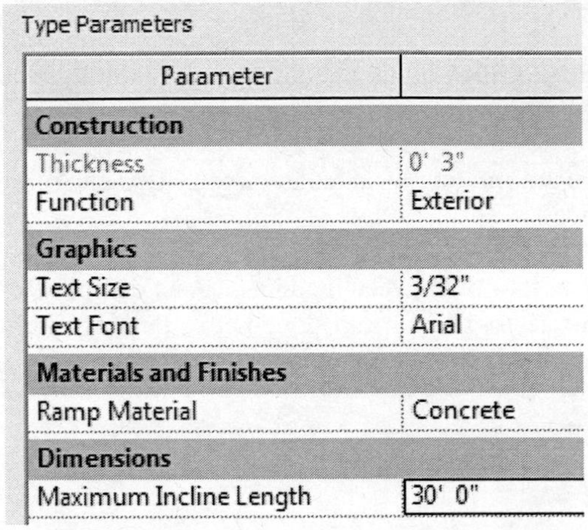 Type Parameters   Set the Function to **Exterior**.

Parameter	
Construction	
Thickness	0' 3"
Function	Exterior
Graphics	
Text Size	3/32"
Text Font	Arial
Materials and Finishes	
Ramp Material	Concrete
Dimensions	
Maximum Incline Length	30' 0"

Set the Ramp Material to **Concrete**.

Set the Maximum Incline Length to **30' 0"**.

7. 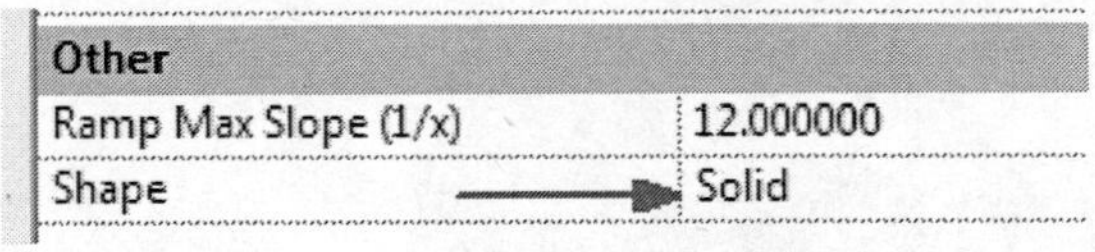
Other	
Ramp Max Slope (1/x)	12.000000
Shape	Solid

Scroll down and set the Shape to **Solid**.

Press **OK**.

8. 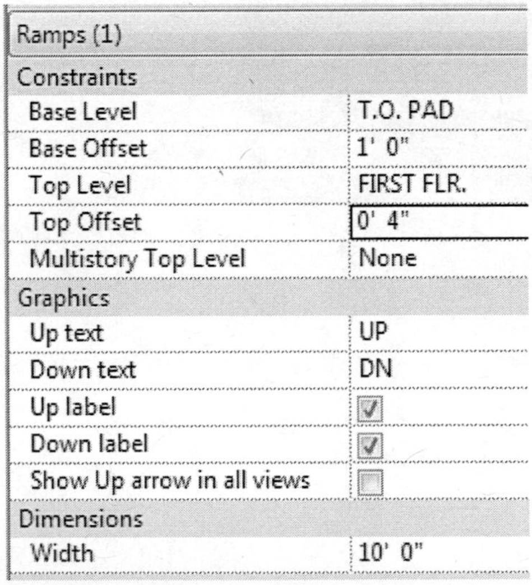
Ramps (1)	
Constraints	
Base Level	T.O. PAD
Base Offset	1' 0"
Top Level	FIRST FLR.
Top Offset	0' 4"
Multistory Top Level	None
Graphics	
Up text	UP
Down text	DN
Up label	☑
Down label	☑
Show Up arrow in all views	☐
Dimensions	
Width	10' 0"

In the Properties pane:

Set the Base Level to **T.O. PAD**.
Set the Base Offset to **1' 0" [0.0]**.
Set the Top Level to **FIRST FLR**.
Set the Top Offset to **0' 4" [100.0]**.
Set the Width to **10' 0" [3050]**.

9. 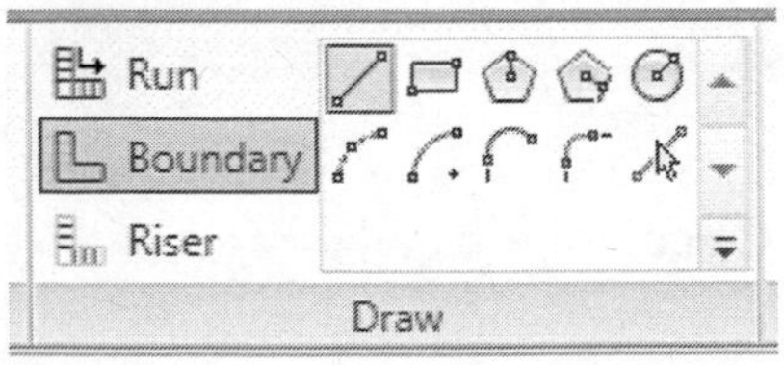
🖽 Run
⌐ Boundary
🖩 Riser
Draw

Enable **Boundary** in the Draw panel.

10. 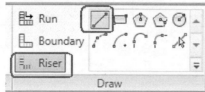 Select the **Pick Line** tool.

11.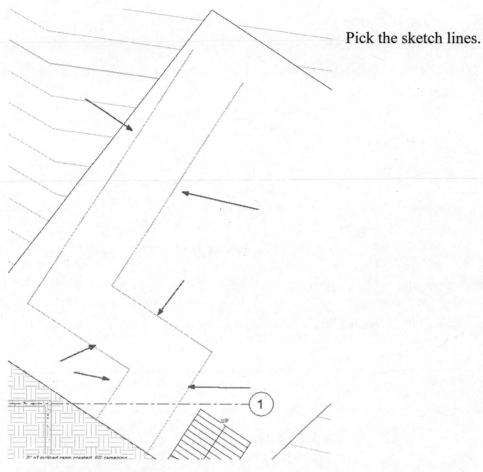

Pick the sketch lines.

12. 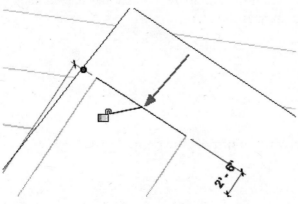 Select the **Riser** tool.

Select the **Line** tool in the Draw panel.

13. Draw a line at the end of the ramp.

14.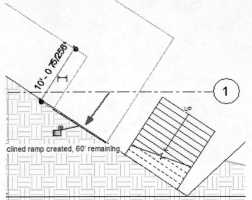

Draw a line at the end of the ramp by the stairs.

The two risers close the boundary.

15.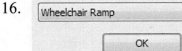

Select **Railing**.

16. Select the **Wheelchair Ramp** from the list.

Press **OK**.

17.

Select the **Green Check** to finish the ramp.

18.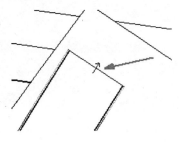

Click on the orientation arrow to flip the direction of the ramp to go up towards the building.

19.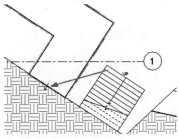

The orientation flip arrow will now move to the top of the ramp near the stairs.

20. 3D Views {3D} Switch to a 3D view so you can inspect the ramp.

21. Close without saving.

Command Exercise

Exercise 4-9– Parking Structure Ramp

Drawing Name: **parking_ramp.rvt**
Estimated Time to Completion: 45 Minutes

*Add a ramp for a parking structure using a floor
Use Shape Editing tools.*

*The Institution of Structural Engineers' excellent publication "Design Recommendations
for Multi-storey and Underground Car Parks" provides detailed information on many
aspects of car park ramp gradients. [www.istructe.org.uk]*

Solution

1.   Structural Plans
     Level 1
     Level 2
     Level 3
     Level 4

Activate the **Level 1 structural plan** under Structural Plans in the Project Browser.

2.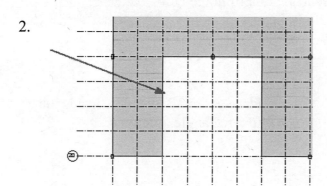

The parking ramp will be placed in the open section indicated.

3.

Select the **Structural Floor** tool from the Structure ribbon.

Floor   Truss   Brace   Bea
                         Syst
   Floor: Structural

4. Floor
   Generic - 12"

Select **Generic – 12″** from the Type Selector on the Properties pane.

5.

Select the Rectangle tool from the Draw panel.

Draw

6.

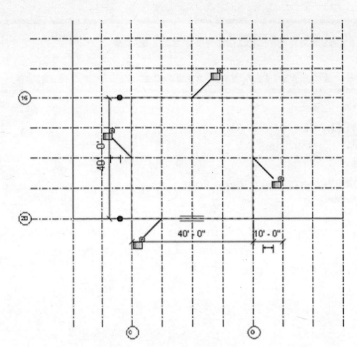

Place a rectangle in the opening of the floor.

The rectangle is placed between C16 and G16 and C20 and G20. Use the Grid Lines to help you place the rectangle.

7.

Select the Rectangle tool from the Draw panel.

8.

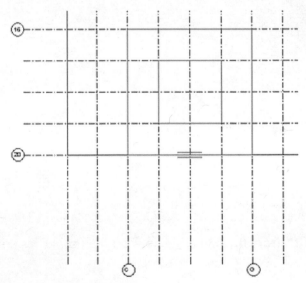

Place a second rectangle inside the first rectangle as shown.

9.

Select the Line tool from the Draw menu.

10. 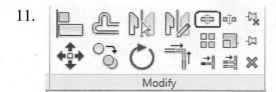 Draw two horizontal lines 6″ [150mm] apart to the right of the bottom of the inner rectangle.

The bottom line is collinear with the inner rectangle's bottom line and the top line is 6″ above the bottom line.

11. 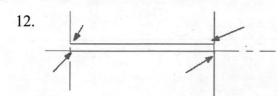 Select the **Split** tool.

12. 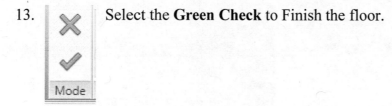 Select the four points indicated. Then, delete the two small vertical lines to create a gap.

13. 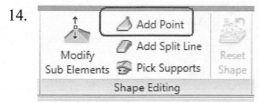 Select the **Green Check** to Finish the floor.

14. With the floor that was just created selected, select the **Add Point** tool on the Shape Editing panel.

15.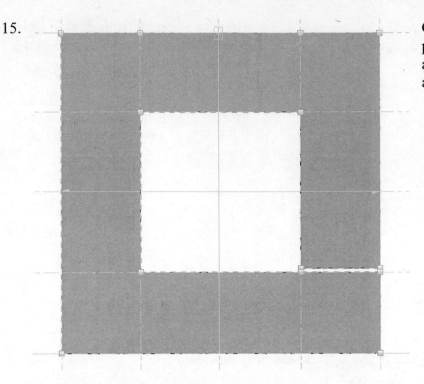

Green points will be placed on each vertex and along the edges automatically.

16. Use **Add Point** to add points at the locations indicated. Each corner should have four points to define a landing.

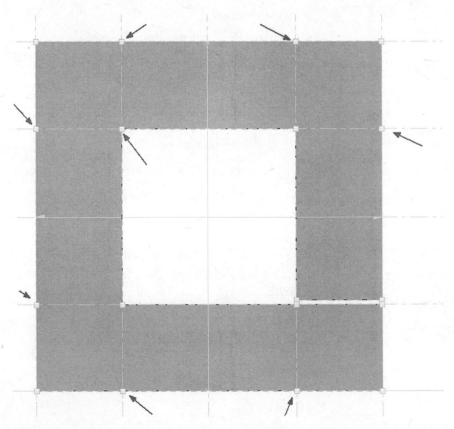

17. ⬡ ▾   Switch to a 3D view.

18. 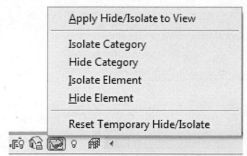 Select the floor that was just placed.

On the View Display bar: select **Isolate Element**.

19. With the floor selected, select the **Modify Sub Elements** tool on the ribbon.

20. Select the point indicated and change the elevation to **2' 0″ [600mm]**.

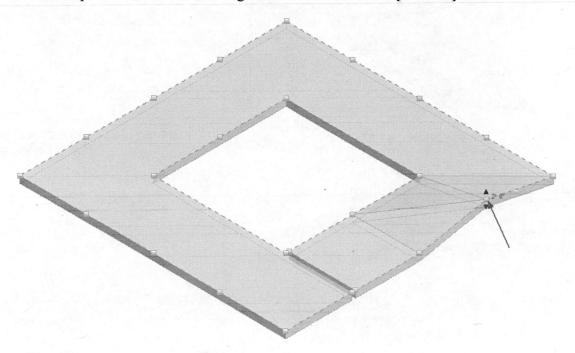

You will see a warning message - ignore it.

21. 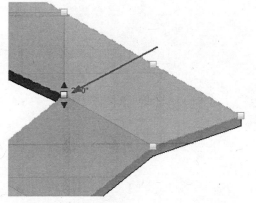 Select the inner point and set the elevation to **2' 0″ [600mm]**.

22. 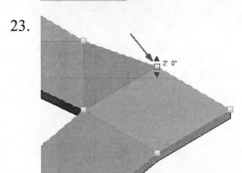 Select the outside corner and set the elevation to **2′ 0″ [600mm]**.

23. 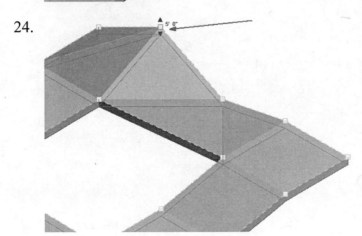 Select the point to the left and set the elevation to **2′ 0″ [600mm]**.

24. Select the next point left and set the elevation to **5′ 0″ [1500mm]**.

25. 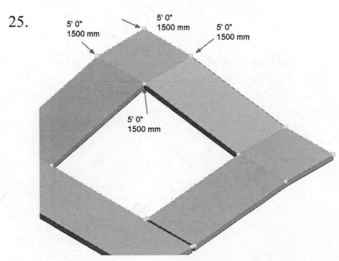 Set the four points indicated to elevation to **5′ 0″ [1500mm]**.

26.

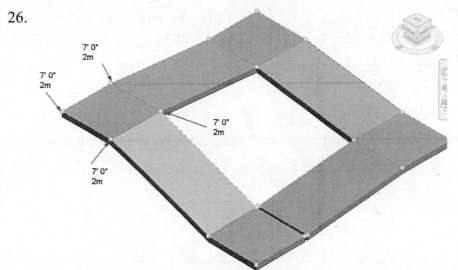

7' 0"
2m

7' 0"
2m

7' 0"
2m

7' 0"
2m

Set the four points indicated to elevation to **7' 0" [2 m]**.

27.

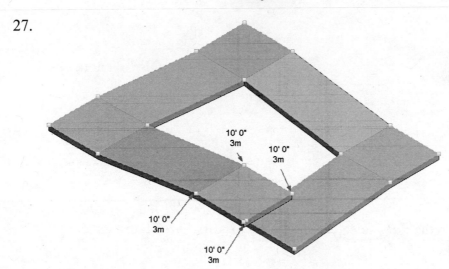

10' 0"
3m

10' 0"
3m

10' 0"
3m

10' 0"
3m

Set the four points indicated to elevation to **10' 0" [3 m]**.

28.

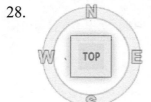

Switch to a Top view using the View Cube.

29.

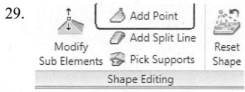

Modify Sub Elements   Add Point   Add Split Line   Pick Supports   Reset Shape

Shape Editing

Select the **Add Point** tool.

30. 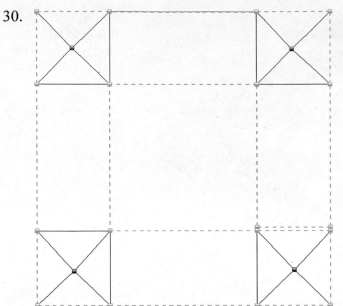 Add four points at the center of each landing area.

31. 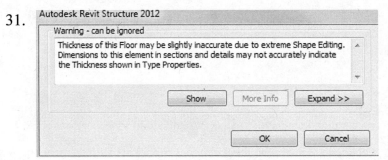 Press **OK** to ignore this warning.

32. Modify Sub Elements

With the floor selected: Select the **Modify Sub Elements** tool on the ribbon.

33. 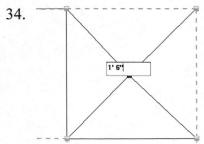 Set the elevation for the left -top point to **4′ 6″ [1.3m]**.

34. Set the elevation for the right -top point to **1′ 6″ [500mm]**.

35. 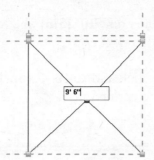 Set the elevation for the right -bottom point to **9′ 6″ [2.8m]**.

36. 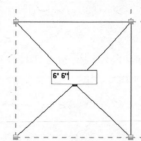 Set the elevation for the left -bottom point to **7′ 6″ [2.2m]**.

Each point is roughly 6"[150mm] below the level to create a drainage area.

37. Switch back to an isometric view.

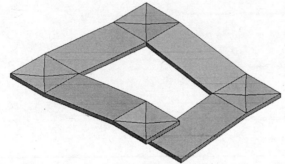

38. 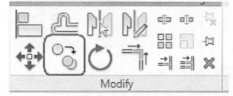 Activate the North Elevation.

39. 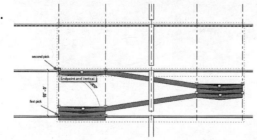 Select the parking ramp floor.

Select the **Copy** tool on the Modify panel.

40. Modify | Floors ☐ Constrain ☐ Disjoin ☑ Multiple   Enable **Multiple** on the Options bar.

41. Select the base point and then a point 10′ above it.

42.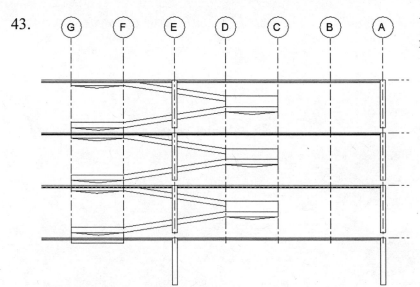
Pick the point **10′ [3m]** above to place the next copy.

Right click and select **Cancel** to exit the command.

43.
You should see three ramps placed.

44. Switch to a 3D view.

45. On the View Display bar: Reset Temporary/Hide Isolate to restore the model.

Hide Element

Reset Temporary Hide/Isolate

46. Orbit the model to inspect the parking structure and the ramp.

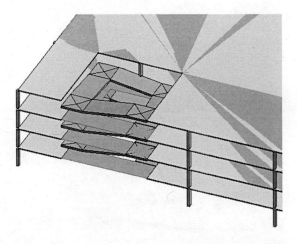

47. Close without saving.

Lesson Five
Tags, Symbols, Legends, and Schedules

Tags display parametric information attached to elements.

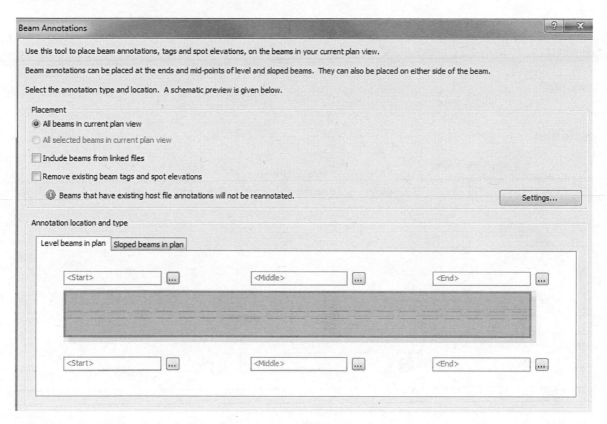

You can control the placement of beam annotations using the Beam Annotations tool on the Annotate ribbon.

Command Exercise

Exercise 5-1 – Create and Use Notes

Drawing Name: **notes.rvt**
Estimated Time to Completion: 15 Minutes

Scope

Copy and paste notes from Microsoft Word into a Legend.

Solution

1. 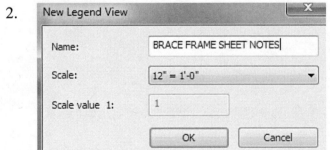 Activate the **View** ribbon.
   Select the **Legend** tool from the Create panel.

2. Type **BRACE FRAME SHEET NOTES.**
   Press **OK.**

New Legend View	
Name:	BRACE FRAME SHEET NOTES
Scale:	12" = 1'-0"
Scale value 1:	1

3. Legends
   BRACE FRAME SHEET NOTES

   The legend will be listed in the Project Browser.
   An empty view will open.

4. **A** Activate the **Annotate** ribbon.
   Text
   Select the **Text** tool from the Text panel.

5. Text
   1/4" Arial Title

   Select the **1/4"Arial Title** text style from the Type Selector list on the Properties pane.

6. **BRACE FRAME SHEET NOTES**
   Left click in the window to place the text.
   Type the title: **BRACE FRAME SHEET NOTES.**
   Left click to finish the text.

7. Text
   1/8" Arial

   Select the 1/8" Arial text from the Type Selector list on the Properties pane.

8. Left click to start the next text.

9. `File name: brace frame sheet notes` Locate the Word document in the class exercise folder named *brace frame sheet notes* and **Open** using Word.

10. Use the **Select All** tool or mouse over all of the text to select.

   - Select All
   - Select Objects
   - Select Text with Similar Formatting

11. Select the **Copy** tool or press **Ctl+C** to copy to the clipboard.

   - Home / Insert
   - Cut
   - Copy
   - Format Painter
   - Clipboard

12. Switch back to Revit.
   Activate the **Annotate** ribbon.
   Select the **Text** tool from the Text panel.

13. **BRACE FRAME** Place the text to start beneath the header text.

14. Select the **Paste from Clipboard** tool or type Ctl+V to paste the selected text.

   - Paste
   - Clipboard

15. **BRACE FRAME SHEET NOTES**
   1. SEE SHEETS S5.06 TO S5.07 FOR BRACE FRAME CONNECTION DETAILS.
   2. SEE X-SX.XX FOR COLUMN SPLICE DETAIL FOR FRAME COLUMNS.
   3. SEE X-SX.XX FOR BASE PLATE DETAILS AT FRAME COLUMNS.
   4. BRACE CONNECTION DETAIL CALLOUTS REFER TO DETAIL NUMBERS ON SHEETS S5.06, S5.06A, & S5.06B. S5.06, S5.06A, & S5.06B CORRESPOND TO STAR SEISMIC CLEVIS PIN CONNECTION, NIPPON CRUCIFORM BOLTED CONNECTION, AND CORE BRACE LUG-TYPE CONNECTION, RESPECTIVELY

   The notes will be pasted into the legend.
   Right click and select **Cancel** to exit the Text command.

16. Use the Numbers format on the ribbon to format the text.

   - None None
   - Bullets
   - Numbers

17. Close without saving.

Command Exercise

Exercise 5-2 – Create and Use Legends

Drawing Name: **legend.rvt**
Estimated Time to Completion: 45 Minutes

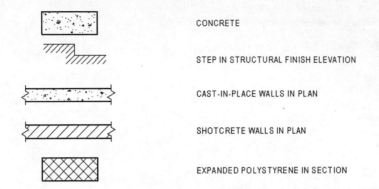

CONCRETE

STEP IN STRUCTURAL FINISH ELEVATION

CAST-IN-PLACE WALLS IN PLAN

SHOTCRETE WALLS IN PLAN

EXPANDED POLYSTYRENE IN SECTION

Scope

Create a Legend using Filled Region, Symbol and Detail Component
Place a Legend on a Sheet

Solution

1. Activate the **View** ribbon.
   Select **Legend→Legend**.

2. Type **MATERIALS**.

   Press **OK**.

3. The legend will be listed in the Project Browser.
   An empty view will open.

4. Activate the **Annotate** ribbon.
Select **Region→Filled** Region.

5. Set the Line Style to **Medium Lines** on the Line Style panel.
Select the **Rectangle** tool on the Draw panel.

6. In the Properties pane:
Set the Filled Region to **1 Concrete**.

7. Draw a rectangle **5′ x 1′ [1500 x 300 mm]**.

8. Select the **Green Check** on the Mode panel to finish the region.

9. Select the **Text** tool from the Text panel on the Annotate ribbon.

10. Set the text to 3/32″ Arial in the Properties pane.

11. CONCRETE Type **CONCRETE** next to the Filled Region.

12. Select the **Symbol** tool from the Symbol panel on the Annotate ribbon.

13. Slab Step Step Down — Select the **Slab Step Step Down** from the Properties pane Type Selector.

14. CONCRETE — Place the symbol below the filled region.

    STEP IN STRUCTURAL FINISH ELEVATION

15. A Text — Add text. Type **STEP IN STRUCTURAL FINISH ELEVATION**.

16. Region / Component / Filled Region — Activate the **Annotate** ribbon.
    Select **Region→Filled** Region.

17. Line Style: Medium Lines / Draw / Line Style — Set the Line Style to **Medium Lines** on the Line Style panel.
    Select the **Rectangle** tool on the Draw panel.

18. Properties / Filled region / Ortho Crosshatch — In the Properties pane:
    Set the Filled Region to **Ortho Crosshatch.**

19. [rectangle] — Draw a rectangle **5′ x 1′ [1500 x 300 mm]**.

20. X / ✓ / Mode — Select the **Green Check** on the Mode panel to finish the region.

21. A Text — Select the **Text** tool from the Text panel on the Annotate ribbon.

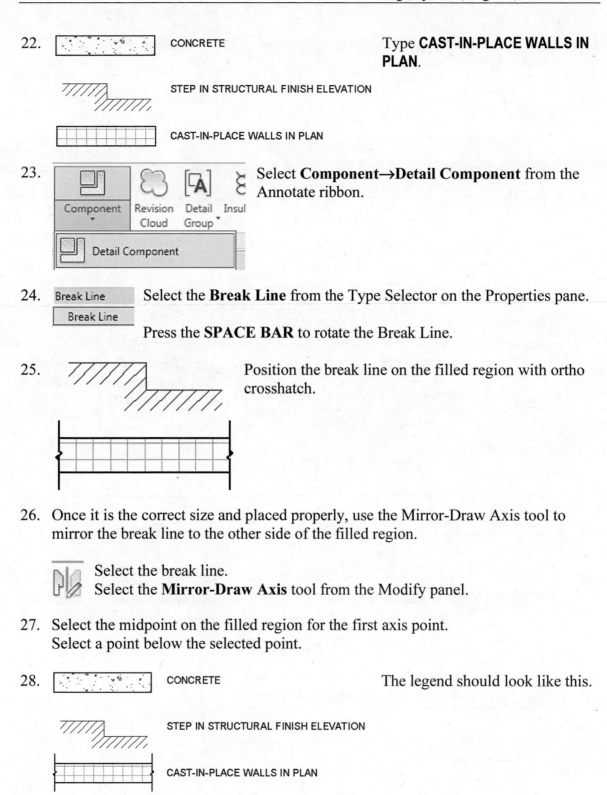

22. CONCRETE

    STEP IN STRUCTURAL FINISH ELEVATION

    CAST-IN-PLACE WALLS IN PLAN

    Type **CAST-IN-PLACE WALLS IN PLAN**.

23. Select **Component→Detail Component** from the Annotate ribbon.

    Component   Revision   Detail   Insul
                Cloud   Group

    Detail Component

24. Break Line

    Break Line

    Select the **Break Line** from the Type Selector on the Properties pane.

    Press the **SPACE BAR** to rotate the Break Line.

25. Position the break line on the filled region with ortho crosshatch.

26. Once it is the correct size and placed properly, use the Mirror-Draw Axis tool to mirror the break line to the other side of the filled region.

    Select the break line.
    Select the **Mirror-Draw Axis** tool from the Modify panel.

27. Select the midpoint on the filled region for the first axis point.
    Select a point below the selected point.

28. CONCRETE

    STEP IN STRUCTURAL FINISH ELEVATION

    CAST-IN-PLACE WALLS IN PLAN

    The legend should look like this.

29. CAST-IN-PLACE WALLS IN PLAN

    Window around the break lines, ortho crosshatch filled region, and text.

30. Use the Copy tool to copy the selected elements to a row below.

31. CONCRETE

    STEP IN STRUCTURAL FINISH ELEVATION

    CAST-IN-PLACE WALLS IN PLAN

    CAST-IN-PLACE WALLS IN PLAN

    Select the copied filled region.

32. 1 Gypsum Plaster

    1 Masonry - Brick

    Set the type to **1 Masonry - Brick** using the Type Selector in the Properties pane.

33. CONCRETE

    STEP IN STRUCTURAL FINISH ELEVATION

    CAST-IN-PLACE WALLS IN PLAN

    SHOTCRETE WALLS IN PLAN

    The filled region updates. Edit the text to: **SHOTCRETE WALLS IN PLAN**.

34. CONCRETE

    STEP IN STRUCTURAL FINISH ELEVATION

    CAST-IN-PLACE WALLS IN PLAN

    SHOTCRETE WALLS IN PLAN

    Copy the top filled region with the concrete pattern along with the text to the row below.

35. Filled region
    Diagonal Crosshatch

    Change the filled region to **Diagonal crosshatch** using the Type Selector in the Properties pane.

36. EXPANDED POLYSTYRENE IN SECTION

    Change the text to: **EXPANDED POLYSTYRENE IN SECTION**

37. CONCRETE

    The completed legend should look like this.

    STEP IN STRUCTURAL FINISH ELEVATION

    CAST-IN-PLACE WALLS IN PLAN

    SHOTCRETE WALLS IN PLAN

    EXPANDED POLYSTYRENE IN SECTION

38. Schedules/Quantities
    Sheets
    S000   New Sheet...
    S0   Type Properties...
                                NOTES

    Highlight **Sheets** in the Project Browser. Right click and select **New Sheet**.

39. Select titleblocks:

    C 17 x 22 Horizontal
    E1 30 x 42 Horizontal : E1 30x42 Horizontal
    None

    Select the **C 17 x 22 Horizontal** title block. Press **OK**.

40. Sheets (all)
    S.1 - Unnamed

    The sheet will appear under Sheets in the Project Browser.

41.
    | Sheet Number | S0.5 |
    | Sheet Name | GENERAL NOTES |
    | Sheet Issue Date | 08/30/10 |

    Scoll down in the Properties pane: Type **GENERAL NOTES** in the Sheet Name field.

42.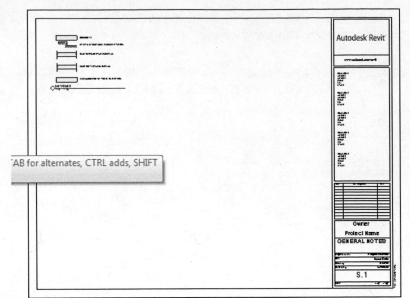

Activate the sheet you created.
Drag and drop the **MATERIALS** legend on to the new sheet.

43. Viewport No Title   Set the Viewport to **Viewport No Title** using the Type Selector on the Properties pane.

44. The legend no longer displays a title.

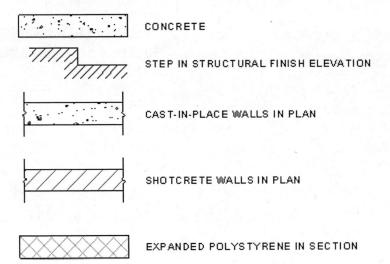

CONCRETE

STEP IN STRUCTURAL FINISH ELEVATION

CAST-IN-PLACE WALLS IN PLAN

SHOTCRETE WALLS IN PLAN

EXPANDED POLYSTYRENE IN SECTION

45. Close without saving.

Command Exercise

Exercise 5-3 – Use Schedule to Change Types

Drawing Name: **schedule1.rvt**
Estimated Time to Completion: 5 Minutes

Scope

Use Schedule to change types.

Solution

1. Schedules/Quantities
   QTO - FRAMING

   Locate the **QTO - FRAMING** Schedule under Schedule/ Quantities in the Project Browser.

   Double click to open the view.

2.

QTO - FRAMING		
Family	Type	Count
Concrete-Rectangular	12 x 24	3
HSS-Hollow Structural	HSS6x6x.250	8
W-Wide Flange	W12x26	34
W-Wide Flange1	W12x26	24
W-Wide Flange	W16X26	30
W-Wide Flange1	W18x35	29
W-Wide Flange	W24x55	4

   Look at the third and fourth rows with W12x26 Type. Note they are both using Wide Flange profiles. It makes more economic sense to switch to the same type.

3.

QTO - FRAMING		
Family	Type	Count
Concrete-Rectangular	12 x 24	3
HSS-Hollow Structural	HSS6x6x.250	8
W-Wide Flange	W12x26	34
W-Wide Flange1	W12x26	24
Concrete-Rectangular Beam	6	30
HSS-Hollow Structural Section	5	29
L-Angle	5	4
W-Wide Flange		
W-Wide Flange1		

   If you click in the column for the Family for the W-Wide Flange1 for the W12 x 26, you will see a drop-down list of all the families used in the schedule.

   Select **Wide Flange** from the list instead of **Wide Flange1**.

4.

QTO - FRAMING		
Family	Type	Count
Concrete-Rectangular	12 x 24	3
HSS-Hollow Structural	HSS6x6x.250	8
W-Wide Flange	W12x26	58
W-Wide Flange	W16X26	30
W-Wide Flange1	W18x35	29
W-Wide Flange	W24x55	4

   The schedule updates with the new quantities and the remaining columns update as well.

5. Close without saving.

Command Exercise

Exercise 5-4 – Export a Schedule

Drawing Name: **schedule1.rvt**
Estimated Time to Completion: 10 Minutes

Scope

Export a schedule

Solution

1. Locate the **QTO - FRAMING** Schedule under Schedule/Quantities in the Project Browser.

   Double click to open the view.

2. 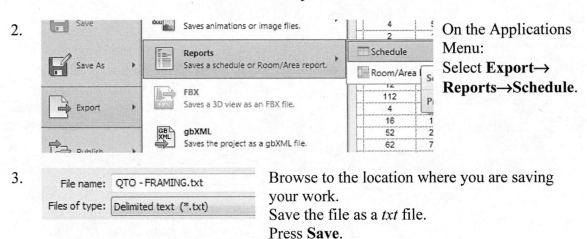 On the Applications Menu:
   Select **Export→ Reports→Schedule**.

3. File name: QTO - FRAMING.txt
   Files of type: Delimited text (*.txt)

   Browse to the location where you are saving your work.
   Save the file as a *txt* file.
   Press **Save**.

4.  Enable **Export column headers**.
   Enable **Multiple rows, as formatted**.
   Set the Field delimiter as **tab**.

   Press **OK**.

5. Launch Excel.

6. 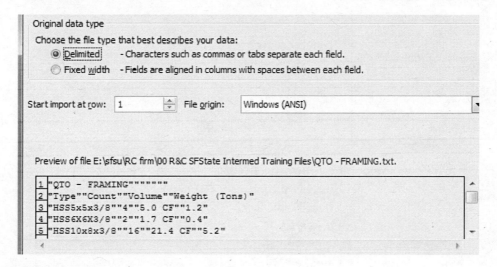 In Excel:

Select **Open**.

7. | Text Files ▾ | Set the file type to **Text Files**.

Otherwise, you won't see the exported schedule.

8. File name: QTO - FRAMING Browse to the location where you saved the file. Press **Open**.

9. A dialog will appear which will preview how your spreadsheet will be formatted.

Original data type

Choose the file type that best describes your data:
- ⊙ Delimited   - Characters such as commas or tabs separate each field.
- ○ Fixed width - Fields are aligned in columns with spaces between each field.

Start import at row: 1   File origin: Windows (ANSI)

Preview of file E:\sfsu\RC firm\00 R&C SFState Intermed Training Files\QTO - FRAMING.txt.

```
1 "QTO - FRAMING"""""""
2 "Type""Count""Volume""Weight (Tons)"
3 "HSS5x5x3/8""4""5.0 CF""1.2"
4 "HSS6X6X3/8""2""1.7 CF""0.4"
5 "HSS10x8x3/8""16""21.4 CF""5.2"
```

Press **Finish**.

10.

	A	B	C	D	E
1	QTO - FRAMING				
2	Type	Count	Volume	Weight (Tons)	
3	HSS5x5x3/8	4	5.0 CF	1.2	
4	HSS6X6X3/8	2	1.7 CF	0.4	
5	HSS10x8x3/8	16	21.4 CF	5.2	
6	HSS12x8x1/2	7	34.6 CF	8.5	
7	HSS12x8x3/8	1	1.8 CF	0.4	
8	W8x10	12	1.4 CF	0.3	
9	W12x19	112	22.2 CF	5.4	
10	W12x26	4	1.3 CF	0.3	
11	W12x35	16	16.5 CF	4	
12	W14x22	52	27.6 CF	6.8	
13	W16x26	62	70.4 CF	17.2	
14	W16x31	29	39.1 CF	9.6	

Your schedule is imported into Excel.

Close without saving.

Command Exercise

Exercise 5-5 – Create and Use a Sheet List

Drawing Name: **sheet_list.rvt**
Estimated Time to Completion: 15 Minutes

Scope

Create a Sheet List
Place on a Sheet

Solution

1. 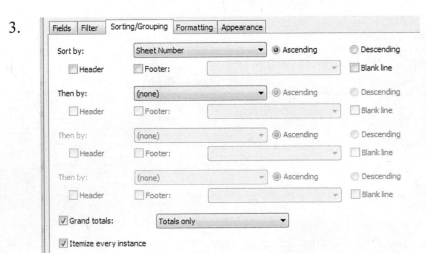 Activate the **View** ribbon.
   Select **Schedules** →**Sheet List** from the Create panel.

2. Select the following fields:

   Sheet Number
   Sheet Name
   Drawn By
   Approved By
   Checked By
   Sheet Issue Date

   (Scheduled fields (in order):)
   Sheet Number
   Sheet Name
   Drawn By
   Approved By
   Checked By
   Sheet Issue Date

3. Enable **Grand Totals** and select **Totals only**.
   Enable **Itemize every instance**.
   Select the Sorting/ Grouping tab.
   Sort by **Sheet Number**.

4.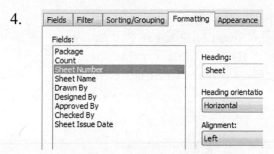

Select the **Formatting** tab.
Set the Heading for Sheet Number to **Sheet**.

5.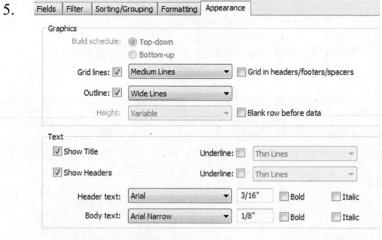

Select the **Appearance** tab.
Enable **Grid Lines**. Set the lines to **Medium Lines**.
Enable **Outline**. Set the lines to **Wide Lines**.
Enable **Show Title**.
Enable **Show Headers**.
Set the Header text to **Arial 3/16″**.
Set the Body text to **Arial Narrow 1/8″**.
Press **OK**.

6.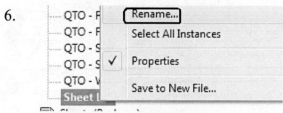

Locate the Sheet List in the Browser.
Right click and select **Rename**.

7.

Type **0 - Sheet List**.
Press **OK**.

8.

Highlight **Sheets** in the Project Browser.
Right click and select **New Sheet**.

9.

Select the Project Titleblock_finish title block.
Press **OK**.

10.

Approved By	Approver
Designed By	Designer
Checked By	Checker
Sheet Number	S-0.0
Sheet Name	SHEET LIST
Sheet Issue Date	12/25/10
Appears In Sheet List	☐
Revisions on Sheet	Edit...
Other	
File Path	
Drawn By	Author
Guide Grid	<None>

In the Properties pane:
Set the Sheet Number to **S-0.00**.
Type **SHEET LIST** for the Sheet Name.
Disable **Appears in Sheet List**.

Press the **Apply** button.

11.
⊞ Sheets (Package)
└─ S000
　　└─ **S0.00 - SHEET LIST** ◄──
　　└─ S0.01 - GENERAL NOTES

The sheet list sheet is listed in the project browser.

12.
⊞ Schedules/Quantities
　└─ **0 - Sheet List** ◄──

Locate the sheet list under Schedules/Quantities.
Drag and drop it onto the sheet.

13. Use the grips to set the column widths.

Command Exercise

Exercise 5-6 – Create a View List

Drawing Name: **view_list.rvt**
Estimated Time to Completion: 10 Minutes

Scope

Create a View List

Solution

1. 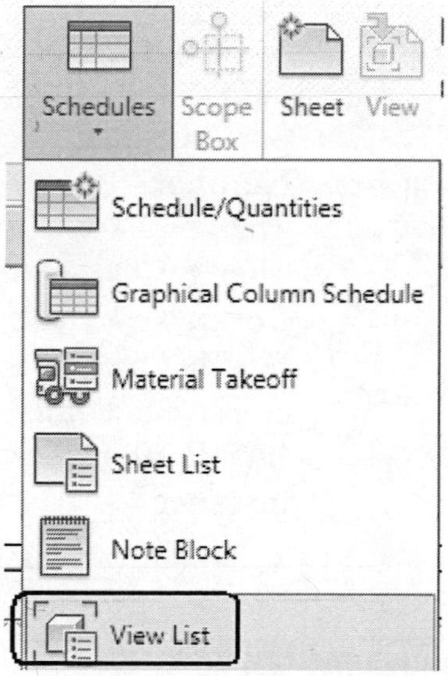 Activate the **View** ribbon.
   Select **Schedules→View List** from the Create panel.

2. 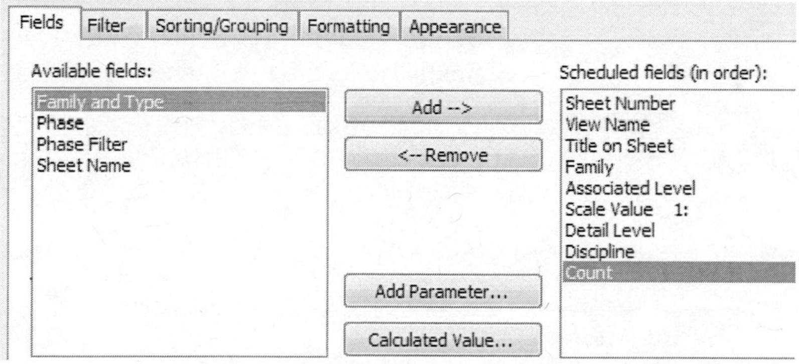 Select the following fields:
   - Sheet Number
   - View Name
   - Title on Sheet
   - Family
   - Associated Level
   - Scale Value 1:
   - Detail Level
   - Discipline
   - Count

3.

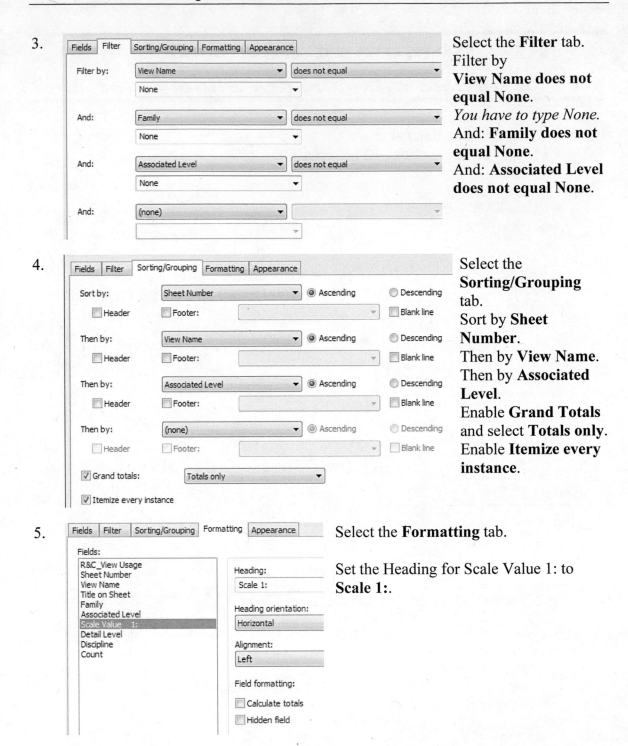

Select the **Filter** tab.
Filter by
View Name does not equal None.
You have to type None.
And: **Family does not equal None.**
And: **Associated Level does not equal None.**

4.

Select the **Sorting/Grouping** tab.
Sort by **Sheet Number.**
Then by **View Name.**
Then by **Associated Level.**
Enable **Grand Totals** and select **Totals only.**
Enable **Itemize every instance.**

5.

Select the **Formatting** tab.

Set the Heading for Scale Value 1: to **Scale 1:.**

6.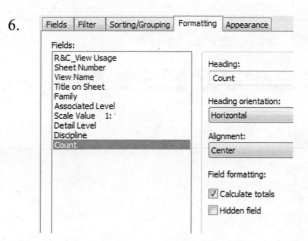

Highlight **Count**.
Enable **Calculate totals**.

7.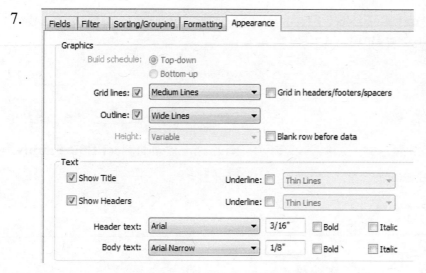

Select the **Appearance** tab.
Enable **Grid Lines**. Set the lines to **Medium Lines**.
Enable **Outline**. Set the lines to **Wide Lines**.
Enable **Show Title**.
Enable **Show Headers**.
Set the Header text to **Arial 3/16″**.
Set the Body text to **Arial Narrow 1/8″**.
Press **OK**.

8.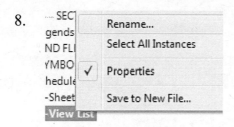

Locate the View List in the Browser.
Right click and select **Rename**.

9.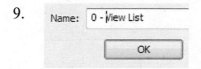

Type **0 - View List**.
Press **OK**.

Command Exercise

Exercise 5-7 – Create a Custom Tag

Drawing Name: **custom_tag.rvt**
Estimated Time to Completion: 10 Minutes

Scope

Create a Custom Tag

Solution

1.   Activate **FIRST FLR.** under the Structural Plans category in the Project Browser.

2.   Select a Structural Framing Tag on the D1 grid.
Right click and select **Edit Family**.

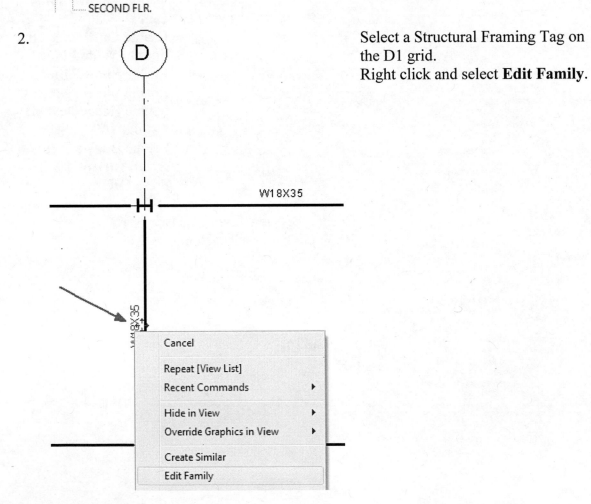

3.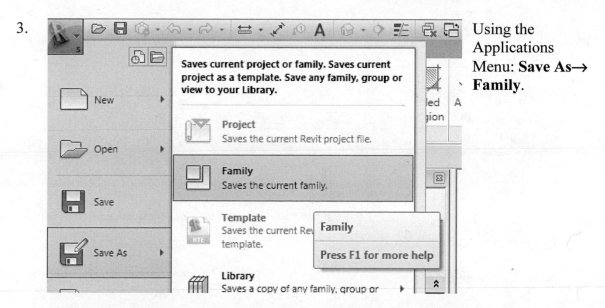

Using the Applications Menu: **Save As→ Family**.

4. File name: Structural Framing Tag with Elevation.rfa

Files of type: Family Files (*.rfa)

Edit the name so it is **Structural Framing Tag with Elevation**. Press **Save**.

5.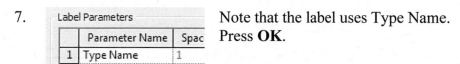

Select the text so it highlights.

6.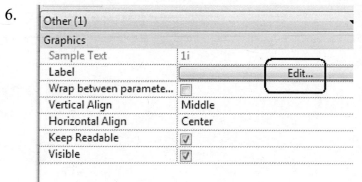

On the Properties pane: Select the **Edit** button in the Label field.

7. Label Parameters

	Parameter Name	Spac
1	Type Name	1

Note that the label uses Type Name. Press **OK**.

8. Label

Activate the **Create** ribbon.
Select the **Label** tool on the Text panel.
Left click below the rectangle in the view.

9. URL
z-Direction Offset Value

Scroll down and select **z-direction Offset Value**.

10. Select the **Add** tool in the middle of the dialog.

11.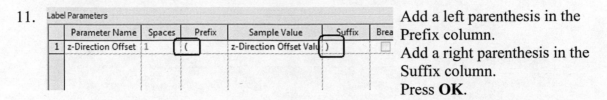

    Add a left parenthesis in the Prefix column.
    Add a right parenthesis in the Suffix column.
    Press **OK**.

12. | 1i |
    |---|

    (z-Direction Offset Value)

    Adjust the position of the label so it appears as shown.

13. Save the file and close.

Command Exercise

Exercise 5-8 – Using a Custom Tag

Drawing Name: **custom_tag.rvt**
Estimated Time to Completion: 5 Minutes

Scope

Load a custom tag.

Solution

1.   Structural Plans
     BASEMENT
     FIRST FLR.
     ROOF
     SECOND FLR.

   Activate **FIRST FLR.** under the Structural Plans category in the Project Browser.

2.   Load Family | Load as Group
     Load from Library

   Activate the **Insert** ribbon.
   Select **Load Family** from the Load from Library panel.

3.   File name: Structural Framing Tag with Elevation
     Files of type: All Supported Files (*.rfa, *.adsk)

   Locate the *Structural Framing Tag with Elevation.*
   Press **Open**.

4.   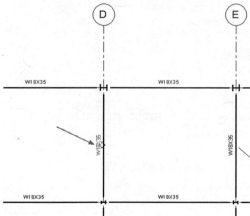 Select the tag indicated.

5.   Structural Framing Tag with Elevation
     Boxed
     Standard
     Structural Framing Tag   Boxed

   Select the **Structural Framing Tag with Elevation Boxed** from the Type Selector on the Properties pane.

6.   The tag updates with the Z-elevation offset information.

Command Exercise

Exercise 5-9 – Framing Schedule

Drawing Name: **parts list.rvt**
Estimated Time to Completion: 45 Minutes

Scope

Create a Framing Schedule

A common complaint among structural users is the necessity to include items such as bolts and stiffeners in schedules without adding them to the model – which would be extremely time-intensive. One work-around would be to export the schedule, add the missing items, and then import the revised Excel spreadsheet. However, Revit does not currently allow users to import Excel spreadsheets. There are add-ins and utilities available to allow Excel-linking, but they cost money. Another method would be to create a project and insert the missing elements into the project and then link it to the active project. You could create a project with just the stiffeners and hardware for each schedule and then re-use the projects as needed.

Solution

1.
   - Views (all)
     - Structural Plans
       - BASEMENT
       - FIRST FLR.
       - ROOF
       - SECOND FLR.
     - 3D Views
       - {3D}

   Activate the **3D** view.

2. Select the structural member indicated.

3.

Dimensions		⌃
Length	16' 5 45/256"	
Volume	0.81 CF	
Identity Data		⌃
Comments		
Mark	C3A	
Phasing		⌃

In the Properties pane:

Scroll down to the Identity Data area.
Note that you can assign a Mark to each structural member.

4.   Activate the Insert ribbon.

Select **Link Revit**.

5.   Locate the **C3-DETAILS** project.
     Press **Open**.

File name: C3-DETAILS
Files of type: RVT Files (*.rvt)
Positioning: Auto - Center to Center

This project has a couple of stiffeners and some bolts loaded into it.

6.   Zoom into where the link is loaded.
     Select it.

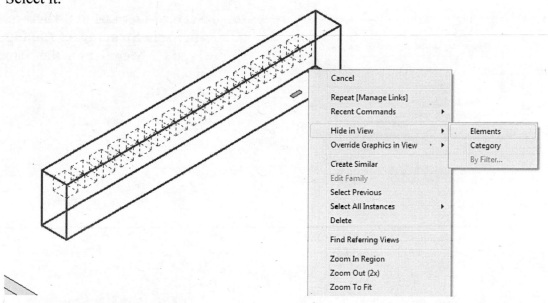

7.   Select the **Bind Link** tool on the ribbon.

This will convert the linked file to a group.

8.   Press **OK**.

Bind Link Options

Include
☑ Attached Details
☐ Levels
☐ Grids

Note: Checking Levels and Grids will create additional uniquely-named levels and grids in addition to those presently in the project.

OK   Cancel

9. 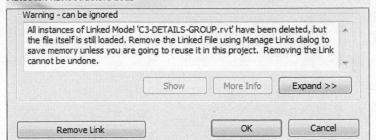 Select **Remove Link**.

Autodesk Revit Structure 2013

Warning - can be ignored

All instances of Linked Model 'C3-DETAILS-GROUP.rvt' have been deleted, but the file itself is still loaded. Remove the Linked File using Manage Links dialog to save memory unless you are going to reuse it in this project. Removing the Link cannot be undone.

Show   More Info   Expand >>

Remove Link   OK   Cancel

10. Schedules ▾   Sheet
    Schedule/Quantities

    Activate the View ribbon.
    Select **Schedules→Schedules/Quantities**.

11. Filter list: Structure

    Category:
    — Landings
    — Runs
    — Supports
    — Structural Columns
    — Structural Connections
    — Structural Fabric Reinforcem.
    — Structural Foundations
    — Structural Framing
    ⊟ — Structural Internal Loads
        — Internal Area Loads
        — Internal Line Loads
        — Internal Point Loads

    Name:
    C3 Members
    ◉ Schedule building components
    ○ Schedule keys
       Key name:

    Phase:
    New Construction

    Set the Filter List to **Structure**.
    Highlight **Structural Framing**.
    Type **C3 Members** in the Name field.
    Press **OK**.

12. Scheduled fields (in order):
    Count
    Mark
    Description
    Cut Length

    Add the following fields:
    - Count
    - Mark
    - Description
    - Cut Length

13. Select available fields from:
    Structural Material

    In the Select available fields from:
    Select **Structural Material** from the down-down list.

14. Fields | Filter | Sorting/Grouping | Formatting | Appearance

    Available fields:
    Structural Material: Material Type
    Structural Material: Minimum tensile strength
    Structural Material: Minimum yield stress
    Structural Material: Poisson ratio X
    Structural Material: Poisson ratio Y
    Structural Material: Poisson ratio Z
    Structural Material: Property Set Name
    Structural Material: Reduction factor for shear
    Structural Material: Resistance calculation strength
    Structural Material: Shear modulus X
    Structural Material: Shear modulus Y
    Structural Material: Shear modulus Z

    Add the **Structural Material: Property Set Name** to the list of Scheduled Fields.

15. 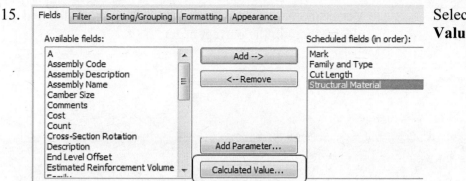 Select the **Calculated Value** button.

16. 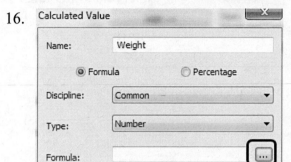 Type **Weight** in the Name field.
Set the Type to **Number**.
Select the **...** button.

17. 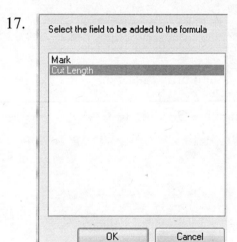 Select **Cut Length** and press **OK**.

18.  In the Formula field, type:
Cut Length/1*490.

This formula calculates pounds (lbs) units.
To calculate metric tonnes use:
*Cut Length/1*1000*

Press **OK**.

19. 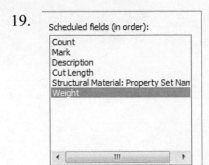 Verify that you have selected the necessary fields and placed them in the correct order.

20.  Select the Filter tab.
Set Filter by: to **Mark**
Contains
Type **C3**.

The schedule will now include only members with C3 as part of their mark value.

21.  Select the Sorting/Grouping tab.
Set Sort by: **Mark**.

The schedule will now sort by the Mark value.

22. 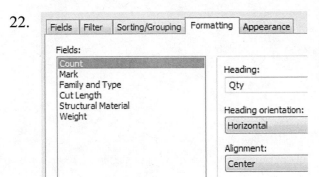 Select the Formatting tab.
Highlight **Count**.
Change the Heading to **Qty**.
Set the Alignment to **Center**.

23. 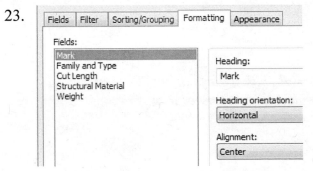 Highlight **Mark**.
Set the Alignment to **Center**.

24.

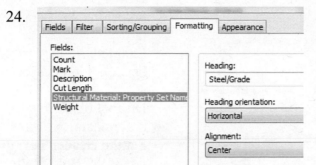

Highlight **Structural Material: Property Name Set**.
Change the Heading to **Steel/Grade**.
Set the Alignment to **Center**.

25.

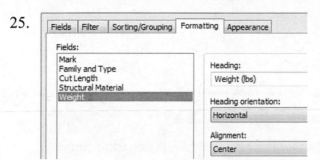

Highlight **Weight**.
Set the Heading to **Weight (lbs)**.
Set the Alignment to **Center**.

26.

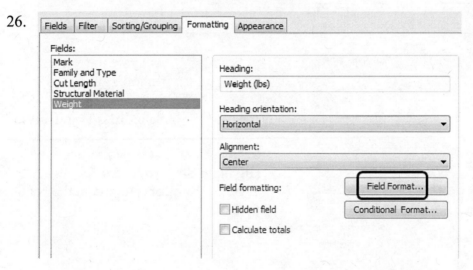

Select the **Field Format** button.

27.

Uncheck **Use default settings**.
Set the Units to **Fixed**.
Set the Rounding to **1 decimal place**.
Press **OK**.

28.

Select the Appearance tab.
Enable Grid in headers/footers/spacers.
Disable blank row before data.
Set the Header Text to **Arial ¼″ Bold Italic**.
Set the Body Text to **Arial Narrow, 1/8″ Italic**.
Press **OK**.

29.

C3 Members					
Qty	Mark	Description	Cut Length	Steel/Grade	Weight (lbs)
1	C3A	W12x26	15' - 1"	ASTM A992	7392.0
1	C3B	W12x26	15' - 8 1/2"	ASTM A992	7699.5
1	C3C	W12x26	15' - 1"	ASTM A992	7392.0

A preview of the schedule appears.

30.

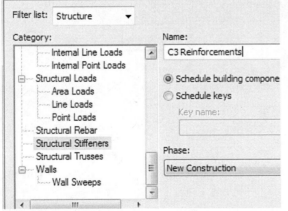

Activate the View ribbon.
Select **Schedules→ Schedules/Quantities**.

31.

Filter list: Structure

Category:
Internal Line Loads
Internal Point Loads
Structural Loads
Area Loads
Line Loads
Point Loads
Structural Rebar
Structural Stiffeners
Structural Trusses
Walls
Wall Sweeps

Name:
C3 Reinforcements

◉ Schedule building compone
◯ Schedule keys
Key name:

Phase:
New Construction

Set the Filter List to **Structure**.
Highlight **Structural Stiffeners**.
Type **C3 Reinforcements** in the Name field.
Press **OK**.

32.

Scheduled fields (in order):

Count
Mark
Description
Length
Material

Select the following fields:
- Count
- Mark
- Description
- Length
- Material

33.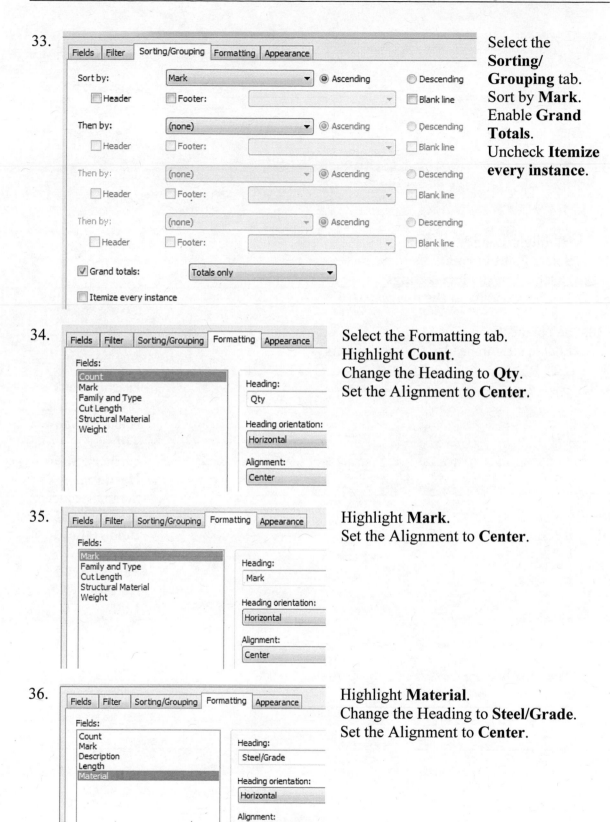

Select the **Sorting/ Grouping** tab. Sort by **Mark**. Enable **Grand Totals**. Uncheck **Itemize every instance**.

34.

Select the Formatting tab. Highlight **Count**. Change the Heading to **Qty**. Set the Alignment to **Center**.

35.

Highlight **Mark**. Set the Alignment to **Center**.

36.

Highlight **Material**. Change the Heading to **Steel/Grade**. Set the Alignment to **Center**.

37.

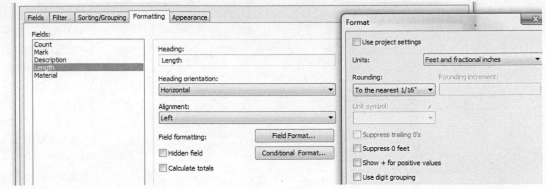

Highlight **Length**.
Select **Field Format**.
Disable **Use project settings**.
Set the rounding **to the nearest 1/16″**.

38. Select the Appearance tab.
Enable Grid in headers/footers/spacers.

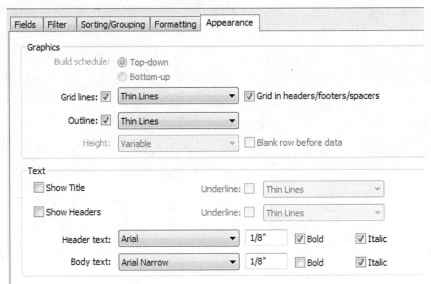

Disable blank row before data.
Uncheck **Show Title**.
Uncheck **Show Headers**.
Set the Header Text to **Arial ¼″ Bold Italic**.
Set the Body Text to **Arial Narrow, 1/8″ Italic**.
Press **OK**.

39. The schedule appears.

14		3/4″ DIA THREADED STUDS	0′ - 3 1/2″	Steel ASTM A36
1	E6	3/8″ X 4″ PLATE	0′ - 11″	Steel ASTM A36
1	S6	3/8″ X 4″ PLATE	0′ - 11″	Steel ASTM A36

40.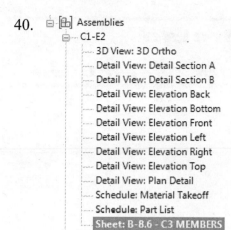

In the Project Browser:
Scroll down to the Assemblies and locate **C1-E2**.
Activate the **Sheet**.

41. Place the Plan Detail on the sheet.

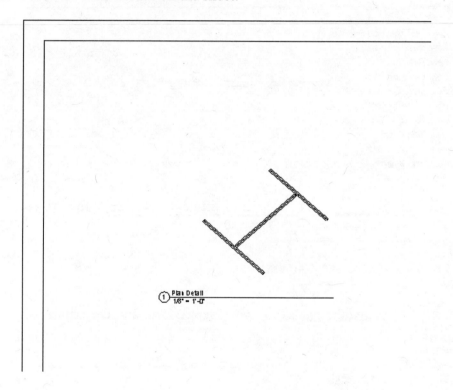

42.

C3 Members					
Qty	Mark	Description	Cut Length	Steel/Grade	Weight (lbs)
1	C3A	W13 x3 6	15' - 1"	ASTM A993	7393.0
1	C3B	W13 x3 6	15' - 8 1/2"	ASTM A993	7699.5
1	C3C	W13 x3 6	15' - 1"	ASTM A993	7393.0
14		3/4" DIA THREADED STUDS	0' - 3 1/2"	Steel ASTM A36	
1	E6	3/8" X 4" PLATE	0' - 11"	Steel ASTM A36	
36	36	3/8" X 4" PLATE	0' - 11"	Steel ASTM A36	

Drag and place the C3 Members schedule on the sheet.
Drag and drop the C3 Reinforcements schedule below it.
Use the grips to adjust the column widths.

43. Save as *ex5-9.rvt*.

Command Exercise

Exercise 5-10 – Parts List in Assemblies

Drawing Name: **assembly parts list.rvt**
Estimated Time to Completion: 40 Minutes

Scope

Modify an Assembly Parts List

1. 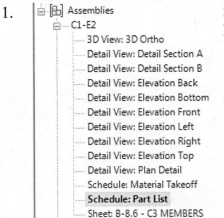 Scroll down the Project Browser and locate the Part List under the C1-E2 assembly.

2. 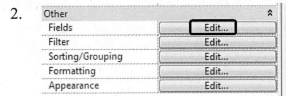 Select **Edit** next to Fields in the Project Browser.

3. Adjust the list so you see Count, Mark, and Description.

    Scheduled fields (in order):

    Count
    Mark
    Description

4. 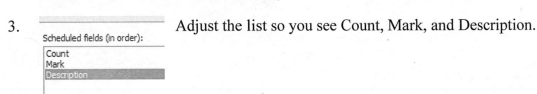 Select **Add Parameter**.

5.

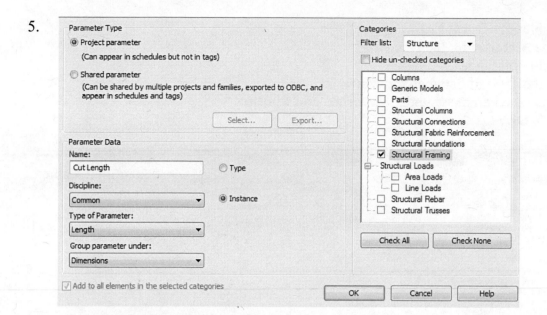

Enable **Structural Framing**.
Type **Cut Length** for the Name.
Enable **Instance**.
Set the Type of Parameter to **Length**.
Group the Parameter under **Dimensions**.
Press **OK**.

6.

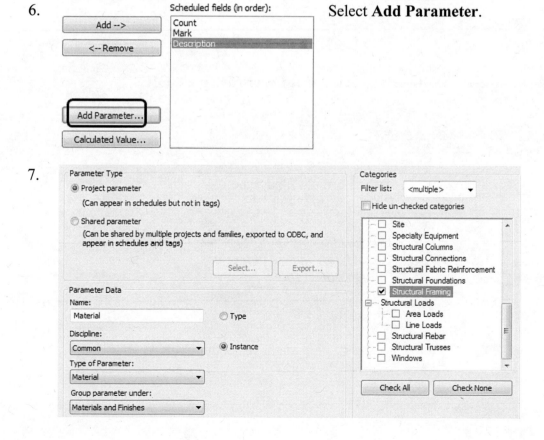

Select **Add Parameter**.

7.

Enable **Structural Framing**.
Type **Material** for the Name.
Enable **Instance**.
Set the Type of Parameter to **Material**.
Group the Parameter under **Materials and Finishes**.
Press **OK**.

8. 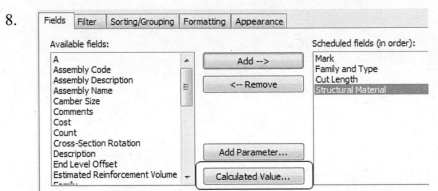 Select the
Calculated Value
button.

9. 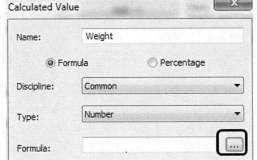 Type **Weight** in the Name field.
Set the Type to **Number**.
Select the **...** button.

10. Select **Cut Length** and press **OK**.

11.  In the Formula field, type:
Cut Length/1*490.

This formula calculates pounds (lbs) units.
To calculate metric tonnes use:
*Cut Length/1*1000*

Press **OK**.

12. Verify that you have set the fields as shown.

13.

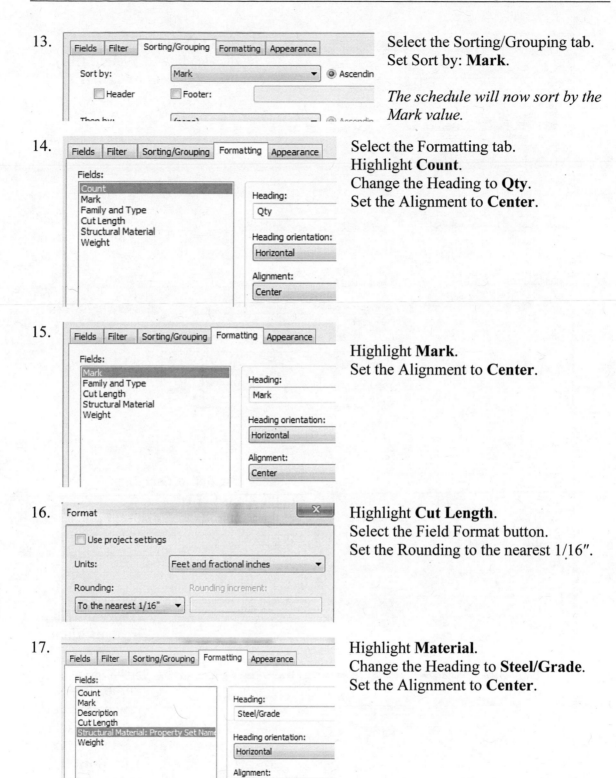

Select the Sorting/Grouping tab.
Set Sort by: **Mark**.

The schedule will now sort by the Mark value.

14.

Select the Formatting tab.
Highlight **Count**.
Change the Heading to **Qty**.
Set the Alignment to **Center**.

15.

Highlight **Mark**.
Set the Alignment to **Center**.

16.

Highlight **Cut Length**.
Select the Field Format button.
Set the Rounding to the nearest 1/16″.

17.

Highlight **Material**.
Change the Heading to **Steel/Grade**.
Set the Alignment to **Center**.

18.

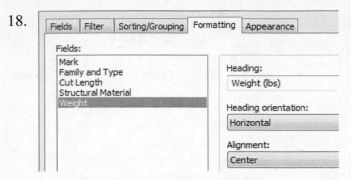

Highlight **Weight**.
Set the Heading to **Weight (lbs)**.
Set the Alignment to **Center**.

19.

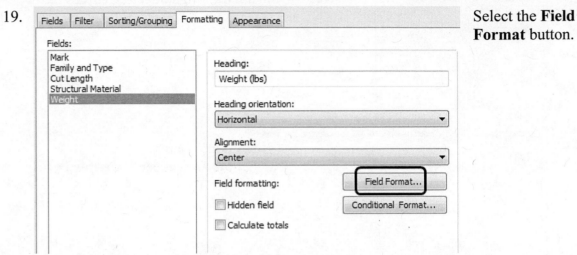

Select the **Field Format** button.

20.

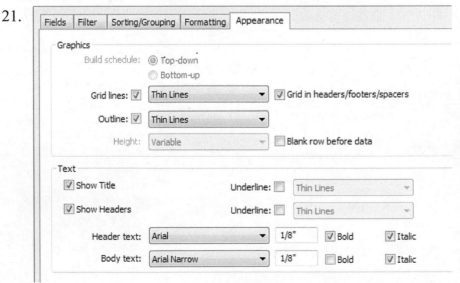

Uncheck **Use default settings**.
Set the Units to **Fixed**.
Set the Rounding to **1 decimal place**.
Press **OK**.

21.

Select the Appearance tab.
Enable Grid in headers/footers/spacers.
Disable blank row before data.
Set the Header Text to **Arial 1/8″ Bold Italic**.
Set the Body Text to **Arial Narrow, 1/8″ Italic**.
Press **OK**.

22. A preview of the schedule appears.

Part List					
Qty	Mark	Description	Cut Length	Steel/Grade	Weight (lbs)
1	C2A				
1	C2B				
1	C2C				

There is a lot of missing information, but we can fix that.

23. ⊟ 🔲 Assemblies   Activate the 3D View under the assembly.
     ⊟ C1-E2
        3D View: 3D Ortho
        Detail View: Detail Section A
        Detail View: Detail Section B
        Detail View: Elevation Back

24. 🗔 Edit Assembly   Select the assembly so it highlights.
     Select **Edit Assembly** from the ribbon.

25. 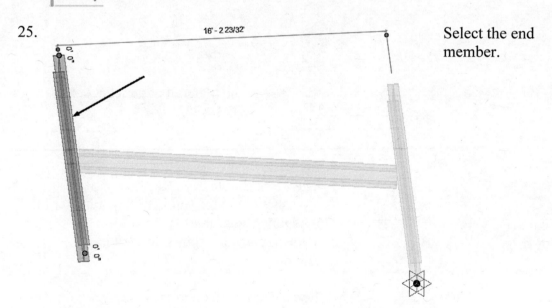 Select the end member.

26.
Dimensions		⌃
Length	16' 8 253/256"	
Volume	0.86 CF	
Cut Length	16' 8 253/256"	
Identity Data		⌃
Assembly Name	C1-E2	
Comments		
Mark	C2A	
Phasing		⌄

Scroll down the Properties pane.
The Mark should be **C2A**.
You should see the Cut Length parameter in the Dimensions area.
Type in the value shown in the Length parameter.

27.
Materials and Finishes		⌃
Structural Material	Metal - Steel - ASTM A992	
Material	Metal - Steel - ASTM A992	

In the Material parameter, select ASTM A992.

28. 🔲 Edit Type   Select **Edit Type**.

29.

Identity Data	
Assembly Code	B10
Keynote	
Model	
Manufacturer	
Type Comments	
URL	
Description	W12x26
Assembly Description	Superstructure

Type **W12x26** in the Description field.
Press **OK**.

Left click anywhere in the display window to release the selection.

30.

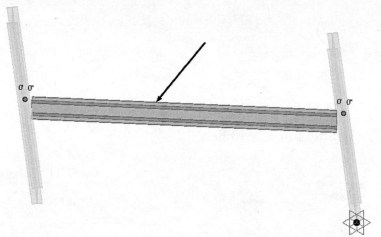

Select the middle bar.

31.

Materials and Finishes		⊗
Structural Material	Metal - Steel - ASTM A992	
Material	Metal - Steel - ASTM A992	
Structural		⊗

In the Material parameter, select ASTM A992.

32.

Enable Analytical Model	☑
Dimensions	
Length	16' 5 45/256"
Volume	0.85 CF
Cut Length	16' 5 45/256"
Identity Data	
Assembly Name	C1-E2
Comments	
Mark	C2B
Phasing	

Scroll down the Properties pane.
The Mark should be **C2B**.
You should see the Cut Length parameter in the Dimensions area.
Type in the value shown in the Length parameter.

Left click anywhere in the display window to release the selection.

33.

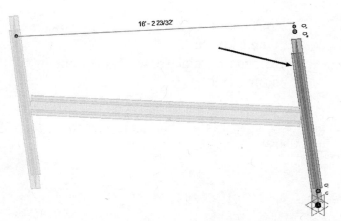

Select the end bar on the right.

34.

Materials and Finishes		☆
Structural Material	Metal - Steel - ASTM A992	
Material	Metal - Steel - ASTM A992	

In the Material parameter, select ASTM A992.

35.

Dimensions	
Length	16' 1 47/128"
Volume	0.81 CF
Cut Length	16' 1 47/128"
Identity Data	
Assembly Name	C1-E2
Comments	
Mark	C2C
Phasing	

Scroll down the Properties pane.
The Mark should be **C2C**.
You should see the Cut Length parameter in the Dimensions area.
Type in the value shown in the Length parameter.

Left click anywhere in the display window to release the selection.

36.

Select **Finish** from the Edit Assembly toolbar.

37.

Part List					
Qty	Mark	Description	Cut Length	Steel/Grade	Weight (lbs)
1	C2A	W12x26	16' - 9"	Metal - Steel - ASTM A992	8207.0
1	C2B	W12x26	16' - 5 3/16"	Metal - Steel - ASTM A992	8051.3
1	C2C	W12x26	16' - 1 3/8"	Metal - Steel - ASTM A992	7895.8

Activate the Part List and you see that it has updated.

38.

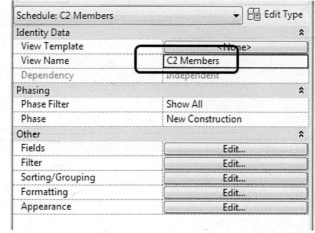

In the Properties pane:
Change the View Name to **C2 Members**.

Note that the title of the Part List updates.

39.

Right click on the **C1-E2** assembly and select **Create Assembly Views**.

40.

View Scale	
Scale:	3/4" = 1'-0" ▼
Scale Value:	16

Views to Create

☐ 3D Ortho	Check All
☐ Plan	Check None
☐ Section A	
☐ Section B	
☐ Elevation Top	
☐ Elevation Bottom	
☐ Elevation Right	
☐ Elevation Left	
☐ Elevation Front	
☐ Elevation Back	
☐ Part List	
☐ Material Takeoff	
☑ Sheet	B 11 x 17 Horizontal ▼

Set the Scale to ¾″ = 1′-0″.
Select **Check None** to uncheck the list of views.
Enable **Sheet**.
Select **B 11 x 17 Horizontal** under the sheet lists.

Press **OK**.

41.

Current Revision	
Approved By	Approver
Designed By	Designer
Checked By	Checker
Sheet Number	B-8.7
Sheet Name	C2 Members ▼
Sheet Issue Date	10/25/12
Appears In Sheet List	☑
Revisions on Sheet	Edit...

In the Properties pane:
Change the sheet name to **C2 Members**.

42.

⊟ 🏠 Assemblies
  ⊟ C1-E2
    ├─ 3D View: 3D Ortho
    ├─ Detail View: Detail Section A
    ├─ Detail View: Detail Section B
    ├─ Detail View: Elevation Back
    ├─ Detail View: Elevation Bottom
    ├─ Detail View: Elevation Front
    ├─ Detail View: Elevation Left
    ├─ Detail View: Elevation Right
    ├─ Detail View: Elevation Top
    ├─ Detail View: Plan Detail
    └─ Schedule: C2 Members

Drag and drop the Plan Detail view onto the sheet.

43.

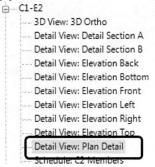

① Plan Detail
  1/8" = 1'-0"

Add the C2 Members Part List to the Sheet.

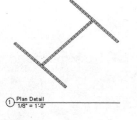

C2 Members					
Qty	Mark	Description	Cut Length	Steel/Grade	Weight (lbs)
1	C2A	W12x26	16'-9"	Metal - Steel - ASTM A992	8207.0
1	C2B	W12x26	16'-5 3/16"	Metal - Steel - ASTM A992	8051.3
1	C2C	W12x26	16'-1 3/8"	Metal - Steel - ASTM A992	7895.8

44. Save as *ex5-10.rvt*.

Command Exercise

Exercise 5-11 – Material Take-Offs

Drawing Name: **material take-off.rvt**
Estimated Time to Completion: 40 Minutes

Scope

Create a material take-off schedule

Material take-off schedules are used for estimating construction and labor costs

1. 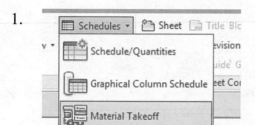 Activate the View ribbon.

   Select **Schedules→Material Takeoff**.

2. 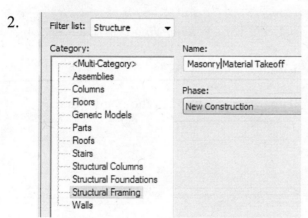 Change the Name to **Masonry Material Takeoff**.
   Highlight **Structural Framing**.

   Press **OK**.

3. 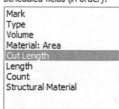 Select the following fields:
   - Mark
   - Type
   - Volume
   - Material: Area
   - Cut Length
   - Length
   - Count
   - Structural Material

4. [Calculated Value...] Select the Calculated Value button.

5.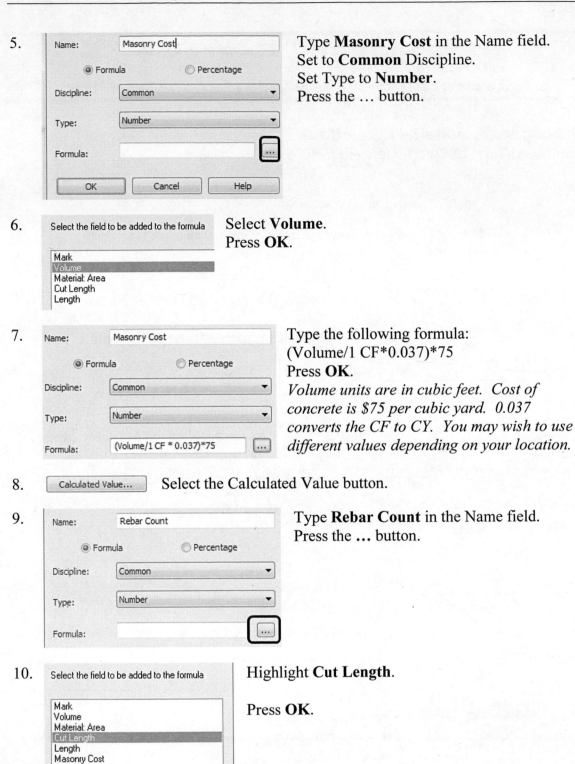

Type **Masonry Cost** in the Name field.
Set to **Common** Discipline.
Set Type to **Number**.
Press the ... button.

6.

Select the field to be added to the formula

Mark
Volume
Material: Area
Cut Length
Length

Select **Volume**.
Press **OK**.

7.

Name: Masonry Cost

○ Formula   ○ Percentage

Discipline: Common

Type: Number

Formula: (Volume/1 CF * 0.037)*75

Type the following formula:
(Volume/1 CF*0.037)*75
Press **OK**.
*Volume units are in cubic feet. Cost of
concrete is $75 per cubic yard. 0.037
converts the CF to CY. You may wish to use
different values depending on your location.*

8.

Calculated Value...

Select the Calculated Value button.

9.

Name: Rebar Count

○ Formula   ○ Percentage

Discipline: Common

Type: Number

Formula:

Type **Rebar Count** in the Name field.
Press the ... button.

10.

Select the field to be added to the formula

Mark
Volume
Material: Area
Cut Length
Length
Masonry Cost

Highlight **Cut Length**.

Press **OK**.

11.

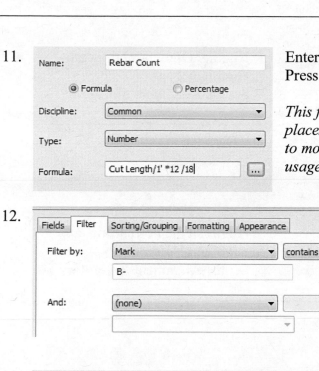

Enter the formula **Cut Length/1'*12/18**. Press **OK**.

This formula converts feet to inches then places rebar every 18 inches. You may wish to modify the formula depending on your usage.

12.

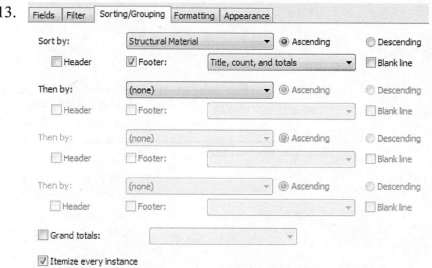

Select the Filter tab. Set the first filter to Mark contains B-.
You will have to type 'B-', which means only elements with a mark containing B- will be included in the schedule.

13.

Select the **Sorting/ Grouping** tab.
Sort by **Structural Material**.
Enable **Footer** and set to **Title, count, and totals**.
Enable **Itemize every instance**.

14.

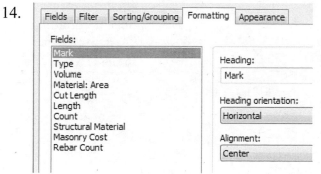

Highlight the Formatting tab.
Highlight **Mark**.
Set the Alignment to **Center**.

15.

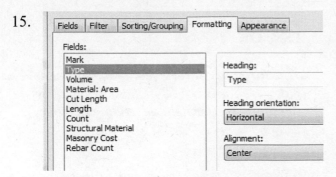

Highlight the Formatting tab.
Highlight **Type**.
Set the Alignment to **Center**.

16.

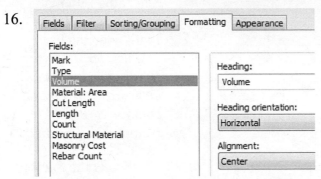

Highlight the Formatting tab.
Highlight **Volume**.
Set the Alignment to **Center**.

17.

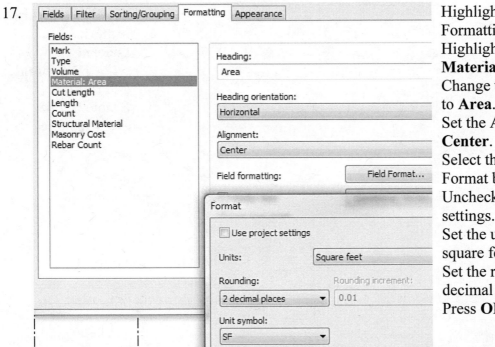

Highlight the Formatting tab.
Highlight **Material:Area**.
Change the Heading to **Area**.
Set the Alignment to **Center**.
Select the Field Format button.
Uncheck use project settings.
Set the units to square feet.
Set the rounding to 2 decimal places.
Press **OK**.

18.

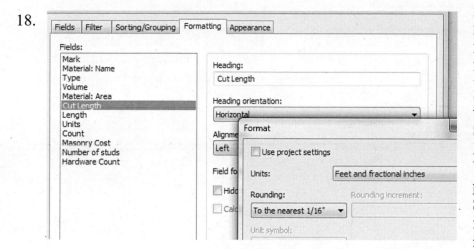

Highlight the Formatting tab. Highlight **Cut Length**. Set the Alignment to **Center**. Select the Field Format button. Uncheck use project settings. Set the units to feet and fractional inches. Set the rounding to nearest 1/16″. Press **OK**.

19.

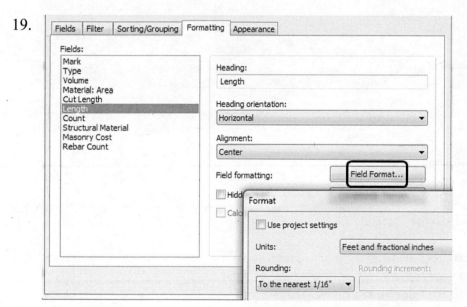

Highlight the Formatting tab. Highlight **Length**. Set the Alignment to **Center**. Select the Field Format button. Uncheck use project settings. Set the units to feet and fractional inches. Set the rounding to nearest 1/16″. Press **OK**.

20.

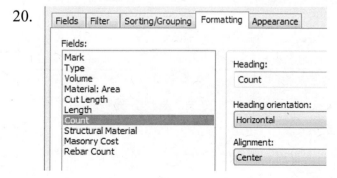

Highlight the Formatting tab. Highlight **Count**. Set the Alignment to **Center**.

21.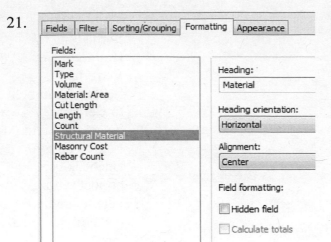

Highlight the Formatting tab.
Highlight **Structural Material**.
Change the Heading to **Material**.
Set the Alignment to **Center**.

22.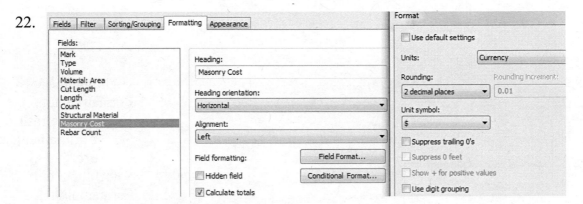

Highlight the Formatting tab.
Highlight **Masonry Cost**.
Set the Alignment to **Left**.
Select the Field Format button.

23. Uncheck **use project settings**.
Set the units to **Currency**.
Set the rounding to **2 decimal places**.
Set the unit symbol to **$**.
Press **OK**.
Enable **Calculate totals**.

24.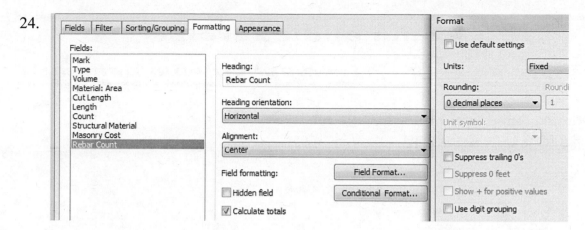

Highlight the Formatting tab.
Highlight **Rebar Count**.
Set the Alignment to **Center**.
Select the Field Format button.

25. Uncheck **use project settings**.
Set the units to **Fixed**.
Set the rounding to **0 decimal places**.
Press **OK**.
Enable **Calculate totals**.

26.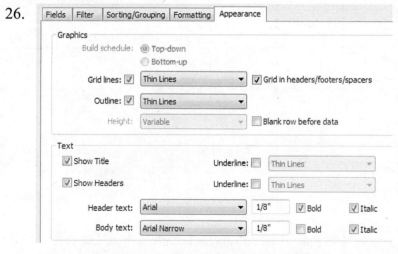

Select the Appearance tab.
Uncheck blank row before data.
Enable Grid in headers/footers/spacers.
Set the Header text to Arial, 1/8″ Bold and Italic.
Set the Body text to Arial Narrow, 1/8″ Italic.
Press OK.

27.

Mark	Type	Volume	Area	Cut Length	Length	Count	Material	Masonry Cost	Rebar Count
B-B	12 x 24	44.08 CF	136.23 SF	22' - 0 7/16"	22' - 5 15/16"	1	Concrete - Cast-in-Place	$122.31	15
B-A.5-2	12 x 24	41.33 CF	127.98 SF	20' - 7 15/16"	21' - 1 7/16"	1	Concrete - Cast-in-Place	$114.68	14
B-A.5	12 x 24	43.99 CF	133.98 SF	21' - 11 15/16"	22' - 9 3/4"	1	Concrete - Cast-in-Place	$122.08	15
B-A.5	12 x 24	43.99 CF	2.00 SF	21' - 11 15/16"	22' - 9 3/4"	1	Concrete - Cast-in-Place	$122.08	15
Concrete - Cast-in-Place Concrete: 4								$481.16	58

The schedule is displayed.

28. Save as *ex5-11.rvt*.

Command Exercise

Exercise 5-12 – Graphical Column Schedule

Drawing Name: column schedule.rvt
Estimated Time to Completion: 40 Minutes

Scope

Create a graphical column schedule

1.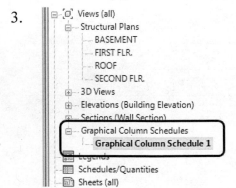
   Go to the View ribbon.
   Select **Schedules→Graphical Column Schedule**.

2.
   A graphical column schedule is automatically generated.

Column Locations	A.5-2	B(-0' - 6")1	B(-0' - 6")-2(0' - 10")	C-1	C(-0' - 6")-2(0' - 10")	C(-0' - 6")-3(0' - 6")	D-1	D

   ROOF 28' - 0"
   SECOND FLR. 14' - 0"
   FIRST FLR. 0' - 0"
   BASEMENT -14' - 0"

3.
   The graphical column schedule is listed in the Project Browser under Graphical Column Schedules.

   - Views (all)
     - Structural Plans
       - BASEMENT
       - FIRST FLR.
       - ROOF
       - SECOND FLR.
     - 3D Views
     - Elevations (Building Elevation)
     - Sections (Wall Section)
     - Graphical Column Schedules
       - **Graphical Column Schedule 1**
     - Legends
     - Schedules/Quantities
     - Sheets (all)

4.

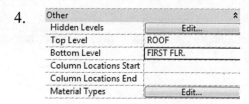

On the Properties pane:
Set the Top Level to ROOF.
Set the Bottom Level to FIRST FLR.
Note how the schedule adjusts.

5.

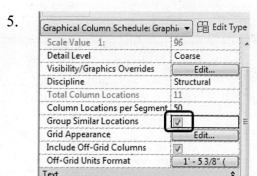

Scroll up in the Project Browser.
Place a check next to Group Similar Locations.
Note how the schedule adjusts.

6.

Graphical Column Schedule: Graphi ▼ Edit Typ
View Scale	1/8" = 1'-0"
Scale Value 1:	96
Detail Level	Medium
Visibility/Graphics Overrides	Edit...
Discipline	Structural

Change the Detail Level to Medium.
Note how the schedule adjusts.

7.

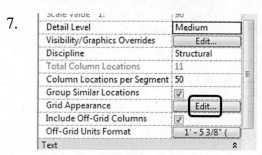

Select Edit next to **Grid Appearance**.

8.

Adjust the values for the
Horizontal widths and
Vertical Heights as shown.
Press **OK**.

9.

Tag
All

Activate the Annotate ribbon.
Select **Tag All**.

10.

Category	Loaded Tags
Structural Column Tags	Structural Column Tag
Structural Foundation Tags	Structural Foundation Tag
Structural Framing Tags	Structural Framing Tag
Structural Framing Tags	Structural Framing Tag : Boxed
Structural Framing Tags	Structural Framing Tag : Standard

◉ All objects in current view
○ Only selected objects in current view
☐ Include elements from linked files

☐ Leader   Leader Length: 1/2"

Tag Orientation: Vertical ▼

Highlight **Structural Column Tag**.
Set the Tag Orientation to **Vertical.**
Press **OK**.

If you forget to set the tag orientation, simply select one tag. Right click and select all instances visible in view. Then change the orientation on the Options bar.

11.

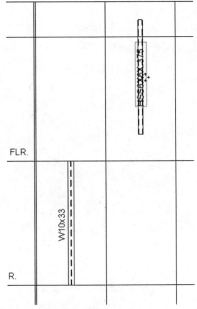

To move the tag:
Hover the mouse over the tag.
Press the TAB key until the tag highlights.
Left click to select and move off the column.

12. Save as *ex5-12.rvt*.

	A.5-2	B (-0' - 6")-1	B (-0' - 6")-2 (0' - 10"), C (-0' - 6")-2 (0' - 10")	C-1, D-1, E-1, F-1, G-1	C (-0' - 6")-3 (0' - 6")	D-2, E-2, F-2	D-3, E-3, F-3	D-4, E-4, F-4	G-2	G-3	G-4	
ROOF 28' - 0"		HSS6X6X.375	HSS6X6X.375	W14x99	HSS6X6X.375	W10x33	W10x33	W14x99	W10x49	W10x49	W10x49	**ROOF** 28' - 0"
SECOND FLR. 14' - 0"	W10x33											**SECOND FLR.** 14' - 0"
FIRST FLR. 0' - 0"												**FIRST FLR.** 0' - 0"
Column Locations												

Command Exercise

Exercise 5-13 – Custom Level Symbol

Drawing Name: **new annotation family**
Estimated Time to Completion: 10 Minutes

Scope

Create a custom level symbol

1. 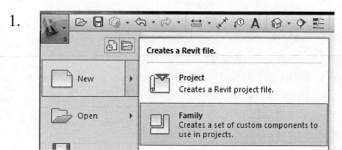 Go to the Application menu.

   Select **New→Family**.

2. Browse to the Annotation folder.
   Select **Level Head**.

3. 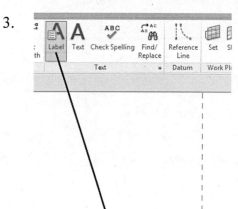 Select the Label tool and place the label above the line.

   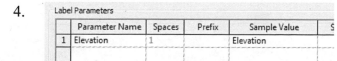

4. Select the **Elevation** parameter.

	Parameter Name	Spaces	Prefix	Sample Value	S
1	Elevation	1		Elevation	

5.  Select the **Format units** icon at the bottom of the dialog.

6. Uncheck **Use project settings**.
Set the Units to **Decimal Feet**.
Set Rounding to **2 decimal places**.
Set Unit symbol to **None**.
Press **OK**.

7. Delete the instructional note and the line.

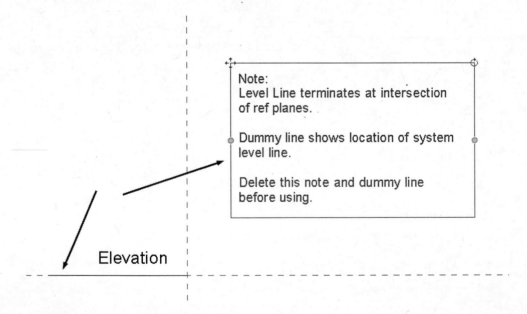

8. Save as *Level- Decimal Feet.rfa*.

Lesson Six
Sections, Elevations, Details, and Drafting Views

> ➢ You can model components that need to be displayed in more than one view and use detail components or sketches to display components that need to be displayed in a single view.
> ➢ Place detail components in views if the components are not going to be displayed in any other view.
> ➢ Overpopulating a design with non-essential details takes time, increases the file size, and slows the performance of the work station...don't add elements you don't need.

Command Exercise

Exercise 6-1 – Use of Cropped Views

Drawing Name: **crop_view.rvt**
Estimated Time to Completion: 5 Minutes

Scope

Use of Crop Regions to define a view

Solution

1. Elevations (Building Elevation)
    Elevation 1 - a
    Elevation 2 - a
    Elevation 3 - a
    Elevation 4 - a

    Activate **Elevation 2-a** under the *Elevations (Building Elevation)* folder in the Project Browser.

2. | Extents | |
    | --- | --- |
    | Crop View | ✓ |
    | Crop Region Visible | ✓ |
    | Annotation Crop | |

    In the Properties Pane:

    Scroll down the window and:
    Enable **Crop View**.
    Enable **Crop Region Visible**.

3. Zoom out.

    Select the viewport rectangle.

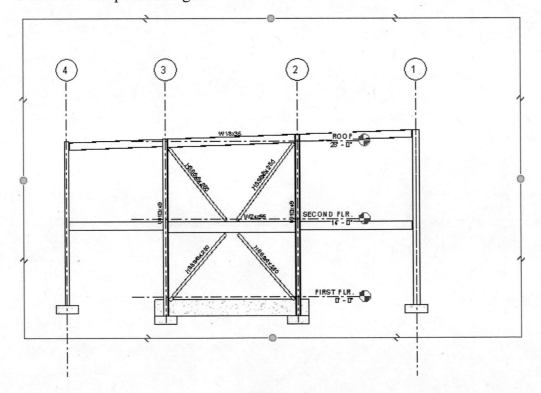

4.

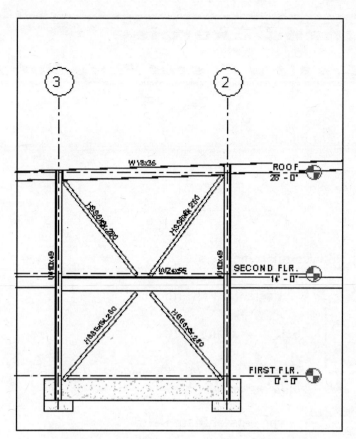

Use the grips to position the viewport so that only the structural columns between Grids 2 and 3 are visible.

5.   1/4" = 1'-0" Select **Hide Crop Region** using the tool in the View Control bar.
Press **OK**.

6.

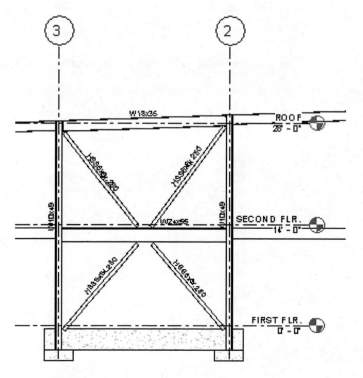

You have created a cropped view of an elevation.

Command Exercise

Exercise 6-2– Create a Gusset Plate Detail

Drawing Name: **new**
Estimated Time to Completion: 90 Minutes

Scope

Create a Drafting View for a Gusset Plate Detail

Solution

1. Start a new project using the Structural Template.

2. Activate the **View** ribbon.

   Select **Drafting View**.

   Drafting Views are not associated with the building model.

3. Type **Gusset Plate Detail**.
   Set the Scale to **1″ = 1′-0″**.
   Press **OK**.

   Name: Gusset Plate Detail
   Scale: 1" = 1'-0"
   Scale value 1: 12

4. Activate the **Annotate** ribbon.

   Select **Component→Detail Component**.

   Component   Revision   Detail   Insu
              Cloud   Group

   Detail Component

5. Select **Load Family** from the Mode panel.

   Load
   Family
   Mode

6. ProgramData
      Autodesk
         RST 2013
            Libraries
               US Imperial
                  Detail Items
                     Div 05-Metals
                        051200-Structural Steel Framing

   Browse to the *051200 Structural Steel Framing* folder under *Detail Items/Div 05-Metals*.

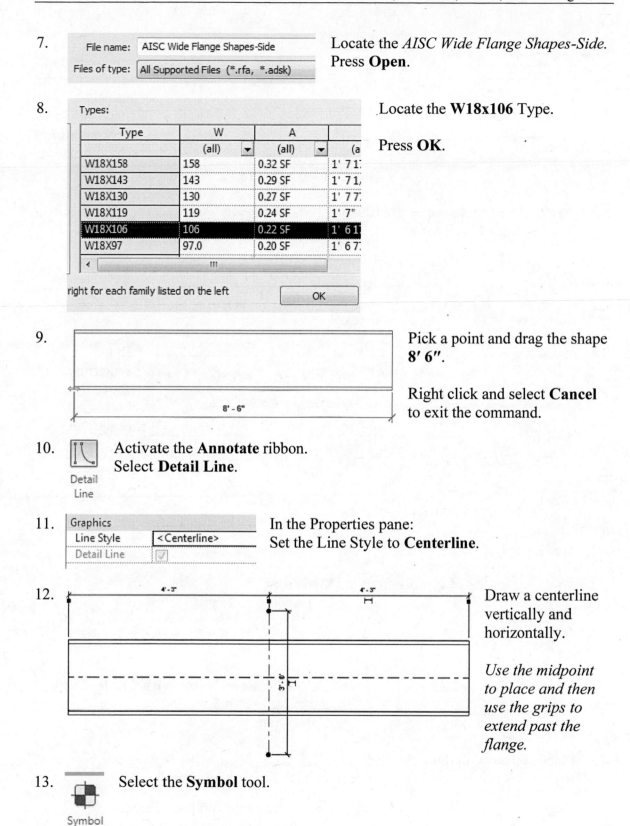

7.

| File name: | AISC Wide Flange Shapes-Side |
| Files of type: | All Supported Files (*.rfa, *.adsk) |

Locate the *AISC Wide Flange Shapes-Side*. Press **Open**.

8.

Types:

Type	W	A	
	(all) ▼	(all) ▼	(a
W18X158	158	0.32 SF	1' 7 1
W18X143	143	0.29 SF	1' 7 1,
W18X130	130	0.27 SF	1' 7 7.
W18X119	119	0.24 SF	1' 7"
W18X106	106	0.22 SF	1' 6 1
W18X97	97.0	0.20 SF	1' 6 7.

right for each family listed on the left

OK

Locate the **W18x106** Type.

Press **OK**.

9. Pick a point and drag the shape **8' 6"**.

Right click and select **Cancel** to exit the command.

8' - 6"

10. Activate the **Annotate** ribbon.
Select **Detail Line**.

Detail Line

11.

Graphics	
Line Style	<Centerline>
Detail Line	☑

In the Properties pane:
Set the Line Style to **Centerline**.

12. Draw a centerline vertically and horizontally.

Use the midpoint to place and then use the grips to extend past the flange.

13. Select the **Symbol** tool.

Symbol

14. Centerline

In the Properties pane:
Select **Centerline** from the Type Selector.

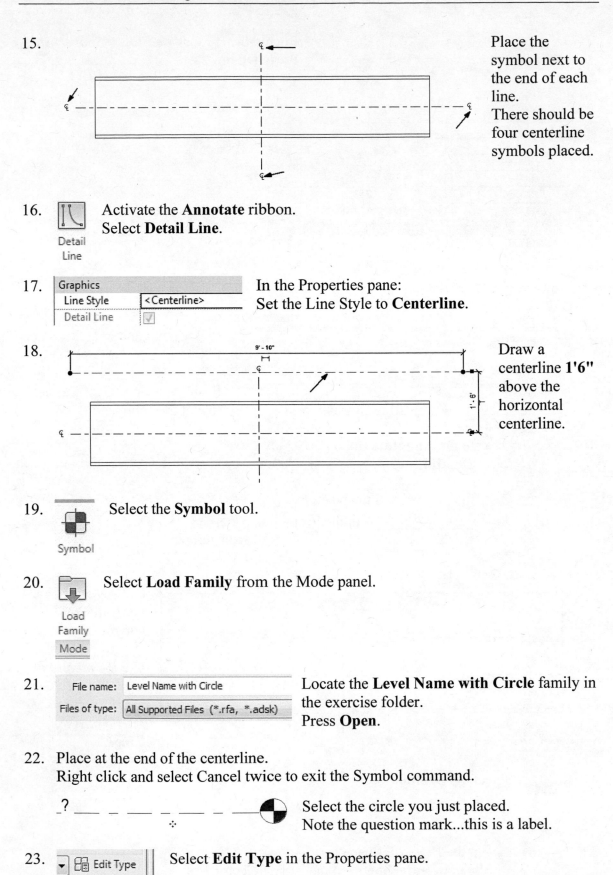

15. Place the symbol next to the end of each line.
There should be four centerline symbols placed.

16. Activate the **Annotate** ribbon.
Select **Detail Line**.

Detail Line

17. In the Properties pane:
Set the Line Style to **Centerline**.

Graphics
Line Style | < Centerline >
Detail Line | ☑

18. Draw a centerline **1'6"** above the horizontal centerline.

19. Select the **Symbol** tool.

Symbol

20. Select **Load Family** from the Mode panel.

Load Family
Mode

21. Locate the **Level Name with Circle** family in the exercise folder.
Press **Open**.

File name: | Level Name with Circle
Files of type: | All Supported Files (*.rfa, *.adsk)

22. Place at the end of the centerline.
Right click and select Cancel twice to exit the Symbol command.

Select the circle you just placed.
Note the question mark...this is a label.

23. Select **Edit Type** in the Properties pane.

Edit Type

24.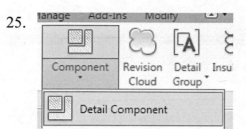

Enter **LEVEL 2,3,5, ROOF** in the Level Name field.
Press **OK**.
Left click in the window to de-select the symbol.

25.

Activate the **Annotate** ribbon.

Select **Component→Detail Component**.

26.

Select **Load Family** from the Mode panel.

27.

Browse to the *Div 01-General* folder under *Detail Components*.

28.

Locate the **Break Line**.
Press **Open**.

29. Place a break line on each side of the flange.
Position as shown.

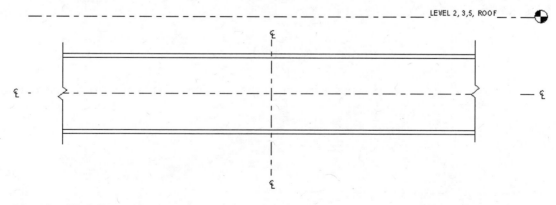

Use the SPACE BAR to rotate the break line.

30.  Activate the **Annotate** ribbon.

    Select **Component→Detail Component**.

31.  Select **Load Family** from the Mode panel.

32. Browse to the *050523-Metal Fastenings* folder under *Detail Items/Div 05-Metals/050500-Common Work Results for Metals*.

33.

| File name: | Steel Plate-Plain-Side-Length |
| Files of type: | All Supported Files (*.rfa, *.adsk) |

Locate the **Steel Plate-Plain-Side-Length** family.
Press **Open**.

34. 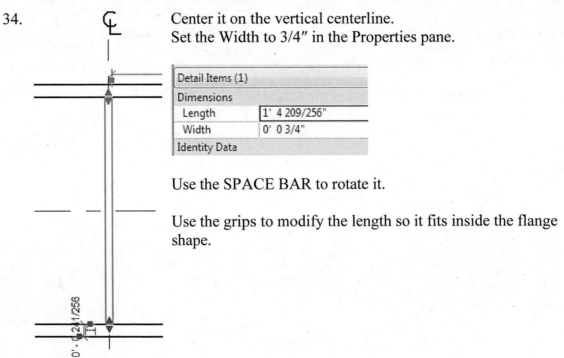 Center it on the vertical centerline.
Set the Width to 3/4″ in the Properties pane.

Detail Items (1)	
Dimensions	
Length	1′ 4 209/256″
Width	0′ 0 3/4″
Identity Data	

Use the SPACE BAR to rotate it.

Use the grips to modify the length so it fits inside the flange shape.

35. Use the Copy tool on the Modify ribbon to copy the steel plate below the flange.

36. Select the vertical centerline.
Select **Bring to Front** on the Arrange panel.

37. 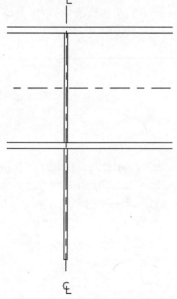 The centerline now appears above the steel plate detail.

38. Select the **Text** tool on the Text panel on the Annotate ribbon.

39. Enable the Leader with shoulder.
Set the format to center horizontal alignment.

40. Point the arrowhead at the intersection of the two centerlines.
Type **W.P.** for the text.

Select **Edit Type** on the Properties pane.

41. Select **Duplicate**.

42. Name the style **Note Dot_Small**.

Press **OK**.

43.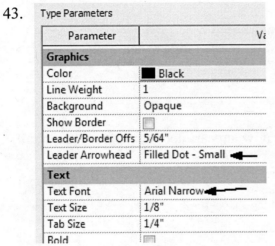

Set the Leader Arrowhead to **Filled Dot-Small**.
Set the Text Font to **Arial Narrow**.
Set the Text Size to **1/8″**.
Set the Tab Size to **1/4″**.

Press **OK**.

44. The note will update.

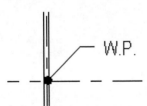

If the note doesn't update, it wasn't selected when you made the change. Simply select the note and apply the new text style using the Type Selector drop-down on the Properties palette.

Right click and select Cancel to exit the Text command.

45. Activate the **Annotate** ribbon.

Select **Component→Detail Component**.

46. Select **Load Family** from the Mode panel.

Load
Family
Mode

47.

| File name: | Bevel Plate Detail 1 |
| Files of type: | All Supported Files (*.rfa, *.adsk) |

Browse to the exercise folder.
Locate the **Bevel Plate Detail 1** family.
Press **Open**.

48. Use the MOVE tool to position so it is centered underneath the flange beam.

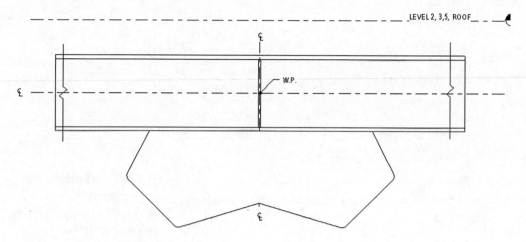

49. Activate the **Annotate** ribbon.

Detail
Line   Select **Detail Line**.

50.

| Line Style: |
| <Centerline> |

Set the Line Style to **Centerline**.

51.

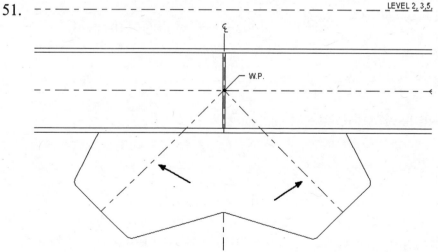

Draw two lines from the midpoints of the bevel legs to the intersection of the centerlines on the flange beam.

52.  Activate the **Annotate** ribbon.

Select **Component→Detail Component**.

53. Select **Load Family** from the Mode panel.

54. | File name: | Gusset Plate Detail 2 |
    | Files of type: | All Supported Files (*.rfa, *.adsk) |

Browse to the exercise folder.
Locate the *Gusset Plate Detail 2* family.
Press **Open**.

55. 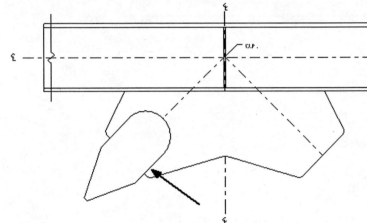 Place the component so it is halfway onto the bevel.

Rotate and align the component using ROTATE and ALIGN on the MODIFY ribbon.

You may need to use the Bring to Front tool to position it properly.

56. 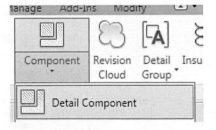 Activate the **Annotate** ribbon.

Select **Component→Detail Component**.

57. Select **Load Family** from the Mode panel.

58. | File name: | Gusset Plate Detail 1 |
    | Files of type: | All Supported Files (*.rfa, *.adsk) |

Browse to the exercise folder.
Locate the *Gusset Plate Detail 1* family.
Press **Open**.

59. 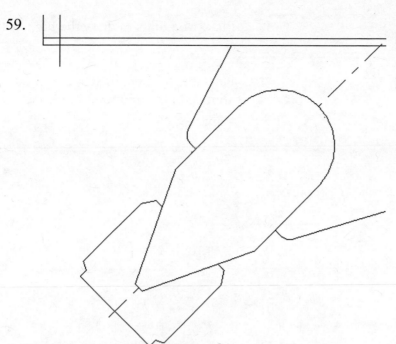 Use the MOVE and ROTATE tools to place the detail component in the proper position.

60. Activate the **Annotate** ribbon.

Select **Component→Detail Component**.

61. Select **Load Family** from the Mode panel.

62. Browse to the *051200-Structural Steel Framing* folder under *Detail Items/Div 05-Metals..*

63. Locate the **AISC Tube Shapes-Side** family. Press **Open**.

File name: AISC Tube Shapes-Side
Files of type: All Supported Files (*.rfa, *.adsk)

64. Highlight **HSS14X14X1/2** Type.

Press **OK**.

Types:

Type	Shape	
	(all) ▾	
HSS14X14X1/2	Square	89.6
HSS14X14X3/8	Square	68.2

65.

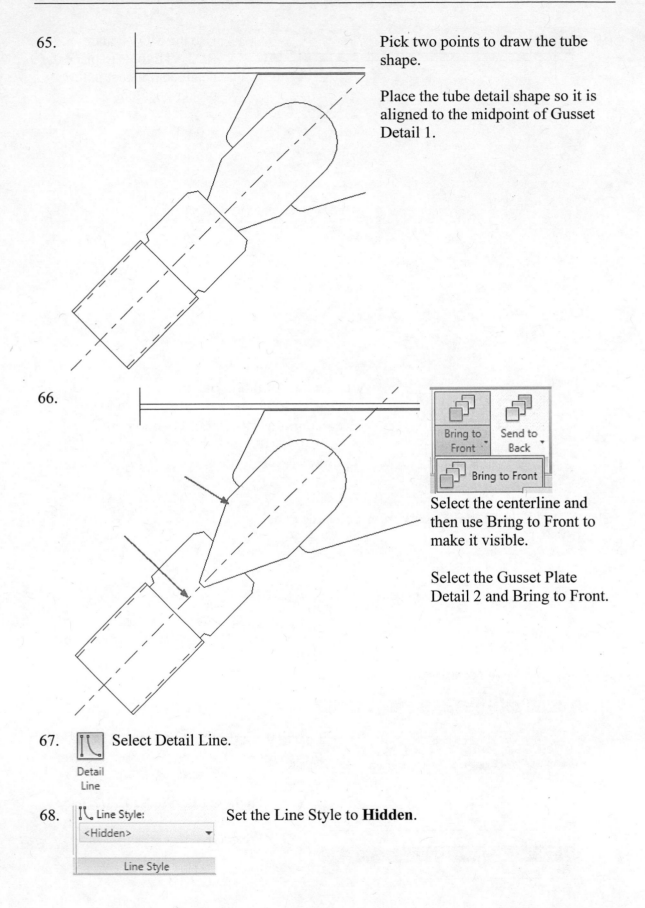

Pick two points to draw the tube shape.

Place the tube detail shape so it is aligned to the midpoint of Gusset Detail 1.

66.

Select the centerline and then use Bring to Front to make it visible.

Select the Gusset Plate Detail 2 and Bring to Front.

67. Select Detail Line.

Detail
Line

68. Line Style:

<Hidden>

Line Style

Set the Line Style to **Hidden**.

69. Select the **Pick Line** tool.

Draw

70. Pick the two hidden edges to add the hidden lines.

Select an edge or a line

71. Select the Steel Plate and use the Bring to Front tool to make it visible.

W.P.

72. Use the grips to size the plate so it extends to both edges of the gusset plate.

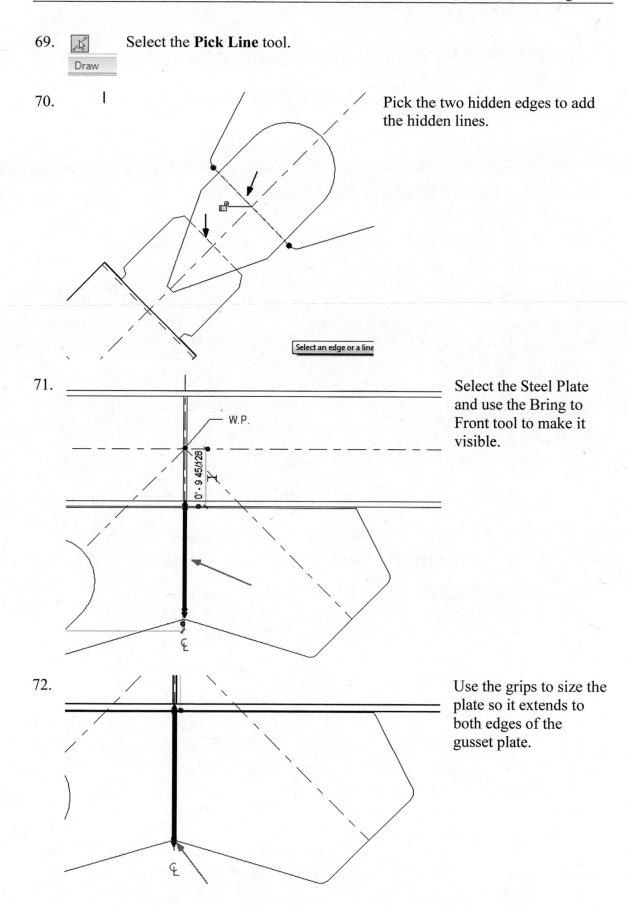

73.  Activate the **Annotate** ribbon.

    Select **Component→Detail Component**.

74. Break Line   Select the **Break Line** from the Properties pane.

75.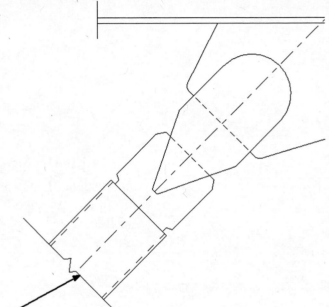

    Place a break line on the end of the tube component.
    Position as shown.

    Use ROTATE on the Modify panel to rotate the break line or use the SPACE BAR.

76. Activate the **Annotate** ribbon.

    Symbol   Select **Symbol**.

77. Centerline   Select the **Centerline** from the Properties pane.

78.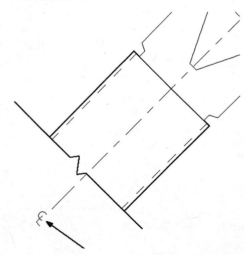

    Place on the centerline on the tube component.

    Use the Rotate tool to position it properly.

79. Activate the **Annotate** ribbon.

Select **Component→Detail Component**.

80. Select **Steel Plate - Plain Side - Length 3/4″** from the Properties pane.

81. Position as shown.

Use ROTATE and resize the length using grips.

82. Activate the **Annotate** ribbon.

Select **Component→Detail Component**.

83. Select **Load Family** from the Mode panel.

84. Browse to the *050523-Metal Fastenings* folder under *Detail Items/Div 05-Metals/050500-Common Work Results for Metals*.

85. 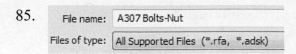 Locate the **A307 Bolts-Nut** family.
Press **Open**.

86. A307 Bolts-Nut 1"   Select **A307 Bolts-Nut 1″** from the Type Selector on the Properties pane.

87. 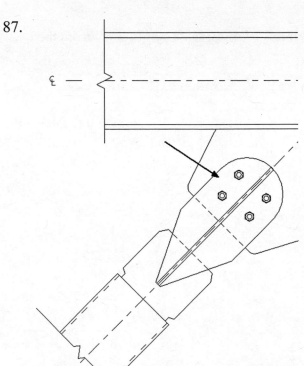 Place four bolts in the pattern shown.

88. 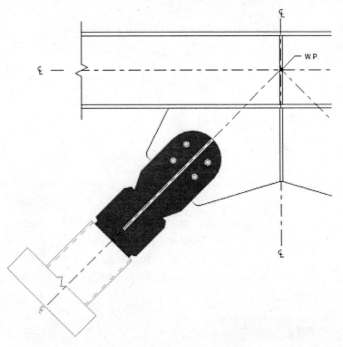 Select all the components placed on the bevel.

Use the **Mirror→Pick Axis** tool to mirror to the other side.

89.

Check the CL symbol that was mirrored.

You will see that the text is backwards. Mirror it around the centerline to orient properly and delete the incorrect centerline symbol.

90. Activate the **Annotate** ribbon.

Symbol   Select **Symbol**.

91. Select **Load Family** from the Mode panel.

Load
Family
Mode

92. Browse to the *Structural* folder under *Annotations*.

ProgramData
Autodesk
RST 2013
Libraries
US Imperial
Annotations
Structural

93. File name: Weld Symbol

Files of type: All Supported Files (*.rfa, *.adsk)

Select the **Weld Symbol** family.

Press **Open**.

94. Weld Symbol Both

Select the **Weld Symbol-Both** from the Type Selector in the Properties pane.

95. Number of Leaders: 1

On the Options bar:
Set the Number of Leaders to **1**.

96.

Structural	
Weld All Around	☐
Top Weld Size	1/2
Top Weld Length	L3
Field Weld	☐
Bottom Weld Size	1/2
Bottom Weld Length	L3

Enter the values shown and adjust the position of the weld symbol.

Uncheck Symbol Left.

97. Place a second weld symbol.

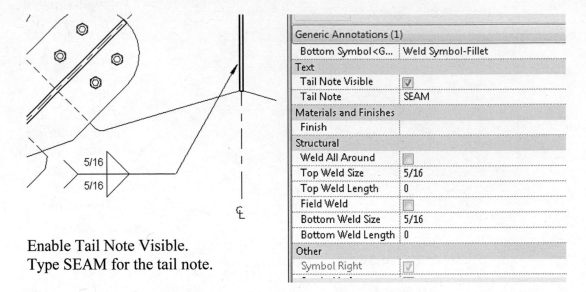

Enable Tail Note Visible.
Type SEAM for the tail note.

Enter the values shown and adjust the position of the weld symbol.

98. Orient the symbols so that they are both using Symbol Right.

Uncheck Symbol Left. Press **Apply**.

99. The completed detail should appear as shown.

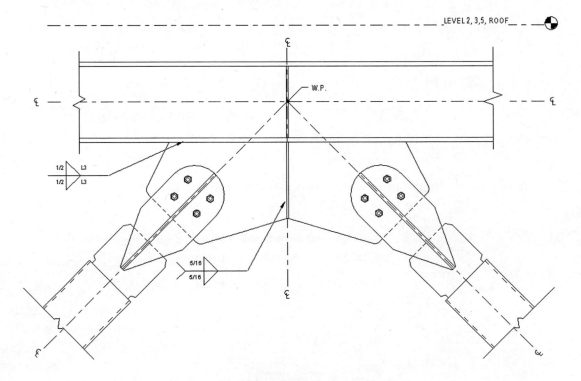

Command Exercise

Exercise 6-3 – Challenge Detail Views

Drawing Name: **Detail Library**
Estimated Time to Completion: 50 Minutes

Scope

Create a set of detail views to be used in a structural project

Solution

S6 DRAFTING VIEW

1.
Name:	S6
Scale:	3/4" = 1'-0"
Scale value 1:	16

Create a drafting view called **S6**.

Set the Scale to **3/4" = 1'-0"**.

2.

ProgramData
  Autodesk
    RST 2013
      Libraries
        US Imperial
          Detail Items
            Div 05-Metals
              050500-Common Work Results for Metals
              050523-Metal Fastenings

Load a Detail Component from 050523-Metal Fastenings.

3.
File name:	Gusset Plate-2 Bevel-Elevation
Files of type:	All Supported Files (*.rfa, *.adsk)

Locate and load Gusset Plate - 2 Bevel Elevation.

4.
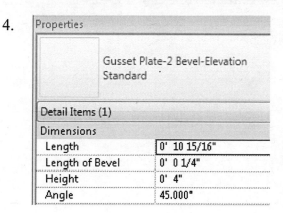

Properties

Gusset Plate-2 Bevel-Elevation
Standard

Detail Items (1)

Dimensions
Length	0' 10 15/16"
Length of Bevel	0' 0 1/4"
Height	0' 4"
Angle	45.000°

Adjust the dimensions of the Gusset Plate in the Properties palette.

Set the Length to 10 15/16".
Set the Length of Bevel to 1/4".
Set the Height to 4".

Press **Apply**.

5.　Add Aligned Dimensions and text.

You will need to create a new dimension family so your dimensions appear correctly.

FOR W12 X 50

6.

Text	
Width Factor	1.000000
Underline	☐
Italic	☐
Bold	☐
Text Size	3/32"
Text Offset	1/16"
Read Convention	Horizontal
Text Font	Arial
Text Background	Opaque
Units Format	1' - 5 5/16"
Show Opening Height	☐
Suppress Spaces	☐

For vertical dimension:
Set Read Convention to Horizontal.
Set Units Format to Round to the nearest 1/16″ and to Fractional Inches.

Format	
☐ Use project settings	
Units:	Fractional inches
Rounding:	Rounding increment:
To the nearest 1/16" ▼	

7.

Identity Data	
View Template	<None>
View Name	S6
Dependency	Independent
Title on Sheet	3/8" STIFFENER PL. ~ S6
Referencing Sheet	
Referencing Detail	

In the Properties Palette:

Set the View Name to S6.
Set the Title on Sheet to 3/8"
STIFFENER PL. ~S6.

E46 DRAFTING VIEW

8.

Name:	E46
Scale:	3/4" = 1'-0"
Scale value 1:	16

Create a drafting view called **E46**.

Set the Scale to **3/4″ = 1′-0″**.

9.
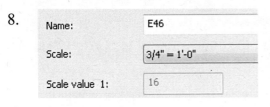

```
ProgramData
  Autodesk
    RST 2013
      Libraries
        US Imperial
          Detail Items
            Div 05-Metals
              050500-Common Work Results for Metals
              050523-Metal Fastenings
```

Load a Detail Component from 050523-Metal Fastenings.

10.

File name:	Gusset Plate-2 Bevel-Elevation
Files of type:	All Supported Files (*.rfa, *.adsk)

Locate and load Gusset Plate - 2 Bevel Elevation.

11.

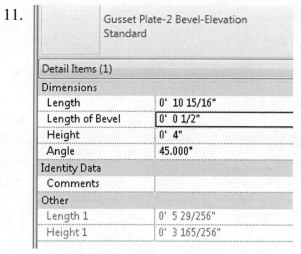

Adjust the dimensions of the Gusset Plate in the Properties palette.

Set the Length to 10 15/16".
Set the Length of Bevel to 1/2".
Set the Height to 4".

Press **Apply**.

12.

Load Detail Component from *050523-Metal Fastenings* under *Detail Items/Div 05 - Metals/ 050500-Common Works Results for Metals.*

13.

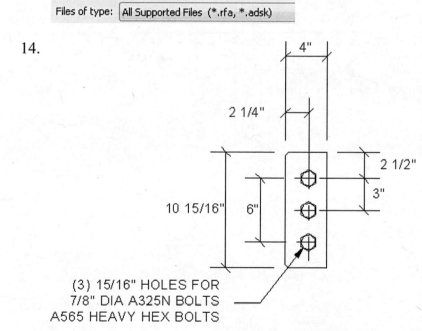

Locate the **A325 Bolts-Head** and **Open**.

14.

Add Aligned Dimensions and text.

Dimension style has been modified to display 1/16" tick marks and 1/16" Arial text.

A center line was added using a detail line.

The note uses 1/16" Arial text and a 1/16" Arrow Filled 30 Degree.

15.

Text	
Width Factor	1.000000
Underline	☐
Italic	☐
Bold	☐
Text Size	3/32"
Text Offset	1/16"
Read Convention	Horizontal
Text Font	Arial
Text Background	Opaque
Units Format	1' - 5 5/16"
Show Opening Height	☐
Suppress Spaces	☐

For vertical dimensions :
Set Read Convention to
Horizontal.
Set Units Format to Round to
the nearest 1/16″.

16.

Identity Data	
View Template	
View Name	E46
Dependency	Independent
Title on Sheet	3/8" PL. ~ E46
Referencing Sheet	
Referencing Detail	

In the Properties Palette:

Set the View Name to E46.
Set the Title on Sheet to 3/8″ PL. ~E46.

E25 DRAFTING VIEW

17.

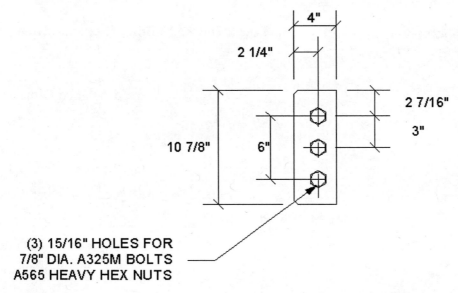

4"

2 1/4"

2 7/16"

3"

10 7/8"   6"

(3) 15/16" HOLES FOR
7/8" DIA. A325M BOLTS
A565 HEAVY HEX NUTS

W12X50 BM.

Identity Data	
View Template	<None>
View Name	E25
Dependency	Independent
Title on Sheet	3/8" PL. ~ E25
Referencing Sheet	
Referencing Detail	

Duplicate the E46 drafting view with
detailing to create the E25 drafting
view.

E47 DRAFTING VIEW

18. Duplicate the E46 drafting view with detailing to create the E47 drafting view.

    Use Detail Component Gusset Plate -3 Bevel - Elevation (included with exercise files).

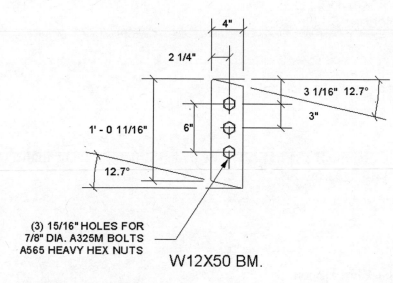

Dimensions have been modified using custom arrowheads and tick marks. Create using Manage→Additional Settings→Arrowheads.

Units have been set to Fractional Inches only for most dimensions.

E15 DRAFTING VIEW

19.

Identity Data	
View Template	<Nc
View Name	E15
Dependency	Independent
Title on Sheet	3/8" PL. ~ E15
Referencing Sheet	

Use Steel Base Top - ½" Detail Component and 7/8" A325N Bolt.

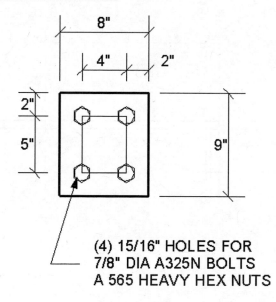

Command Exercise

Exercise 6-4 – Create a Wall Section

Drawing Name: **wall_section.rvt**
Estimated Time to Completion: 50 Minutes

Scope

Create a section view of a wall

Solution

1. Open the **BASEMENT** view under Structural Plans in the Project Browser.

   Views (all)
   Structural Plans
   BASEMENT
   FIRST FLR.
   ROOF
   SECOND FLR.

2. Activate the **View** ribbon.

   Section   Select the **Section** tool from the Create panel.

3. Section
   Wall Section   Verify that Wall Section is active in the Properties pane.

4. 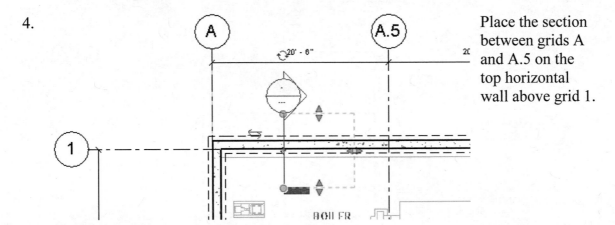   Place the section between grids A and A.5 on the top horizontal wall above grid 1.

5.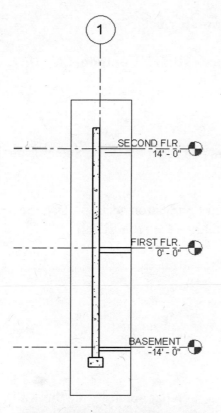

Double click on the grid bubble to activate the view.

Adjust the crop region so the view displays only the wall section.

Hide the Crop Region to turn off the visibility of the region rectangle.

6.

Activate the **Annotate** ribbon.

Select **Component→Detail Component**.

7. Break Line   Select **Break Line** from the Properties panel.

8.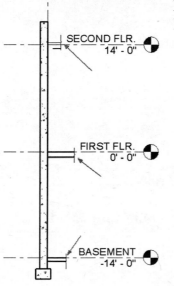

Rotate the break line and position it on the floors at each level.

9.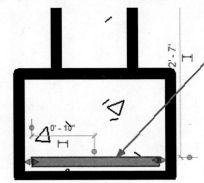

Activate the **Annotate** ribbon.

Select **Component→Detail Component**.

10. Reinf Bar Elevation #11

Select the **Reinf Bar Elevation #11** from the Type Selector on the Properties pane.

11.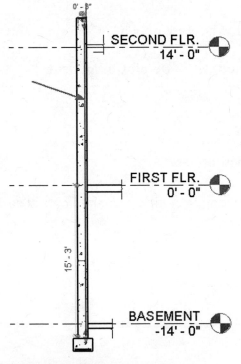

Place in the Wall Foundation section. Use the grips to shorten or lengthen the rebar detail.

12.

Place a second rebar detail inside the wall. Use the SPACE BAR to rotate the rebar detail.
Use the grips to lengthen the detail.

13.

Activate the **Annotate** ribbon.

Select **Component→Detail Component**.

14. 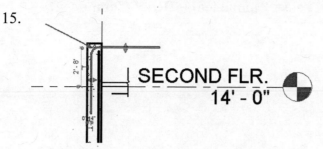 Reinf Bar Bend 9-11 #11 Select the **Reinf Bar Bend 9-11 #11** from the Type Selector on the Properties pane.

15. Place the detail as shown.

16. Adjust the lengths of the bar sides in the Properties pane.

Dimensions	
L1	0' 8"
L2	32' 0"

Set L1 to **0' 8"**.
Set L2 to **32' 0"**.

17. Apply   Press the **Apply** button at the bottom of the Properties pane to see how the rebar size adjusts.

18. 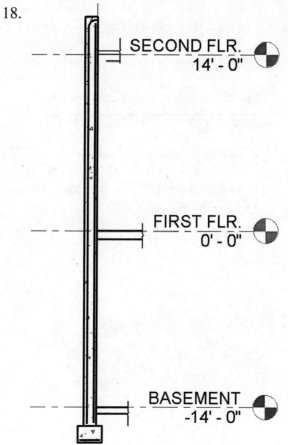 The detail view so far includes a few rebar details and break lines.

19. Activate the **Annotate** ribbon.

Select **Component→Detail Component**.

20. Select **Load Family**.

21. Browse to *321600-Curbs and Gutters* under *Detail Items/Div 32-Exterior Improvements*.

22. Locate **Concrete Curbs and Gutters - Section**.
Press **Open**.

23. Select the **6″ Concrete Curb and Gutter** from the Type Selector on the Properties pane.

24. 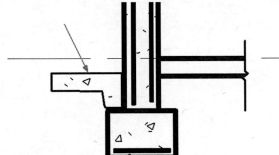 Place in the view.

Use the SPACE BAR to rotate and position the detail.

25. Select **Filled Region** from the Annotate ribbon.

26. 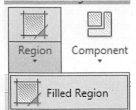 Set the Line Style to **Thin Lines**.

27. ☑ Chain   Offset: 0' 0"   ☐ Radius: 1' 0"   Enable **Chain** on the Options bar.

28. 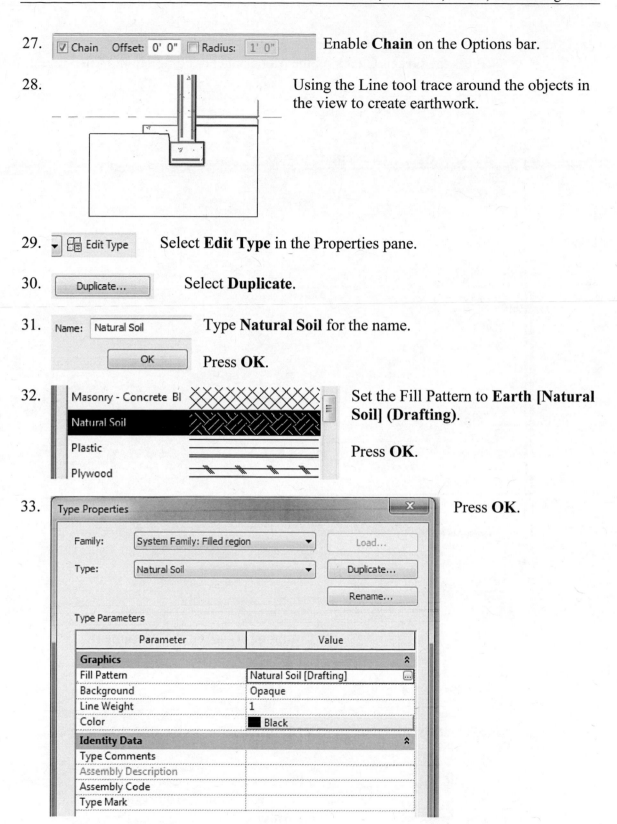   Using the Line tool trace around the objects in the view to create earthwork.

29. ▾ 🔲 Edit Type   Select **Edit Type** in the Properties pane.

30. Duplicate...   Select **Duplicate**.

31. Name: Natural Soil   Type **Natural Soil** for the name.

    OK   Press **OK**.

32. Masonry - Concrete Bl   Set the Fill Pattern to **Earth [Natural**
    Natural Soil   **Soil] (Drafting)**.
    Plastic   Press **OK**.
    Plywood

33.

Parameter	Value
Graphics	
Fill Pattern	Natural Soil [Drafting]
Background	Opaque
Line Weight	1
Color	Black
Identity Data	
Type Comments	
Assembly Description	
Assembly Code	
Type Mark	

Press **OK**.

Type Properties

Family: System Family: Filled region   Load...
Type: Natural Soil   Duplicate...
      Rename...

Type Parameters

*Note: There are several custom hatch patterns in this project file. Use **Transfer Project Standards** on the Manage ribbon to export custom fill patterns from one project to another.*

34. Press the **Green Check** on the Mode panel to complete the filled region.

35. Our section view so far.

SECOND FLR.
14' - 0"

FIRST FLR.
0' - 0"

BASEMENT
-14' - 0"

36. Activate the **Annotate** ribbon.

Select **Component →Detail Component**.

Detail Component

37. Break Line1
Break Line

Select **Break Line** from the Type Selector on the Properties pane.

38. 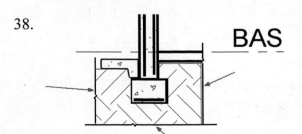 Place two additional break lines on the sides of the earthwork. Adjust the sizes and positions.

BAS

39. Activate the **Annotate** ribbon.

Select **Component→Repeating Detail Component**.

40. Select **#4@12″ O.C.** from the Type Selector on the Properties pane.

41.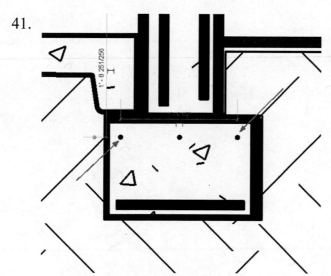

Select a point above the horizontal rebar on the left.
Drag a horizontal line to the right.
Pick a point above the right end of the horizontal rebar.

You should see an array of rebar in section view.

42. Activate the **Annotate** ribbon.

Select **Component→Repeating Detail Component**.

43. Select **Edit Type** from the Properties pane.

44. Select **Duplicate**.

45. Name: #8@18″ O.C.

Type **#8@18″O.C.**
Press **OK**.

46.

Pattern	
Detail	Reinf Bar Section1 : #_8
Layout	Fixed Distance
Inside	☐
Spacing	1' 6"
Detail Rotation	None

Set the Detail to **Reinf Bar Section: #8**.
Set the Layout to **Fixed Distance**.
Set the Spacing to **1′ 6″**.
Press **OK**.

47.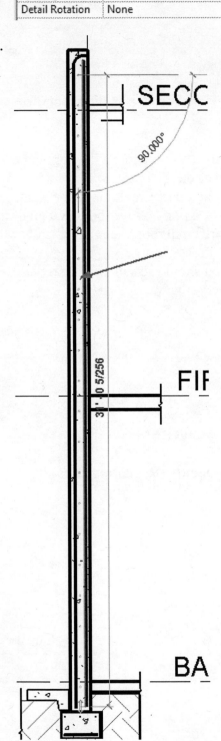

Place vertically to the right of the bent rebar detail on the wall.

48. **A**   Activate the **Annotate** ribbon.
Text   Select the **Text** tool on the Text panel.

49.   Text   Select the **1/8″ Arial** style from the Type Selector on the Properties
  1/8" Arial   pane.

50.   Add notes to identify the rebar.

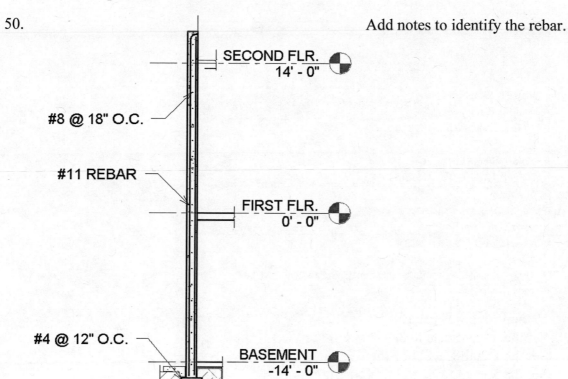

51.

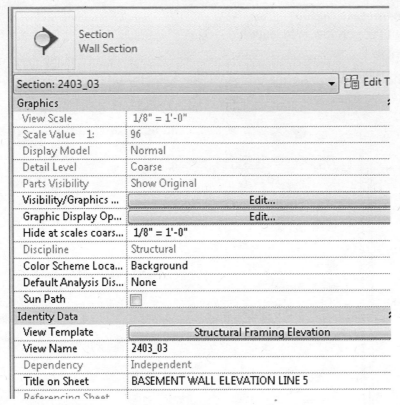

In the Properties pane:
Set the View Scale to **3/16″ = 1′-0″**.
Set the Detail Level to **Fine**.
Set the Visual Style to **Hidden Line**.

Set the View Name to **S403_03**.
Set the Title on Sheet to **BASEMENT WALL ELEVATION LINE 5**.
Set the Default View Template to **Structural Framing Elevation.**

Disable **Crop Region Visible**.

Press **Apply**.

52. Close without saving.

Command Exercise

Exercise 6-5 – Save a Drafting View

Drawing Name: **save_view.rvt**
Estimated Time to Completion: 5 Minutes

Scope

Save a Drafting View

Solution

1. 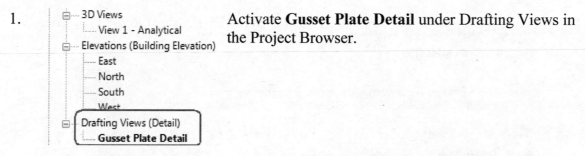 Activate **Gusset Plate Detail** under Drafting Views in the Project Browser.

2. 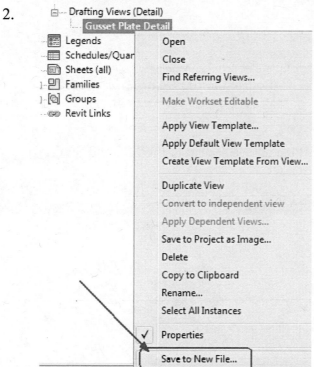 Highlight **Gusset Plate Detail**. Right click and select **Save to New File**.

3.
File name:	Gusset Plate Detail
Files of type:	Project Files (*.rvt)

   Browse to your work folder.

   The file is saved with the view name.
   Press **Save**.

4. Close the file without saving.

Command Exercise
Exercise 6-5 – Import a Drafting View

Drawing Name: **import_drafting_view**
Estimated Time to Completion: 5 Minutes

Scope

Import a Drafting View

Solution

1.   `...... C3 Reinforcements`   Activate **B-8.6-C3 MEMBERS** sheet in the Project
          Sheets (all)   Browser.
          B-8.6 - C3 MEMBERS
          Families

2. Activate the **Insert** ribbon.
   Select **Insert from File→ Insert Views from File**.

3. Locate the file *Detail Library*.
   Press **Open**.

   File name: Detail Library
   Files of type: All Supported Files (*.rvt, *.adsk)

4. Place a check next to the E25 and S6 drafting views.

   Press **OK**.

   Views:
   Show all views and sheets

   ☐ Drafting View: E15
   ☑ Drafting View: E25
   ☐ Drafting View: E46
   ☐ Drafting View: E47
   ☑ Drafting View: S6

5. Press **OK**.

   Duplicate Types

   The following Types already exist but are different. The Types from the project into which you are pasting will be used.

   Callout Tag : Callout Head w 1/8" Corner Radius
   Drafting View : Detail
   Section Tag : Section Head - No Arrow, Section Tail - Filled Horizontal
   Viewport : Title w Line

   OK   Cancel

6.   ⊟ Drafting Views (Detail)
              E25
              S6

The drafting views are now imported and listed in the Project Browser.

7.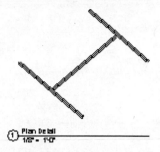

Activate **B-8.6-C3 MEMBERS** sheet in the Project Browser.

8.

Drag and drop the two drafting views onto the sheet below the schedule.

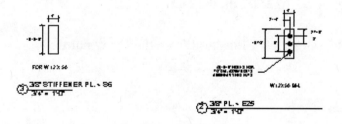

9.   Highlight/select the **E25** drafting view.

Identity Data	⌃
View Template	<None>
View Name	E6
Dependency	Independent
Title on Sheet	3/8" PL. ~ E6
Sheet Number	B-8.6
Sheet Name	C3 MEMBERS

In the Properties pane:
Change the View Name to **E6**.
Change the Title on Sheet to **3/8″ PL.~ E6**.

Notice that the view updates.

10.   Save as *ex6-6.rvt*.

Command Exercise

Exercise 6-7 – Use of Scope Boxes

Drawing Name: **scope_boxes.rvt**
Estimated Time to Completion: 30 Minutes

Scope

Use of scope boxes

Scope boxes are used to control the visibility of grid lines and levels in views.

Solution

1. Structural Plans
    Level 1
    Level 1 - Analytical
    Level 2
    Level 2 - Analytical

    Activate **Level 1** under the *Structural Plans* folder in the Project Browser.

2.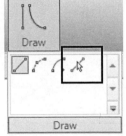
    Level   Grid
    Datum

    Activate the **Structure** ribbon.

    Select the **Grid** tool from the Datum panel.

3. Offset: 2 0"

    Set the Offset to **2′ 0″** on the Options bar.

4. Draw

    Draw

    Select the **Pick Lines** tool from the Draw panel.

5.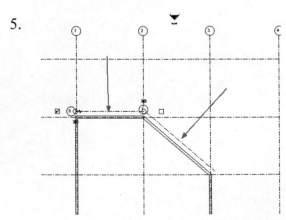

    Place two grid lines using the exterior side of the structural walls to offset.

6.

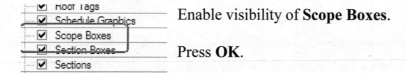

Re-label the grid bubbles so that the horizontal grid line is 0.1 and the angled grid line is 0.2.
Enable bubbles on both ends.

7. Type **VV** to launch the Visibility/Graphics dialog.

Activate the **Annotation Categories** tab.

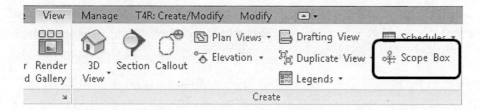

Enable visibility of **Scope Boxes**.

Press **OK**.

8. Activate the **View** ribbon.

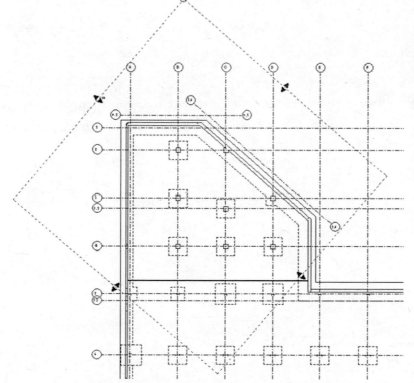

Select the **Scope Box** tool from the Create panel.

9.

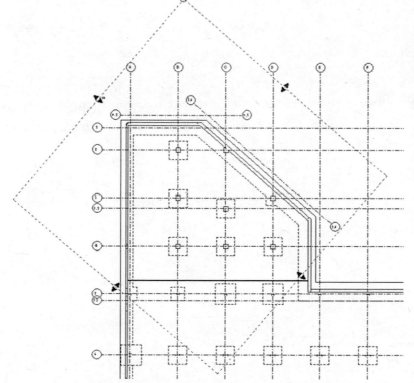

Place the scope box.

Use the Rotate icon on the corner to rotate the scope box into position.

Use the blue grips to control the size of the scope box.

10. Select the scope box.
    In the Properties pane:

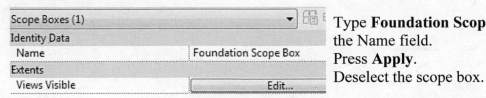

Type **Foundation Scope Box** in
the Name field.
Press **Apply**.
Deselect the scope box.

11.

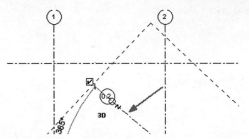

Select the grid line labeled **0.2**.

12.

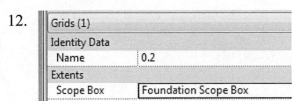

In the Properties pane:

Set the Scope Box to **Foundation Scope
Box**, the scope box which was just placed.

13.

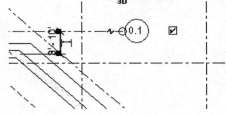

Select the grid line labeled **0.1**.

14. In the Properties pane:

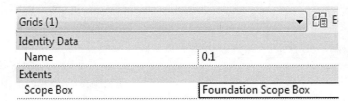

Set the Scope Box to
Foundation Scope Box, the
scope box which was just
placed.

15.

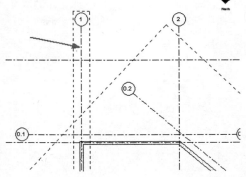

Select the grid line labeled **1**.

16. In the Properties pane:

Identity Data	
Name	1
Extents	
Scope Box	Foundation Scope Box

Set the Scope Box to **Foundation Scope Box**, the scope box which was just placed.

17.

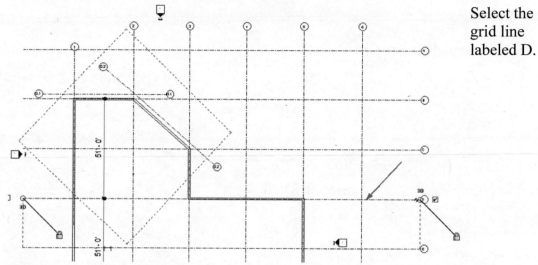

Select the grid line labeled D.

18.

Grids (1)	
Identity Data	
Name	D
Extents	
Scope Box	Foundation Scope Box

In the Properties pane:

Set the Scope Box to **Foundation Scope Box**, the scope box which was just placed.

19. Select the Scope Box.

Extents	
Views Visible	Edit...

Select **Edit** next to Views Visible in the Properties pane.

20. Scroll through the list.

Click on the column headers to change the sort order.

View Type	View Name	Automatic visibility	Override
3D View	View 1 - Analytical	Visible	None
3D View	{3D}	Visible	None
Elevation	South	Invisible	None
Elevation	West	Invisible	None
Elevation	East	Invisible	None
Elevation	North	Invisible	None
Structural Plan	Level 1	Visible	None
Structural Plan	Level 2	Visible	None
Structural Plan	Level 2 - Analytical	Visible	None
Structural Plan	Level 1 - Analytical	Visible	None

You will note the views where the associated datums are invisible or visible.

21. Set the **LEVEL 2** Structural Plan Override Invisible.

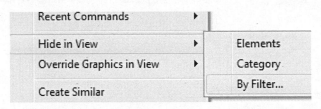

Elevation	North	Invisible	None
Structural Plan	Level 1	Visible	None
Structural Plan	Level 2	Visible	Invisible
Structural Plan	Level 2 - Analytical	Visible	None
Structural Plan	Level 1 - Analytical	Visible	None

Press **OK**.

22. Select the scope box.

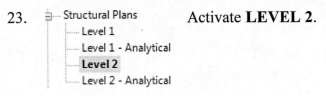

Right click and select **Hide in View→Elements**.

The scope box is no longer visible in the view.

23.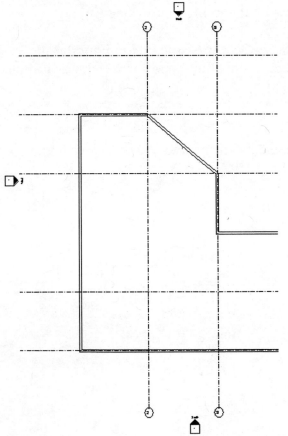

Activate **LEVEL 2**.

Structural Plans
— Level 1
— Level 1 - Analytical
— **Level 2**
— Level 2 - Analytical

24.

The grid lines and scope box are not visible.

Note only the grid lines attached to the scope box are set to invisible in the view.

25. Close without saving.

Command Exercise

Exercise 6-8 – Assembly Views

Drawing Name: **assembly views.rvt**
Estimated Time to Completion: 60 Minutes

Scope

Create views for assemblies.
Create a sheet.
Place views on a sheet.
Tag the framing members.
Modify the tag family.
Add parts list and material take off to sheet.

Solution

1. ⊟ ⊞ Assemblies
       ⊞— C1-E2
        — C3-E4
        — E1-G2
        — E3-G4

    In the Project Browser:

    Scroll down to the Assemblies.
    There are several assemblies listed.

2. ⊟ ⊞ Assemblies
       ⊞— C1-E2
        — C3-E4
        — E1-G2
        — E3-G4

    Click the plus symbol next to the first assembly.

3. ⊟— C1-E2
       — **3D View: 3D Ortho**
       — Detail View: Detail Section A
       — Detail View: Detail Section B
       — Detail View: Elevation Back
       — Detail View: Elevation Bottom
       — Detail View: Elevation Front
       — Detail View: Elevation Left
       — Detail View: Elevation Right
       — Detail View: Elevation Top
       — Detail View: Plan Detail
       — Schedule: Material Takeoff
       — Schedule: Part List
       — Sheet: A101 - Sheet

    There is a list of all available views for the assembly.

4.

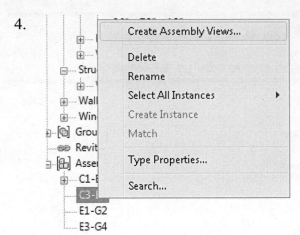

Highlight the C3-E4 assembly.

Right click and select **Create Assembly Views**.

5.

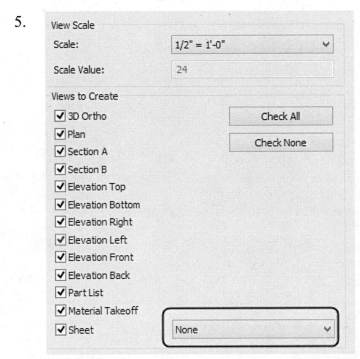

Select the drop-down next to Sheet to assign a sheet to the views.

6.

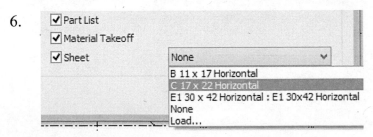

Select the C-size sheet.

Press **OK**.

7. ⊟ C3-E4
  ····· 3D View: 3D Ortho
  ····· Detail View: Detail Section A
  ····· Detail View: Detail Section B
  ····· Detail View: Elevation Back
  ····· Detail View: Elevation Bottom
  ····· Detail View: Elevation Front
  ····· Detail View: Elevation Left
  ····· Detail View: Elevation Right
  ····· Detail View: Elevation Top
  ····· **Detail View: Plan Detail**
  ····· Schedule: Material Takeoff
  ····· Schedule: Part List
  ····· Sheet: A101 - Sheet

Expand the assembly in the Project Browser.
The views, schedules, and sheet are listed below the assembly.

8. C3-E4
  ····· **3D View: 3D Ortho**
  ····· Detail View: Detail Section A
  ····· Detail View: Detail Section B

Activate the 3D View.

9. 🔲 Edit Assembly

Select the assembly.

Select **Edit Assembly**.

10.

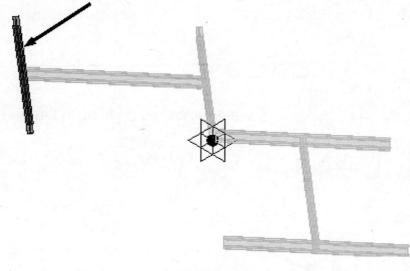

Select the member shown.

11. In the Properties pane:
Under Structural, set the Number of Studs to **10**.

Structural		⌃
Stick Symbol Location	Center of Geometry	
Start Connection	None	
End Connection	None	
Cut Length	16' 8 253/256"	
Structural Usage	Joist	
Camber Size		
Number of studs	10	
Enable Analytical Model	☑	
Dimensions		⌃

12.

Identity Data	
Assembly Name	C3-E4
Comments	
Mark	E4A
Phasing	

Scroll down and set the Mark to **E4A**.

13.

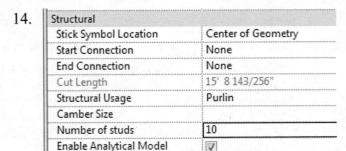

Select the member shown.

14.

Structural	
Stick Symbol Location	Center of Geometry
Start Connection	None
End Connection	None
Cut Length	15' 8 143/256"
Structural Usage	Purlin
Camber Size	
Number of studs	10
Enable Analytical Model	☑

In the Properties pane:
Under Structural, set the Number of Studs to **10**.

15.

Identity Data	
Assembly Name	C3-E4
Comments	
Mark	E4B
Phasing	

Scroll down and set the Mark to **E4B**.

16.

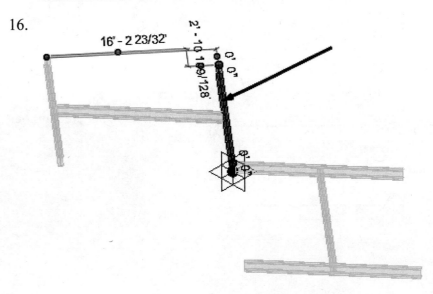

Select the member shown.

17.

Structural	
Stick Symbol Location	Center of Geometry
Start Connection	None
End Connection	None
Cut Length	15' 9 169/256"
Structural Usage	Joist
Camber Size	
Number of studs	10 ←
Enable Analytical Model	☑
Dimensions	
Length	16' 1 47/128"
Volume	0.85 CF
Identity Data	
Assembly Name	C3-E4
Comments	
Mark	E4C ←

In the Properties pane:
Under Structural, set the Number of Studs to **10**.

Scroll down and set the Mark to **E4C**.

18.

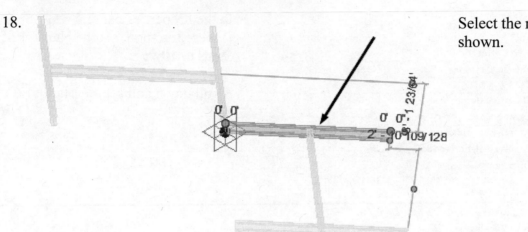

Select the member shown.

19.

Structural Framing (Joist) (1)	▾	⊞ Edit Typ
Start Connection	None	
End Connection	None	
Cut Length	15' 9 169/256"	
Structural Usage	Joist	
Camber Size		
Number of studs	10 ←	
Enable Analytical Model	☑	
Dimensions		⌃
Length	16' 1 47/128"	
Volume	0.85 CF	
Identity Data		⌃
Assembly Name	C3-E4	
Comments		
Mark	E4D ←	
Phasing		⌃
Phase Created	New Construction	

In the Properties pane:
Under Structural, set the Number of Studs to **10**.

Scroll down and set the Mark to **E4D**.

20.

Select the member shown.

21.

Structural	
Stick Symbol Location	Center of Geometry
Start Connection	None
End Connection	None
Cut Length	15' 8 143/256"
Structural Usage	Purlin
Camber Size	
Number of studs	10
Enable Analytical Model	☑
Dimensions	
Length	16' 5 45/256"
Volume	0.85 CF
Identity Data	
Assembly Name	C3-E4
Comments	
Mark	E4E

In the Properties pane:
Under Structural, set the Number of Studs to **10**.

Scroll down and set the Mark to **E4E**.

22.

Select the member shown.

23.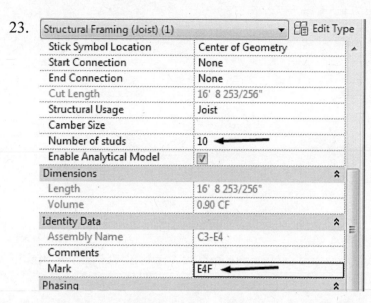

In the Properties pane:
Under Structural, set the
Number of Studs to **10**.

Scroll down and set the Mark to
E4F.

24.

Select **Finish** from the Edit Assembly toolbar.

25.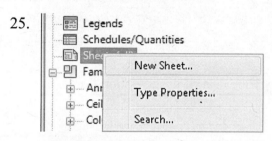

Highlight Sheets in the Project Browser.
Right click and select **New Sheet**.

26.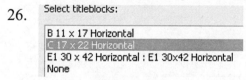

Highlight the **C-size** sheet.
Press **OK**.

27.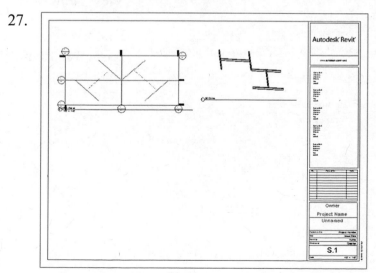

Drag and drop the 3D view and
Plan Detail view on the sheet.
Set the scale of the views to
1/8″ = 1′-0″.

28.

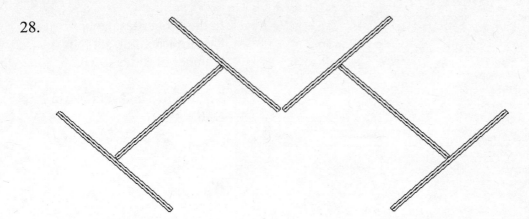

Activate the Plan Detail view.
Turn off the visibility of elevations and sections using the Visibility/Graphics dialog.
Set the Detail Level to Medium.

29.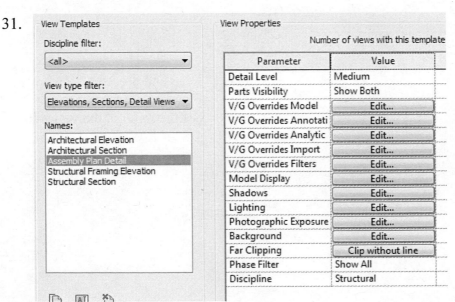

Activate the View ribbon.
Select **Create Template from Current View**.

This saves your view settings to a template.

30. New View Template

Name: Assembly Plan Detail

OK

Type **Assembly Plan Detail** in the Name field.

Press **OK**.

31.

View Templates

Discipline filter:

<all>

View type filter:

Elevations, Sections, Detail Views

Names:

Architectural Elevation
Architectural Section
Assembly Plan Detail
Structural Framing Elevation
Structural Section

View Properties

Number of views with this template

Parameter	Value
Detail Level	Medium
Parts Visibility	Show Both
V/G Overrides Model	Edit...
V/G Overrides Annotati	Edit...
V/G Overrides Analytic	Edit...
V/G Overrides Import	Edit...
V/G Overrides Filters	Edit...
Model Display	Edit...
Shadows	Edit...
Lighting	Edit...
Photographic Exposure	Edit...
Background	Edit...
Far Clipping	Clip without line
Phase Filter	Show All
Discipline	Structural

The template is now listed in the View Templates dialog.
Highlight the **Assembly Plan Detail** template.
Press **OK**.

32.

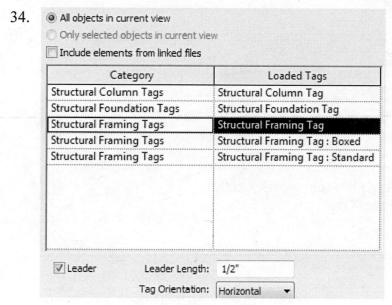

Identity Data		⌃
View Template	Assembly Plan Detail	
View Name	Plan Detail	
Dependency	Independent	
Title on Sheet		

The template is assigned to the view in the Properties pane.

33. Activate the Annotate ribbon.
Select **Tag All**.

Tag All

34.

☑ All objects in current view
○ Only selected objects in current view
☐ Include elements from linked files

Category	Loaded Tags
Structural Column Tags	Structural Column Tag
Structural Foundation Tags	Structural Foundation Tag
Structural Framing Tags	**Structural Framing Tag**
Structural Framing Tags	Structural Framing Tag : Boxed
Structural Framing Tags	Structural Framing Tag : Standard

☑ Leader   Leader Length: 1/2"
Tag Orientation: Horizontal

Highlight **Structural Framing Tag**.
Enable **Leader**.
Press **OK**.

35. 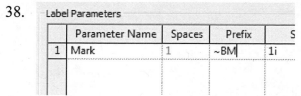 Select one of the tags.

36. Select **Edit Family** on the ribbon.

Edit Family
Mode

37. Select the **Label** tool from the ribbon.

Label

38.

Label Parameters

	Parameter Name	Spaces	Prefix	S
1	Mark	1	~BM	1i

Left click below the existing label.
Assign the parameter **Mark**.
In the Prefix column, type ~BM.

(Include a space after BM to ensure there is space between ~BM and the Mark.)

39. ☐ 1i ☐   Position the second label as shown.

~BM 1i

40. ⊞   Select Family Types from the ribbon.

41. 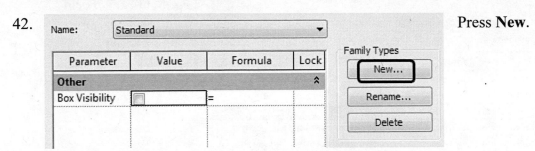   Note that there are currently three types of tags available in this family.

42. 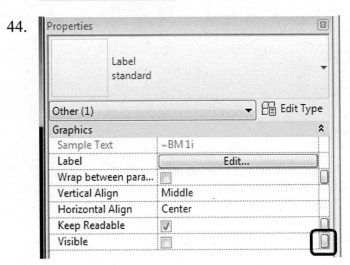   Press **New**.

43. Name: Standard with Mark   Type **Standard with Mark**.

OK   Press **OK**.

44.

Properties

Label
standard

Other (1)   ⊞ Edit Type

Graphics   ≫

Sample Text	~BM 1i
Label	Edit...
Wrap between para...	☐
Vertical Align	Middle
Horizontal Align	Center
Keep Readable	☑
Visible	☐

Select the Mark label.
Select the small button in the Properties pane.

45.

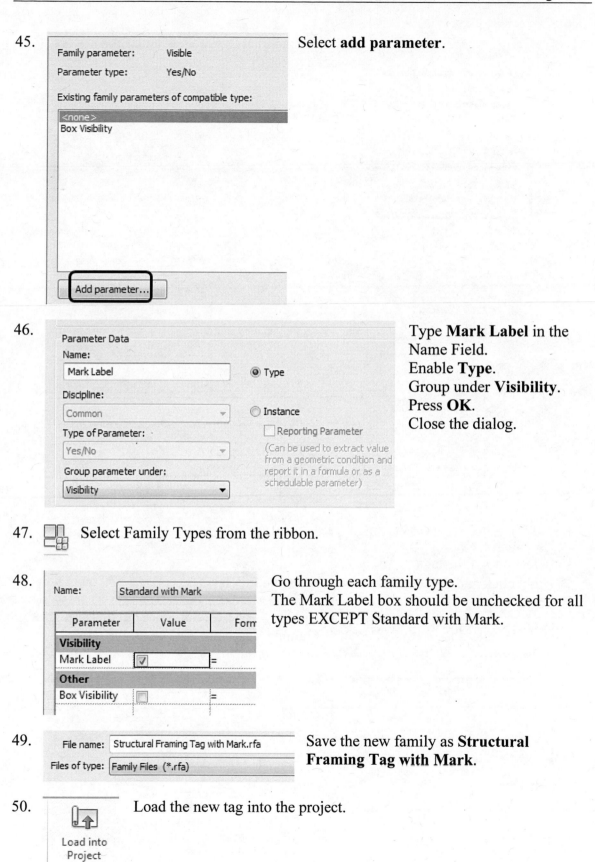

Family parameter: Visible

Parameter type: Yes/No

Existing family parameters of compatible type:

<none>
Box Visibility

Add parameter...

Select **add parameter**.

46.

Parameter Data

Name:

Mark Label   ● Type

Discipline:

Common   ○ Instance

Type of Parameter: ☐ Reporting Parameter

Yes/No   (Can be used to extract value
from a geometric condition and
report it in a formula or as a
schedulable parameter)

Group parameter under:

Visibility

Type **Mark Label** in the
Name Field.
Enable **Type**.
Group under **Visibility**.
Press **OK**.
Close the dialog.

47.   Select Family Types from the ribbon.

48.

Name: Standard with Mark

Parameter	Value	Form
Visibility		
Mark Label	☑	=
Other		
Box Visibility	☐	=

Go through each family type.
The Mark Label box should be unchecked for all
types EXCEPT Standard with Mark.

49.

File name: Structural Framing Tag with Mark.rfa

Files of type: Family Files (*.rfa)

Save the new family as **Structural
Framing Tag with Mark**.

50.

Load into
Project

Family Editor

Load the new tag into the project.

51.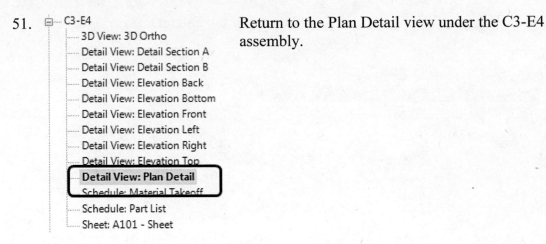

Return to the Plan Detail view under the C3-E4 assembly.

52.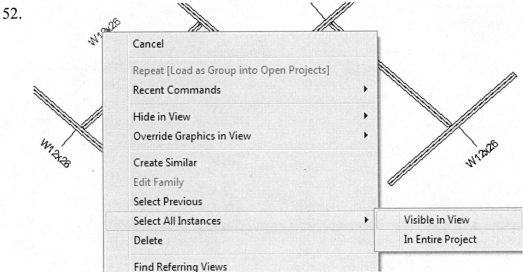

Select one of the tags.

Right click and **Select all instances→Visible in View**.

53.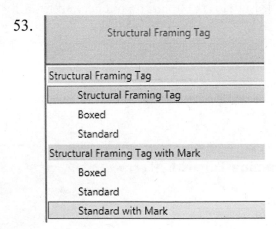

Use the Type Selector to assign the Structural Framing Tag with Mark to all the tags.

54. See if you can use the jogs on the leaders to reposition the tags as shown.

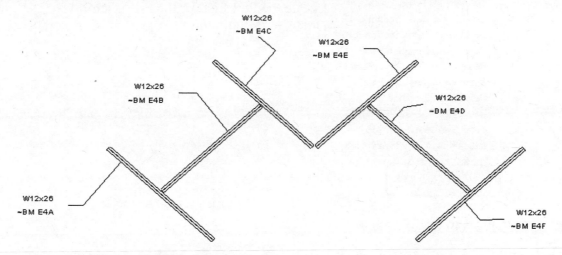

55.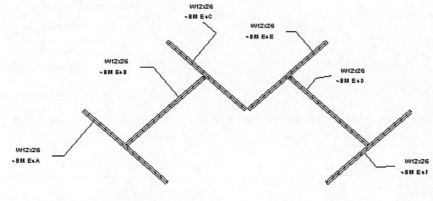

Activate the sheet. Change the name of the view to: W12x26 – E4 Assy

56.

Designed By	Designer
Checked By	Checker
Sheet Number	B-8.9
Sheet Name	E4 ASSY
Sheet Issue Date	10/26/12

Change the Sheet Number to B-8.9.
Change the name of the Sheet to E4 ASSY.

57.
- ⊟ C3-E4
  - 3D View: 3D Ortho
  - Detail View: Detail Section A
  - Detail View: Detail Section B
  - Detail View: Elevation Back
  - Detail View: Elevation Bottom
  - Detail View: Elevation Front
  - Detail View: Elevation Left
  - Detail View: Elevation Right
  - Detail View: Elevation Top
  - Detail View: W12x26 -E4 ASSY
  - Schedule: Material Takeoff
  - Schedule: Part List
  - Sheet: A101 - Sheet
- E1-G2

In the Project Browser:
Locate the Material Takeoff for the E4 Assembly.
Drag and drop it onto the sheet.

58.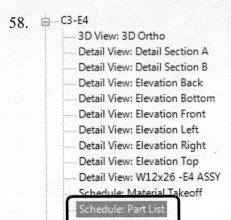

In the Project Browser:
Locate the Part List for the E4 Assembly.
Drag and drop it onto the sheet.

59. Our sheet so far.

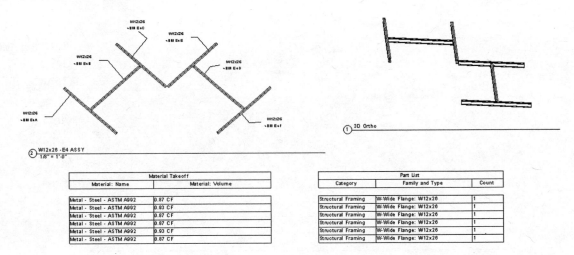

Material Takeoff	
Material: Name	Material: Volume
Metal - Steel - ASTM A992	0.87 CF
Metal - Steel - ASTM A992	0.93 CF
Metal - Steel - ASTM A992	0.87 CF
Metal - Steel - ASTM A992	0.87 CF
Metal - Steel - ASTM A992	0.93 CF
Metal - Steel - ASTM A992	0.87 CF

Part List		
Category	Family and Type	Count
Structural Framing	W-Wide Flange: W12x26	1
Structural Framing	W-Wide Flange: W12x26	1
Structural Framing	W-Wide Flange: W12x26	1
Structural Framing	W-Wide Flange: W12x26	1
Structural Framing	W-Wide Flange: W12x26	1
Structural Framing	W-Wide Flange: W12x26	1

What would you change on the sheet to make it comply with the way your company works?

60. Save as *ex6-8.rvt*.

Lesson Seven

Collaboration

> ➢ Views, schedules, and sheets can all be exported as dxf, dwg and dgn formats.
> ➢ When you export a 3D view, the actual 3D model will be exported.
> ➢ Before you export a model to be used in AutoCAD, specify the layer settings to be used.

Command Exercise

Exercise 7-1 – Import a CAD file

Drawing Name: **import_cad.rvt**
Estimated Time to Completion: 10 Minutes

Scope

Import a CAD File

Solution

1. 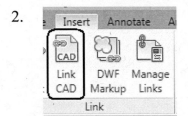 Activate **Level 1** under the Structural Plans category in the Project Browser.

2.  Activate the **Insert** ribbon.
   Select **Link CAD** from the Link panel.

3. Locate the *slab_check.dwg* file.
   Set Colors to **Preserve**.
   Set Layers to **All**.

File name:	slab_check	
Files of type:	DWG Files (*.dwg)	

Colors:	Preserve		Positioning:	Auto - Center to Center
Layers/Levels:	All		Place at:	Level 1
Import units:	Auto-Detect	1.000000		☑ Orient to View
	☑ Correct lines that are slightly off axis		Open	Cancel

4. Set Import Units to **Auto-Detect**.
   Set Positioning to **Auto - Center to Center**.
   Press **Open**.

5.

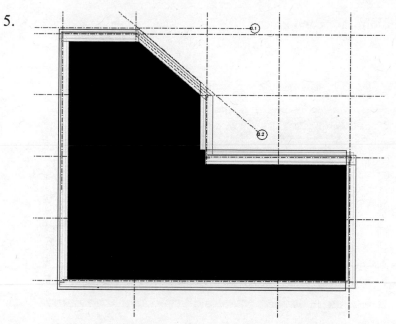

Position the imported file over the existing view. Left click to place.

Left click anywhere in the drawing area to release the selection.

6. Select **Manage Links** on the Link panel.

Manage
Links

7.

| Revit | CAD Formats | DWF Markups | Point Clouds |

Linked File	Status	Positions Not Saved	Size	Saved Path
slab_check.dwg	Loaded	☐	61.4 KB	slab_check.dwg

Note that the link is shown.
Press **OK**.

8. Type **VV** to launch the Visibility/Graphics dialog.
Select the **Imported Categories** tab.
Locate the slab_check.dwg file.

☑ Show imported categories in this view

Visibility	Projection/Surface		Halftone
	Lines	Patterns	
☑ Imports in Families			☐
☑ slab_check.dwg			☐
☑ 0			
☑ A-ANNO-SYMB			
☑ A-WALL-PATT			
☑ S-FNDN			
☑ S-FNDN-FTNG-UNDERLAY			
☑ S-GRID			
☑ SLAB	Override...		

Expand the category.
The layers are listed.

9. Left click in the Lines column for each layer.
    Select **Override**.

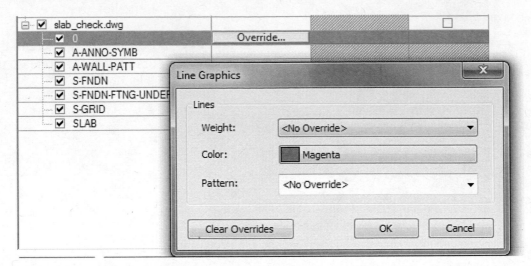

Set the color to **Magenta**.
Press **OK**.

You can also use the CTRL and SHIFT keys to select more than one layer.

10.

Visibility	Projection/Surface	
	Lines	Patterns
☑ Imports in Families		
☐ ☑ slab_check.dwg		
☑ 0		
☑ A-ANNO-SYMB		
☑ A-WALL-PATT		
☑ S-FNDN		
☑ S-FNDN-FTNG-UNDERLAY		
☑ S-GRID		
☑ SLAB		

Verify that all layers for the dwg file have been set to Magenta. Press **OK**.

11.

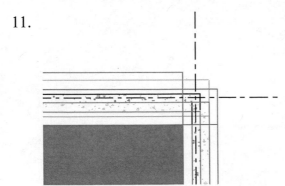

Zoom in and note that the slab edges do not align.
This would need to be corrected.

Students always ask how do we correct this? Well, part of collaboration means notifying the sender about the discrepancy and then figuring out how to fix the problem. Each situation is different, but knowing how to bring in an AutoCAD file and checking it against the Revit model is the first step.

Command Exercise
Exercise 7-2 – Export to DXF

Drawing Name: **export.rvt**
Estimated Time to Completion: 10 Minutes

Scope

Export to DXF

Solution

1.  Go to the **Application Menu**.
Select **Export→CAD Formats→ DXF Files**.

2. 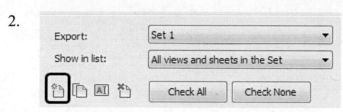 By default, only the current view or sheet will be exported.
To DXF the entire project:
Select **New Set**.

3.  Type **Main Project**.
Press **OK**.

4. You will now see a list of all sheets and views available for export.

Include	Type	Name
☐	⌂	Elevation: SOUTH ELEVATI...
☐	⌂	3D View: View 1 - Analytical
☐	▥	Structural Plan: S201 GROU...
☐	▥	Structural Plan: S202 MEZZ...
☐	▥	Structural Plan: Level 2 - An...
☐	▥	Structural Plan: Level 1 - An...
☐	▥	Structural Plan: S202 TOP O...
☐	▥	Structural Plan: S200 TOP O...

5. 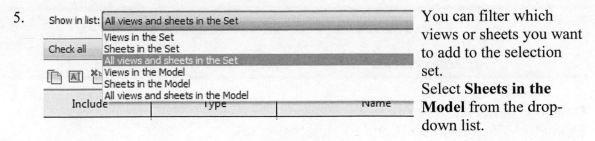   You can filter which views or sheets you want to add to the selection set.
Select Sheets in the Model from the drop-down list.

6. 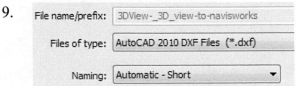   Select **Check all**.
This will add all sheets in the project to the Main Project set for export.

7.   The dialog should look like this.

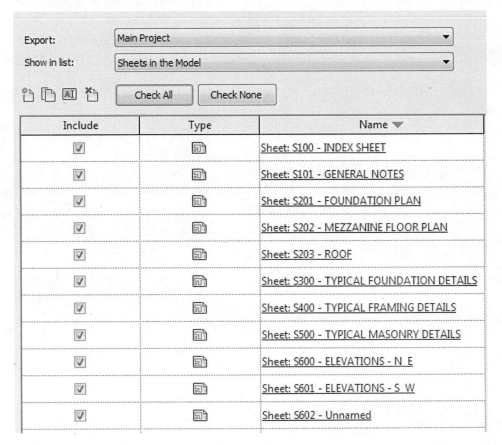

| Export: | Main Project | |
| Show in list: | Sheets in the Model | |

Include	Type	Name ▼
☑		Sheet: S100 - INDEX SHEET
☑		Sheet: S101 - GENERAL NOTES
☑		Sheet: S201 - FOUNDATION PLAN
☑		Sheet: S202 - MEZZANINE FLOOR PLAN
☑		Sheet: S203 - ROOF
☑		Sheet: S300 - TYPICAL FOUNDATION DETAILS
☑		Sheet: S400 - TYPICAL FRAMING DETAILS
☑		Sheet: S500 - TYPICAL MASONRY DETAILS
☑		Sheet: S600 - ELEVATIONS - N E
☑		Sheet: S601 - ELEVATIONS - S W
☑		Sheet: S602 - Unnamed

8.   Next...   Select **Next**.

9.

File name/prefix:	3DView-_3D_view-to-navisworks
Files of type:	AutoCAD 2010 DXF Files (*.dxf)
Naming:	Automatic - Short

When exporting to a CAD format or DWF, specify a name or prefix for the exported files. In the Export dialog, under Naming, set Long or Short for the option:

- *Automatic - Long (Specify prefix)*. Manually specify a prefix in the File name/prefix field or accept the default, which uses the format:

Revit Sheet/View: Project Name-View Type-View Name

- *Automatic - Short*. Revit Structure determines the name automatically and adds a prefix to the file name of the current view or multiple views and sheets. The format is:

Revit Sheet: Sheet Name or Revit View: View Type-View Name

Set the Naming to **Automatic- Short**.

Press **OK**.

10. Files of type: | AutoCAD 2013 DXF Files (*.dxf)

         AutoCAD 2013 DXF Files (*.dxf)
         AutoCAD 2010 DXF Files (*.dxf)
    Naming: AutoCAD 2007 DXF Files (*.dxf)
         AutoCAD 2004 DXF Files (*.dxf)
         AutoCAD 2000 DXF Files (*.dxf)

Note that you can export out down to Version 2000.

11. S100   Browse to the folder where you are storing your work files.

S101

S201   You should see the dxf files there.

S202

S203

S300

S400

S500

S600

S601

S602

Command Exercise

Exercise 7-3 – Check Coordination Views

Drawing Name: **coord-review.rvt**
Estimated Time to Completion: 5 Minutes

Scope

Use Coordination Review to determine if linked files have changed.

Solution

1. Elevations (Building Elevation)
    EAST ELEVATION
    NORTH ELEVATION
    SOUTH ELEVATION
    WEST ELEVATION

    Activate **EAST ELEVATION** under ELEVATIONS in the Project Browser.

2. Home Insert Annotate Analyze

    Link Revit Link CAD DWF Markup Point Cloud Manage Links

    Activate the **Insert** ribbon.

    Select the **Manage Links** tool.

3. Activate the **Revit** tab.

    | Revit | CAD Formats | DWF Markups | Point Clouds |

Linked File	Status	Reference Type	Positions Not Saved	Saved Path	Path Type
coord-review-link.rvt	Loaded	Overlay	☐	coord-review-link.rvt	Relative

    There is a Revit file linked to this file.
    Highlight this file.

4. Reload From... Select the **Reload From** button.

5. File name: coord-review-link
    Files of type: RVT Files (*.rvt)

    Locate the *coord-review-link* file.
    Press **Open**.
    Press **OK** to close the dialog.

6. Structural Plans
    Level 1 - Analytical
    Level 2 - Analytical
    S200 TOP OF PIER
    S201 GROUND FLOOR
    S202 MEZZANINE
    S202 TOP OF TIMBER TRUSSES
    S203 ROOF / APEX OF WALL

    Activate the **S202 MEZZANINE** Structural Plan in the Project Browser.

7.  Activate the **Collaborate** ribbon.

Select **Copy/Monitor→Select Link** from the Coordinate panel.

8. Pick in the window to select the linked file.

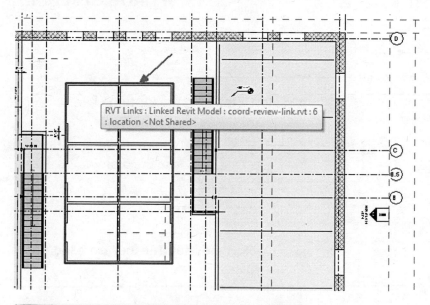

Look for the tooltip as you mouse over the model to see that you are hovering over the linked file.

9.  If the link is selected properly, this toolbar will appear in the ribbon.

10. 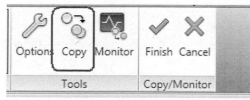 Activate the **EAST ELEVATION** in the Project Browser.

11. 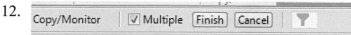 Select the **Copy** tool on the ribbon.

12. On the Options bar:
Enable **Multiple**.

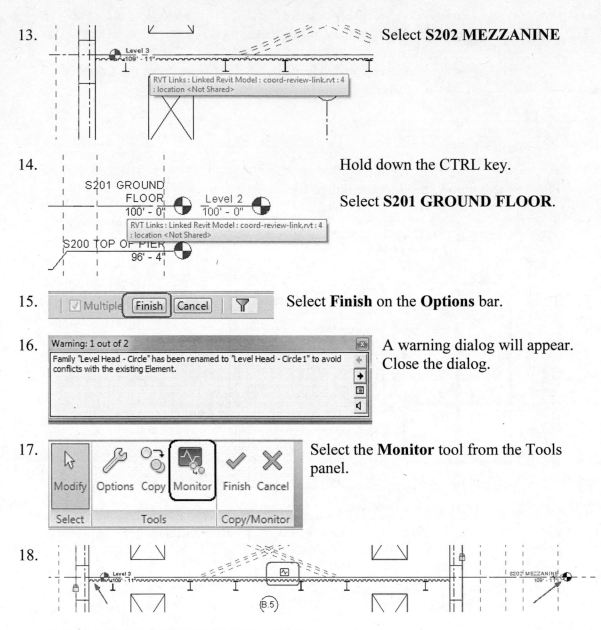

13.   Select **S202 MEZZANINE**

14.   Hold down the CTRL key.

Select **S201 GROUND FLOOR**.

15.   Select **Finish** on the **Options** bar.

16.   A warning dialog will appear. Close the dialog.

Warning: 1 out of 2

Family "Level Head - Circle" has been renamed to "Level Head - Circle 1" to avoid conflicts with the existing Element.

17.   Select the **Monitor** tool from the Tools panel.

18.

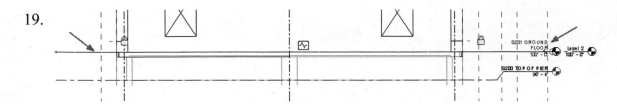

Select the S202 MEZZANINE level.
Select the Level 3 level.
You should see a Monitor symbol appear on the level.

19.

Select the S201 GROUND FLOOR level.
Select the Level 2 level.
You should see a Monitor symbol appear on the level.

20.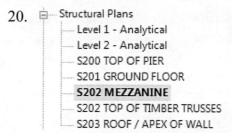

Activate the **S202 MEZZANINE** Structural Plan in the Project Browser.

21.

Select the **Copy** tool on the ribbon.

22.

On the Options bar:
Enable **Multiple**.

23.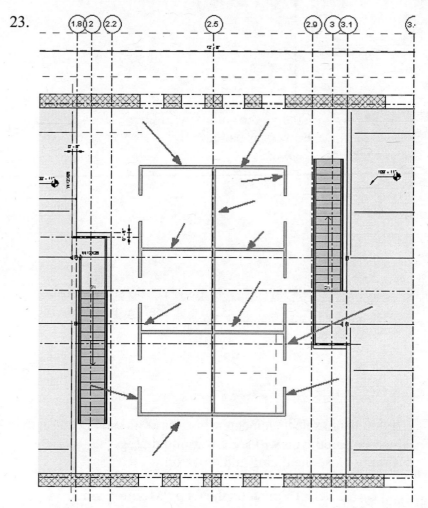

Hold down the CTRL key.

Select the walls in the linked file.

24. Select **Finish** on the **Options** bar.

25.

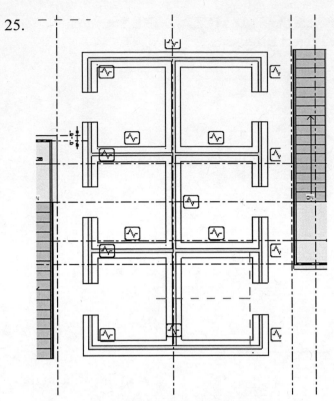

Monitor symbols will appear next to each of the selected walls.

26.

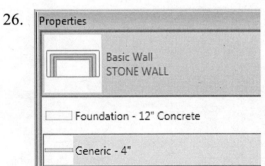

Change the wall type to Generic – 4″ in the Properties panel.

27.

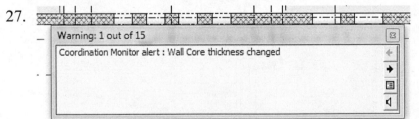

If you see a warning dialog, just close it.

28.

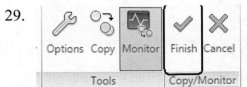

If you try to select elements which have already been set to be monitored, you will see a warning dialog.
Simply close the dialog and move on.

29.

Select **Finish** on the Copy/Monitor panel.

30. Activate the **Insert** ribbon.

Select **Manage Links** from the Link panel.

31. Select the **Revit** tab.
Highlight the *coord-review-link* file.

32. Select **Reload From**.

33. Locate the *coord-review-link_revised* file.
Press **Open**.

34. A dialog will appear indicating that there have been changes which require a Coordination Review.

Press **OK**.

35. Note that the revised file has replaced the previous link.
This is similar to when a sub-contractor or other consultant emails you an updated file for use in a project.
Press **OK**.

36. Activate the **Collaborate** ribbon.
Select **Coordination Review→Select Link** from the Coordinate panel.

37. 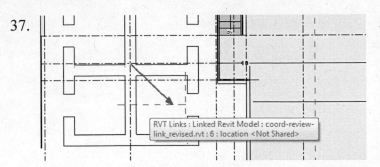 Select the linked file in the drawing window.

The reference plane indicated resides in the linked file so is an easy object to select.

38. 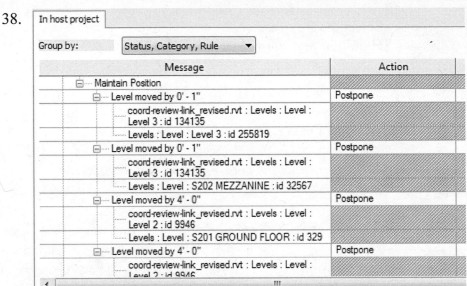 Expand the list of changes in the dialog.

39. 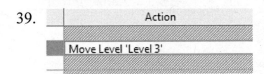 For the first change:
In the Action column: Select **Move Level 3**.

Press the **Add Comment** button.

40. 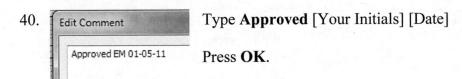 Type **Approved** [Your Initials] [Date]

Press **OK**.

41. 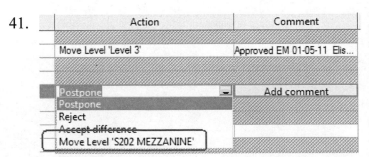 For the second change:
In the Action column: Select
Move Level S202 MEZZANINE.

Press the **Add Comment** button.

42. Edit Comment

Approved EM 01-05-11|

Type **Approved** [Your Initials] [Date]

Press **OK**.

43. 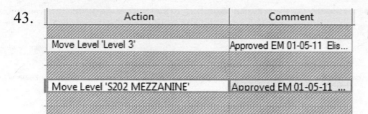   The dialog updates with the changes.

44.

Show:

☑ Postponed   ☑ Rejected

[Show]   [Create Report]

Select **Create Report**.

45. File name: coord-revew

Save as type: Revit Coordination Report (*.html)

Note the folder where the report will be saved.
Press **Save**.

46. Press **OK** to close the Coordination Review dialog box.

47.   🔘 coord-revew   Locate the report you created and double click on it to open.

     📄 coord-revew

Revit Coordination Report

In host project

New/Unresolved	Levels	Maintain Position	Level moved by 4' - 0"	Levels : Level : Level 2 : id 257565 coord-review-link_revised.rvt : Levels : Level : Level 2 : id 9946
New/Unresolved	Levels	Maintain Position	Level moved by 0' - 1"	Levels : Level : Level 3 : id 257566 coord-review-link_revised.rvt : Levels : Level : Level 3 : id 134135
New/Unresolved	Levels	Maintain Position	Level moved by 0' - 1"	Levels : Level : S202 MEZZANINE : id 32567 coord-review-link_revised.rvt : Levels : Level : Level 3 : id 134135
New/Unresolved	Walls	Maintain wall elevation/height	Wall Elevations are different	Walls : Basic Wall : Generic - 4" : id 257844 coord-review-link_revised.rvt : Walls : Basic Wall : Generic - 4" : id 135458
New/Unresolved	Walls	Maintain wall elevation/height	Wall Elevations are different	Walls : Basic Wall : Generic - 4" : id 257845 coord-review-link_revised.rvt : Walls : Basic Wall : Generic - 4" : id 135658
New/Unresolved	Walls	Maintain wall elevation/height	Wall Elevations are different	Walls : Basic Wall : Generic - 4" : id 257846 coord-review-link_revised.rvt : Walls : Basic Wall : Generic - 4" : id 135715
New/Unresolved	Walls	Maintain wall elevation/height	Wall Elevations are different	Walls : Basic Wall : Generic - 4" : id 257847

48. Close the file without saving.

Command Exercise

Exercise 7-4 – Interference Checking

Drawing Name: **interference_structural.rvt**
Estimated Time to Completion: 5 Minutes

Scope

Using Linked Files
Checking for Interference

Solution

1. 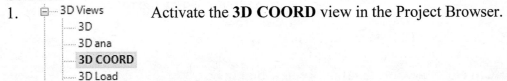 Activate the **3D COORD** view in the Project Browser.

2.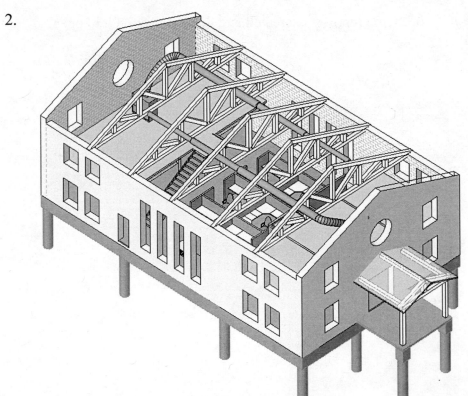

If you inspect the model, you should see some ductwork and some office cubicles.

3.  Activate the Insert ribbon.
Select **Manage Links**.

4.

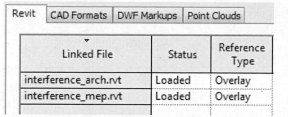

Note there are two files listed.
If the files are not loaded, you can reload them from the Exercise Files that come with the text.

Press **OK**.

5.

Activate the Collaborate ribbon.
Select **Interference Check→Run Interference Check**.

6.

Interference Check

Categories from

Current Project

Categories from

interference_mep.rvt

☐ Doors	☑ Duct Fittings
☐ Floors	☑ Ducts
☐ Railings	☑ Flex Ducts
☐ Roofs	☑ Mechanical Equipment
☐ Stairs	
☐ Structural Columns	
☑ Structural Framing	
☑ Chord	
☑ Girder	
☑ Horizontal Bracing	
☑ Joist	
☑ Kicker Bracing	
☑ Other	
☑ Purlin	
☑ Vertical Bracing	
☑ Web	
☐ Walls	
☐ Windows	

On the left pane:
Set Categories from: Current Project.
Enable Structural Framing and all the items below it.
On the right pane:
Set Categories from: *interference_mep.rvt*.
Enable all the listed items.
Press OK.

7.

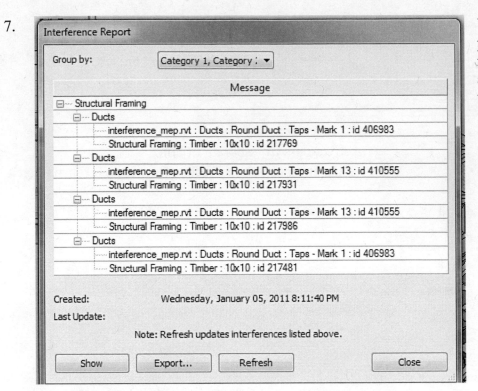

You will see a preview of a report of all areas where there are interference issues.

8.

Highlight the first item in the list.

9.

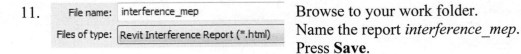

The elements which are conflicting will highlight in the display window.

10. Export...   Select the **Export** button.

11. File name: interference_mep
    Files of type: Revit Interference Report (*.html)

    Browse to your work folder.
    Name the report *interference_mep*.
    Press **Save**.

12. interference_mep
    interference_mep

    Locate the report in your work folder.
    Double click on it to open.

13. You can see the report.

Interference Report

Interference Report Project File: E:\Schroff\Revit Structure 2012 Basics\exercise files\interference_structural.rvt
Created: Wednesday, January 05, 2011 8:11:40 PM
Last Update:

	A	B
1	Structural Framing : Timber : 10x10 : id 217481	interference_mep.rvt : Ducts : Round Duct : Taps - Mark 1 : id 406983
2	Structural Framing : Timber : 10x10 : id 217769	interference_mep.rvt : Ducts : Round Duct : Taps - Mark 1 : id 406983
3	Structural Framing : Timber : 10x10 : id 217931	interference_mep.rvt : Ducts : Round Duct : Taps - Mark 13 : id 410555
4	Structural Framing : Timber : 10x10 : id 217986	interference_mep.rvt : Ducts : Round Duct : Taps - Mark 13 : id 410555

End of Interference Report

This report can be attached to an email or printed out.

14. [Close] Close the Interference Report window.

15. 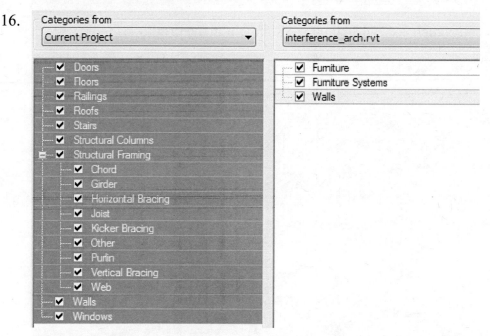 Activate the Collaborate ribbon.
Select **Interference Check→Run Interference Check**.

16.

On the left pane:
Set Categories from: Current Project.
Enable all the listed items.
On the right pane:
Set Categories from: *interference_arch.rvt*.
Enable all the listed items.
Press **OK**.

17. 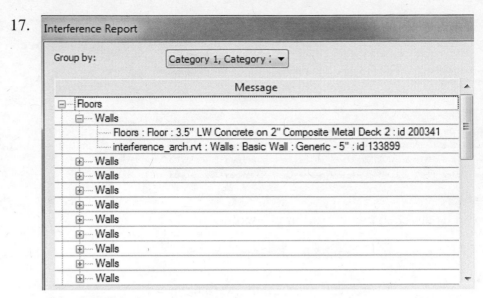 You will see a preview of a report of all areas where there are interference issues.

18. Highlight the first item in the list.

19. The elements which are conflicting will highlight in the display window.

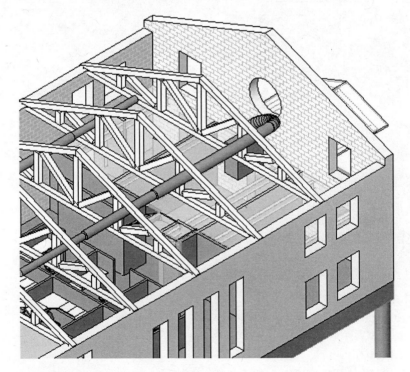

20. Close the report window.

21. Close the file without saving.

Lesson Eight
Structural Analysis

➢ Apply the proper view template to your analytical views to ensure the best results
➢ Views and View Templates are not linked. If you modify a view template, you need to reload it into the view in order for the new settings to be applied.
➢ You can run automatic checks on your analytic model to see if members are supported properly.
➢ Consistency checks identify possible discrepancies between the physical and analytical model.

Revit Structure automatically creates an analytical model of your structure. This analytical model is a simplified 3D representation consisting of simple geometry, material properties, and loads. The physical model is used for modeling and documentation, while the analytical model is used for structural analysis.

The analytical model can be exported to third party analytical applications. You can also perform basic analytical checks within Revit Structure. Autodesk also has a software called Robot Structural Analysis which is used for structural analysis of Revit projects. In this lesson, some of the exercises use the structural extensions to analyze the model. These extensions are available to users who are on subscription only.

➢ To eliminate or reduce duplicate nodes align or lock structural elements to grids, levels, and named reference planes.
➢ In order to ensure structural analysis data is reliable, eliminate any warning errors
➢ Use the Analytical Adjust tool to align structural elements with walls and other elements

There are three load types available in Revit Structure: point, line and area. Loads can be applied by selecting a host, such as a beam or joist, or by creating a sketch. You can also generate load cases, such as snow loads or wind loads.

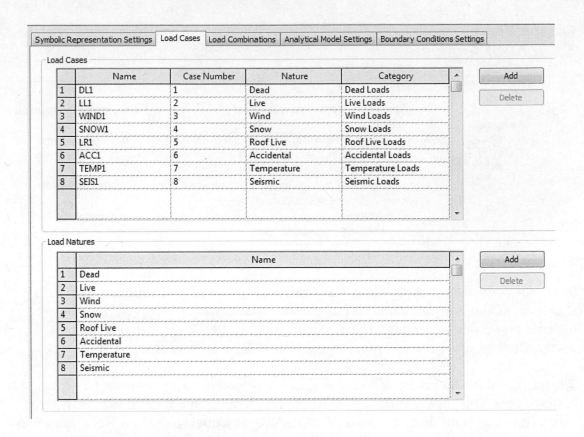

Command Exercise

Exercise 8-1 – Analytical Views

Drawing Name: **new**
Estimated Time to Completion: 40 Minutes

Scope

Defining Analytical and Model view templates for a Project

Solution

1. Start a **New Project** using the default template.

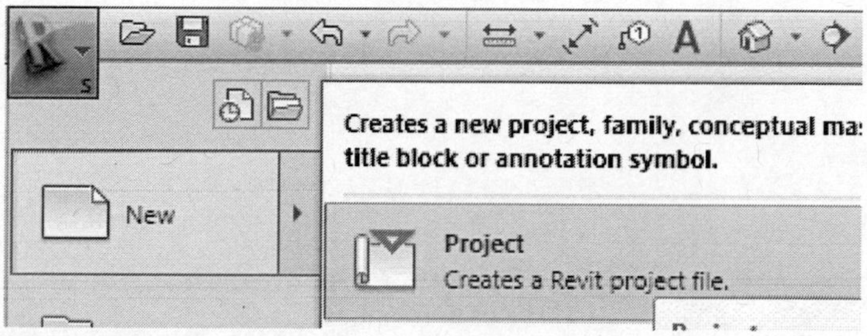

2. Press **OK** when the dialog appears.

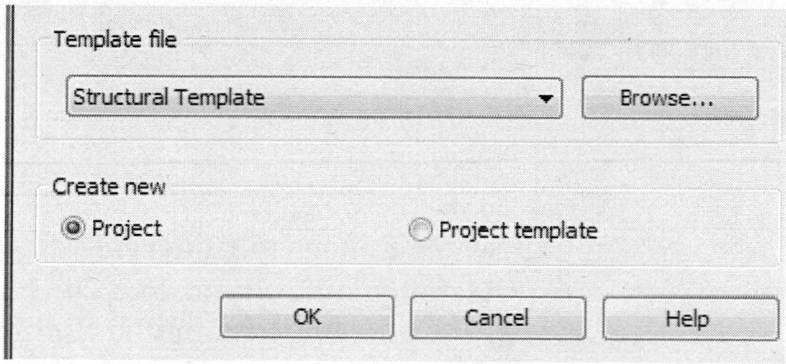

3. Activate the **Level 1 Structural Plan** in the Project Browser.

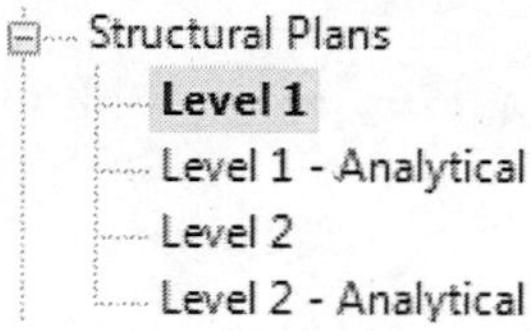

   Structural Plans
   Level 1
   Level 1 - Analytical
   Level 2
   Level 2 - Analytical

4. Activate the **Structure** ribbon.

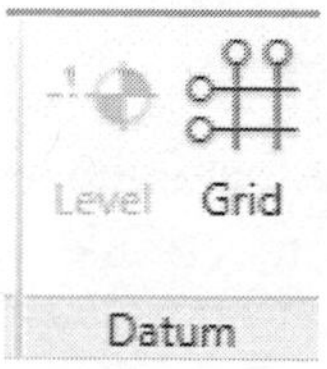

   Select the **Grid** tool from the Datum panel.

5.

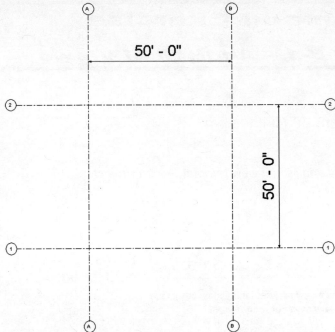

Create a square grid with two horizontal and two vertical grid lines.

Label the vertical grid lines A and B.

Label the horizontal grid lines 1 and 2.

Space the grid lines **50′ 0″ [15240 mm]** apart.

6.

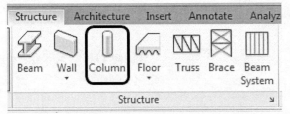

Select the **Column** tool.

7.

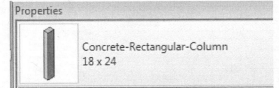

In the Type Selector:
Set the Column to **Concrete - Rectangular-Column 18 x 24 [M_Concrete-Rectangular-Column: 450 x 600 mm]**.

8.

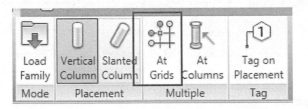

Select **At Grids** on the ribbon.

9.

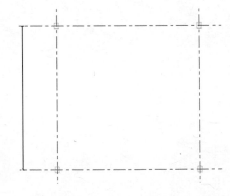

Hold down the CTRL key and select each grid to place columns at all the grid intersections.

The columns will preview to indicate their placement.

10. 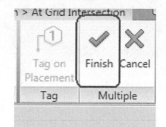 Press **Finish** on the ribbon.

Right click to cancel the command.

11.  Window around the columns so they are selected.

12. In the Properties pane:

Set the Top Level to **Level 2**.

Constraints	
Column Location...	
Base Level	Level 1
Base Offset	-9' 0"
Top Level	Level 2
Top Offset	0' 0"
Column Style	Vertical
Moves With Grids	☑
Room Bounding	☑

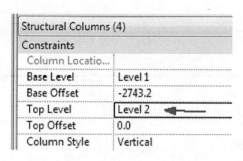

Structural Columns (4)	
Constraints	
Column Locatio...	
Base Level	Level 1
Base Offset	-2743.2
Top Level	Level 2
Top Offset	0.0
Column Style	Vertical

13.  Activate **Level 2** in the Project Browser.

Structural Plans
  Level 1
  Level 1 - Analytical
  Level 2
  Level 2 - Analytical

14. Select the **Beam** tool.

Home Insert

Beam Wall

15.  In the Type Selector:
Set the Column to **W-Wide Flange W14 x 30 [UB-Universal Beam: 305x165x40UB]**.

W-Wide Flange
W14X30

16. Select the **On Grids** tool.

17. 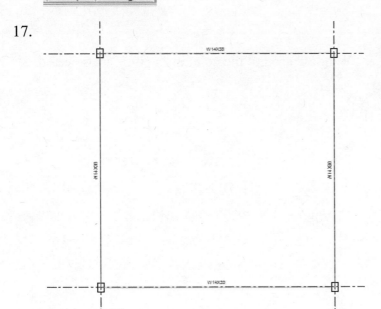 Hold down the CTRL key and select all four grid lines.

The beams will preview their placement.

18. 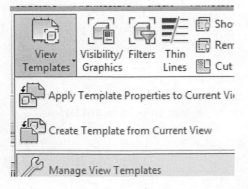 Select the **Finish** tool.

Right click and select **Cancel** to exit the command.

19. Level 2
    Level 2 - Analytical
    Activate the **Level 2- Analytical** in the Project Browser.

20. 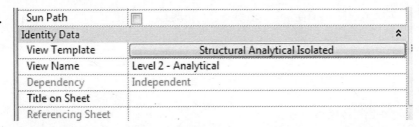 Set the Default View Template to **Structural Analytical Isolated**.

21. Activate the **View** ribbon.

Select **View Template→Manage View Templates**.

22. 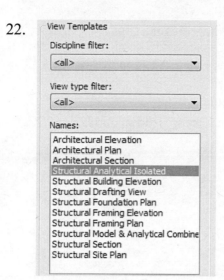 Highlight **Structural Analytical Isolated**.

23. 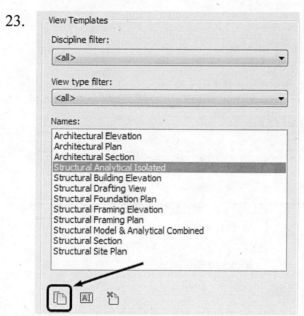 Select **Duplicate**.

24. Name: Structural Analytical Plan

Type **Structural Analytical Plan**.

Press **OK**.

25.

Parameter	Value	Inclu
View Scale	1/8" = 1'-0"	✓
Scale Value 1:	96	
Display Model	Normal	✓
Detail Level	Coarse	✓
Parts Visibility	Show Original	✓
V/G Overrides Model	Edit...	✓
V/G Overrides Annotation	Edit...	✓
V/G Overrides Analytical Model	Edit...	✓
V/G Overrides Import	Edit...	✓
V/G Overrides Filters	Edit...	✓
Model Display	Edit...	✓
Shadows	Edit...	✓

View Properties

Number of views with this template assigned: 1

Select Edit next the **V/G Overrides Model**.

26.

On the Model Categories tab:

Enable **Show model categories in this view**.

Under Structural Columns:
Uncheck Hidden Faces, Hidden Lines, and Stick Symbols.

27.

On the Model Categories tab:

Under Structural Framing:

Uncheck everything but Rigid Links.

Press **Apply** and **OK**.

28.

Highlight **Structural Analytical Isolated**.

Select **Duplicate.**

29.

Type **Structural Analytical Stick**.

Press **OK**.

30.

Architectural Section
Structural Analytical Normal
Structural Analytical Stick
Structural Building Elevation
Structural Drafting View

Highlight **Structural Analytical Stick**.

31.

View Properties

Number of views with this template assigned: **0**

Parameter	Value	Inclu
View Scale	1/8" = 1'-0"	☑
Scale Value 1:	96	
Display Model	Normal	☑
Detail Level	Coarse	☑
Parts Visibility	Show Original	☑
V/G Overrides Model	Edit...	☑
V/G Overrides Annotation	Edit...	☑
V/G Overrides Analytical Model	Edit...	☑
V/G Overrides Import	Edit...	☑
V/G Overrides Filters	Edit...	☑
Model Display	Edit...	☑
Shadows	Edit	☑

Select Edit next the **V/G Overrides Model**.

32.

☑ Show model categories in this view

Visibility	Projection/Surfac	
	Lines	Patt
⊞ ☐ Rooms		
☐ Security Devices		
⊞ ☐ Shaft Openings		
⊞ ☐ Site		
⊞ ☐ Spaces		
⊞ ☐ Specialty Equipment		
☐ Sprinklers		
⊞ ☐ Stair System		
⊞ ☐ Stair System-Landings		
⊞ ☐ Stair System-Runs		
⊞ ☐ Stair System-Steps		
⊞ ☐ Stair System-Stringers		
⊞ ☐ Stairs		
⊞ ☐ Structural Area Reinfor...		
⊞ ☐ Structural Beam Systems		
⊞ ☐ Structural Columns		
☐ Structural Connections		
⊞ ☐ Structural Foundations		
⊞ ☐ Structural Framing		
⊞ ☐ Structural Path Reinfor...		
☐ Structural Rebar		
☐ Structural Stiffeners		
⊞ ☐ Structural Trusses		
☐ Telephone Devices		
⊞ ☐ Topography		
⊞ ☐ Walls		Hid
⊞ ☐ Windows		
⊞ ☐ Wires		

On the Model Categories tab:

None

Select **None** so that nothing is checked.

If the None button doesn't work, just go through and uncheck everything.

Press **OK**.

33. 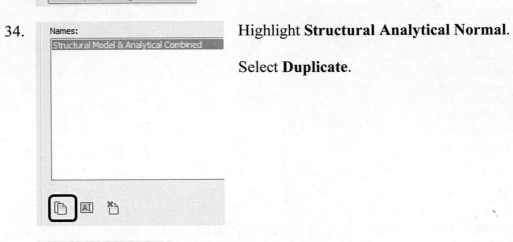 Under View Type filter:
Select **3D Views, Walkthroughs**.

34. Highlight **Structural Analytical Normal**.

Select **Duplicate**.

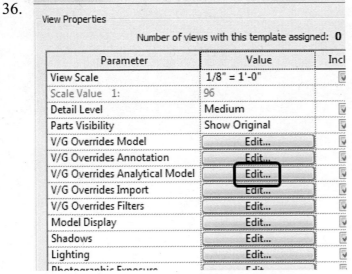

35. Name: 3D-Model   Type **3D-Model** for the name.

OK   Press **OK**.

36. Select Edit next the **V/G Overrides Analytical Model**.

View Properties

Number of views with this template assigned: **0**

Parameter	Value	Incl
View Scale	1/8" = 1'-0"	☑
Scale Value 1:	96	
Detail Level	Medium	☑
Parts Visibility	Show Original	☑
V/G Overrides Model	Edit...	☑
V/G Overrides Annotation	Edit...	☑
V/G Overrides Analytical Model	Edit...	☑
V/G Overrides Import	Edit...	☑
V/G Overrides Filters	Edit...	☑
Model Display	Edit...	☑
Shadows	Edit...	☑
Lighting	Edit...	☑
Photographic Exposure	Edit...	

37.

| Model Categories | Annotation Categories | Analytical Model Categories | Imported (|

☑ Show analytical model categories in this view

Filter list: Structure ▼

Visibility	Projection/Su	
	Lines	Patterns
⊞ ☐ Analytical Beams		
⊞ ☐ Analytical Braces		
⊞ ☐ Analytical Columns		
☐ Analytical Floors		
☐ Analytical Foundation Slabs		
☐ Analytical Isolated Foundations		
☐ Analytical Links		
☐ Analytical Nodes		
☐ Analytical Wall Foundations		
☐ Analytical Walls		
☐ Boundary Conditions		
⊞ ☐ Structural Internal Loads		
⊞ ☐ Structural Load Cases		
⊞ ☐ Structural Loads		

Uncheck all the categories.

Press **Apply** and **OK**.

38.

☑ Structural Beam Systems	
⊟ ☑ Structural Columns	
☑ Hidden Faces	
☑ Hidden Lines	Ove
☐ Rigid Links	
☐ Stick Symbols	
☑ Structural Connections	

Activate the Model Categories tab.
Under Structural Columns:

Enable Hidden Faces and Hidden Lines.

39.

⊞ ☑ Structural Foundations	
⊟ ☑ Structural Framing	
☑ Chord	
☑ Girder	
☑ Hidden Faces	
☑ Hidden Lines	
☑ Horizontal Bracing	
☑ Joist	
☑ Kicker Bracing	
☑ Other	
☑ Purlin	
☑ Rigid Links	
☐ Stick Symbols	
☑ Vertical Bracing	
☑ Web	Override...
⊞ ☑ Structural Path Reinfor	

Under Structural Framing:

Uncheck Stick Symbols.
All other items should be enabled.

Press **OK**.

Close the View Templates dialog.

40. Activate a **3D View**.

41.

| Copy to Clipboard |
| Rename... |
| Select All Instances |
| ✓ Properties |
| Save to New File... |
| Search... |

Highlight the **{3D}** view in the Project Browser.

Right click and select **Rename**.

42. 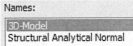 Type **3D-Model** in the name field.

Press **OK**.

43. 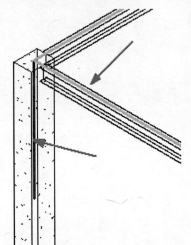 If you zoom in, you should see some blue and orange lines.

These are the analytical elements.

44. 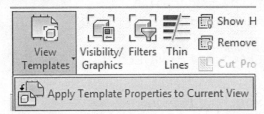 Activate the **View** ribbon.

Select **View Templates→Apply Template Properties to Current View**.

45. Select **3D-Model**.
Press **Apply** Properties and **OK**.

46.
Identity Data	
View Name	3D- Model
Dependency	Independent
Title on Sheet	
Default View Template	3D-Model

In the Project Browser, set the Default View Template to **3D-Model**.

47. 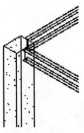 The stick elements are no longer visible.

48.

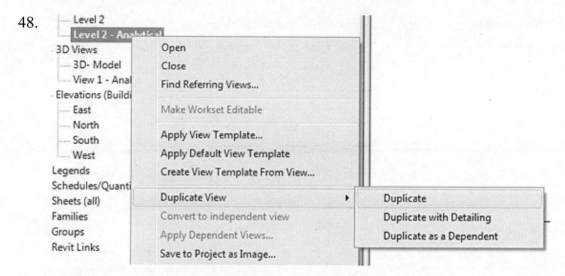

Highlight **Level 2- Analytical**.
Right click and select **Duplicate View→Duplicate**.

49.

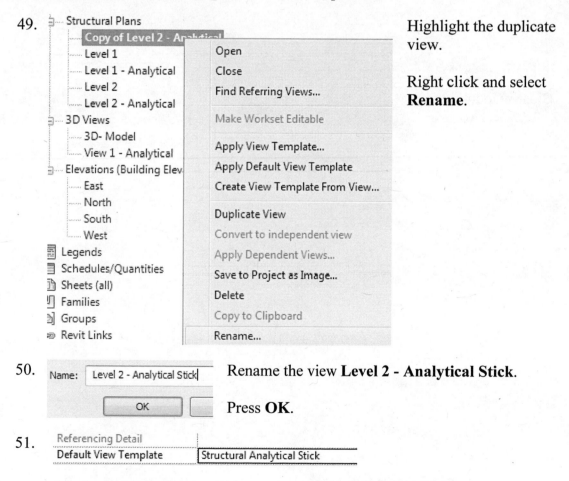

Highlight the duplicate view.

Right click and select **Rename**.

50.

Name: Level 2 - Analytical Stick

OK

Rename the view **Level 2 - Analytical Stick**.

Press **OK**.

51.

Referencing Detail

Default View Template | Structural Analytical Stick

Set the Default View Template to **Structural Analytical Stick**.

52.   The view should update to display only the stick elements.

53.   Close without saving.

Command Exercise

Exercise 8-2 – Analytical Adjust

Drawing Name: **adjust.rvt**
Estimated Time to Completion: 5 Minutes

Scope

> *Use Analytical Adjust to align a beam.*

Solution

1. Structural Plans
   Level 1
   Level 1 - Analytical
   Level 2
   Level 2 - Analytical
   Level 2 - Analytical Stick

   Activate **Level 2-Analytical Structural Plan** in the Project Browser.

2.
   Activate the **Analyze** ribbon.

   We want to join the ends of the two horizontal beams using the Analytical Adjust tool.

3.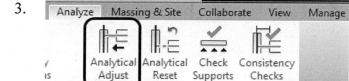

   Activate the Analyze ribbon.

   Select the **Analytical Adjust** tool.

4.

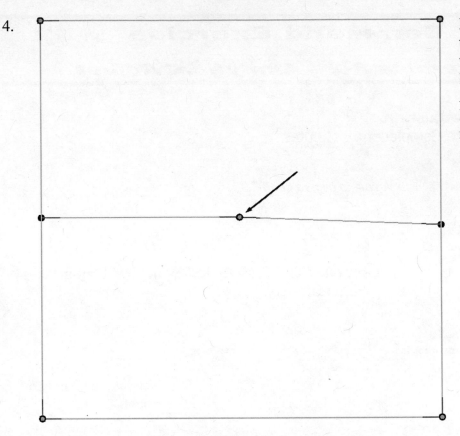

If you mouse over the middle dot, it will display a label saying Analytical node. Left click on the node.

5.

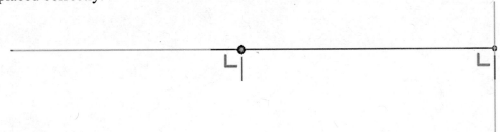

You will see a perpendicular tool on the node.
Select the far right end point of the right beam and adjust the position so it is aligned with the left horizontal beam.

6. You should see a perpendicular symbol at both end points of the right beam when it is placed correctly.

7. Select **Finish**.

Wall Adjustment | Openings | Analytical Link | Finish | Cancel

Edit Analytical Model

8. Close without saving.

Command Exercise

Exercise 8-3 – Load Takedown

Drawing Name: **load-take-down_1.rvt**
Estimated Time to Completion: 25 Minutes

Scope

Create a Load Case
Apply an area load
Apply a line load

Solution

1. Activate **View 1 - Analytical** under the 3D Views category in the Project Browser.

   Level 2 - Analytical
   3D Views
   View 1 - Analytical

2. Activate the **Analyze** ribbon.

   Select **Load Cases** in the Loads panel.

   Structure Architecture Insert Annotate Analyze

   Loads Load Cases Load Combinations Boundary Conditions Anal Ad

   Loads Boundary Conditions

3.

   Load Cases

	Name	Case Number	Nature	Category
1	DL1	1	Dead	Dead Loads
2	LL1	2	Live	Live Loads
3	WIND1	3	Wind	Wind Loads
4	SNOW1	4	Snow	Snow Loads
5	LR1	5	Roof Live	Roof Live Loads
6	ACC1	6	Accidental	Accidental Loads
7	TEMP1	7	Temperature	Temperature Loads
8	SEIS1	8	Seismic	Seismic Loads

   Add
   Delete

   In the Load Cases area:

   Select the **Add** button.

4.

	Name	Case Number
1	DL1	1
2	LL1	2
3	WIND1	3
4	SNOW1	4
5	LR1	5
6	ACC1	6
7	TEMP1	7
8	SEIS1	8
9	Roof Hung ←	9

Type **Roof Hung** for the Name.

Note that Revit automatically assigns the next case number to this load case. This is a read-only property you cannot change it.

5.

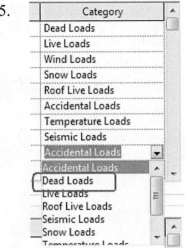

Under the Category column:

Set the new case load to **Dead Loads**.

6.

	Name		Add
1	Dead		Delete
2	Live		
3	Wind		
4	Snow		
5	Roof Live		
6	Accidental		
7	Temperature		
8	Seismic		

In the Load Natures area:

Select the **Add** button.

7.

Load Natures	
1	Dead
2	Live
3	Wind
4	Snow
5	Roof Live
6	Accidental
7	Temperature
8	Seismic
9	Roof Hung

Change the name to **Roof Hung**.

Press **OK** to close the dialog.

8. Activate the **Analyze** ribbon.

Select **Loads** in the Loads panel.

9. The ribbon displays the different types of loads that can be applied.
Select **Hosted Area Load**.

10. Area Loads
Area Load 1

In the Properties panel:
Note that the Area Load is called Area Load 1.

11. Select the slab edge.

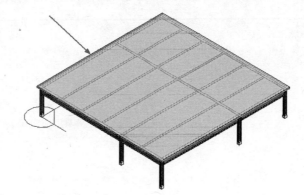

12.

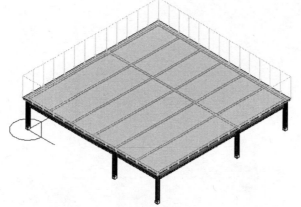

An area load will automatically appear in the display window.

13.

New Area Loads	
Area Loads	
Area Load 1	
Identity Data	
Description	
Comments	
Structural Analysis	
Is Reaction	☐
Load Case	LL1 (2)
Orient to	Host workplane
Fx 1	0.0000 ksf
Fy 1	0.0000 ksf
Fz 1	-0.0300 ksf
Fx 2	0.0000 ksf

Change the value for the Fz1 force to -**0.0300ksf**.

ksf stands for kilos per square foot.

Select the **Apply** button to apply the new value.

14. Structural Plans
 Level 1
 Level 1 - Analytical
 Level 2
 Level 2 - Analytical

Activate the **Level 2 - Analytical Structural Plan** in the Project Browser.

15. Activate the **Analyze** ribbon.

dify | Loads

Select **Loads** in the Loads panel.

16. Point Load | Line Load | Area Load | Hosted Point Load | Hosted Line Load | Hosted Area Load

Loads

Select the **Line Load** tool on the ribbon.

17.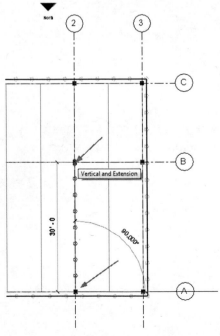

Draw a line from the intersection of Grid 2 and Grid A (A2) to the intersection of Grid 2 and Grid B (B2)

18.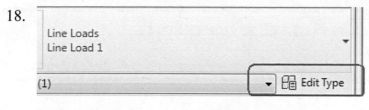

In the Properties pane:
Select **Edit Type**.

19. Duplicate...   Select **Duplicate**.

20. Name: Wind Load

Enter **Wind Load**.

Press **OK**.
Press **OK** to close the Type Properties dialog.

21.

Structural Analysis	
Is Reaction	☐
Load Case	WIND1 (3)
Orient to	Workplane
Fx 1	0.040 kip/ft
Fy 1	0.000 kip/ft
Fz 1	0.000 kip/ft

In the Properties pane:

Set the Load Case to WIND1 (3).
Set Fx1 to 0.04 kip/ft.
Set Fy1 to 0.00 kip/ft.
Set Fz1 to 0.00 kip/ft.

22. Level 2 - Analytical
    3D Views
    View 1 - Analytical

Activate **View 1 - Analytical** under the 3D Views category in the Project Browser.

23. You should see the area load and the line load that was placed.

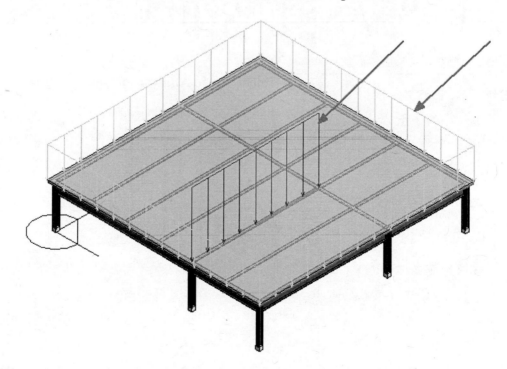

This model is ready to be exported to an outside application for analysis.

24. Close without saving.

Command Exercise

Exercise 8-4 – Static Analysis of Slabs

Drawing Name: **load-take-down_2.rvt**
Estimated Time to Completion: 30 Minutes

Scope

Modify structural members

In order to do this lesson, you need to download and install the Revit Structure Extensions. Note that if you are using 2011, you need to download and install the 2011 extensions. If you are using 2013, you need to download and install the 2013 extensions. Revit Extensions are available free to Autodesk customers on subscription. Contact your reseller for more information.

Solution

1. Extensions   Activate the **Extensions** tab on the ribbon.

2. 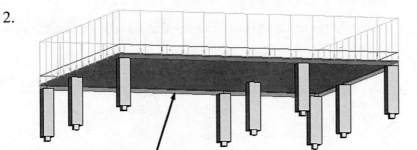 Select the slab in the display area.

3. 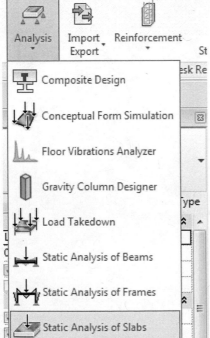 Select **Static Analysis of Slabs** under **Analysis**.

4.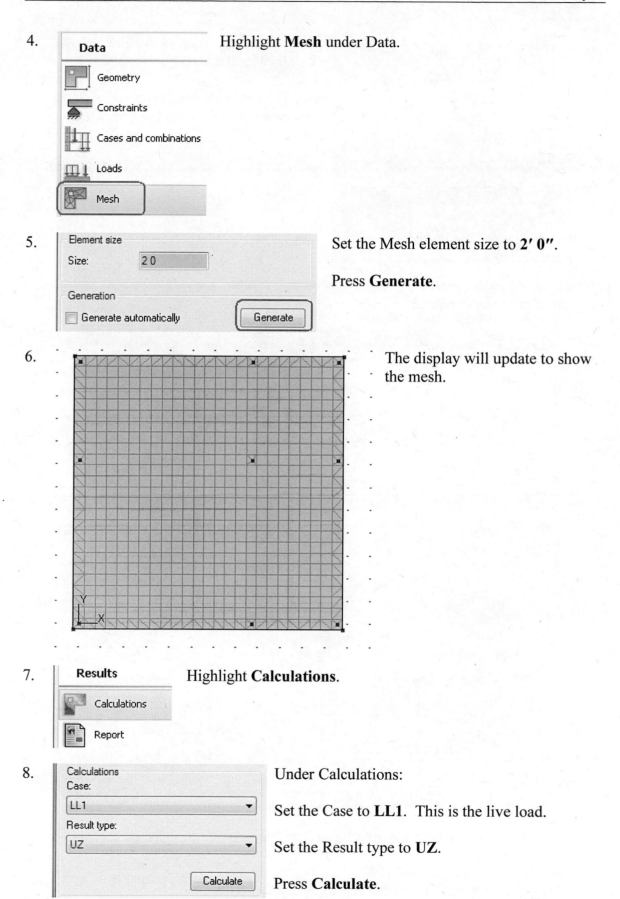

Highlight **Mesh** under Data.

5. Set the Mesh element size to **2′ 0″**.

Press **Generate**.

6. The display will update to show the mesh.

7. Highlight **Calculations**.

8. Under Calculations:

Set the Case to **LL1**. This is the live load.

Set the Result type to **UZ**.

Press **Calculate**.

9.

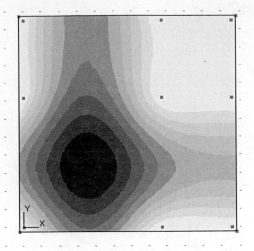

The display changes to show the displacements.

The extension has performed a finite element analysis on the geometry.

10. Select the **Reactions** tab.

		X	Y	FZ	RFix	RFiy
▶	1	0' - 0"	0' - 0"	30.89 kip	0.00 kip*ft	0.00 kip*ft
	2	0' - 0"	30' - 0"	63.13 kip	0.00 kip*ft	0.00 kip*ft
	3	0' - 0"	48' - 0"	13.44 kip	0.00 kip*ft	0.00 kip*ft
	4	32' - 0"	0' - 0"	62.29 kip	0.00 kip*ft	0.00 kip*ft
	5	32' - 0"	30' - 0"	147.54 kip	0.00 kip*ft	0.00 kip*ft
	6	32' - 0"	48' - 0"	30.32 kip	0.00 kip*ft	0.00 kip*ft
	7	48' - 0"	0' - 0"	7.94 kip	0.00 kip*ft	0.00 kip*ft

Tabs: Extreme values | Reactions | Displacements (characteristic points) | Internal forces (characteristic points)

11.

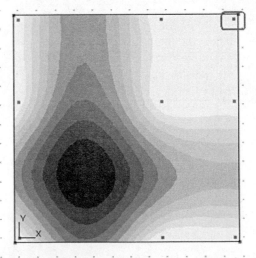

Click on the column located in the upper right.

12.

	8	48' - 0"	30' - 0"	19.69 kip	0.00 kip*ft	0.00 kip*ft
	9	48' - 0"	48' - 0"	-0.24 kip	0.00 kip*ft	0.00 kip*ft

Row 9 will highlight to identify the data associated with the selected column.

13. Note the Fz value is **-0.24 kip**.
This indicates that the column is being lifted up by the load.

14. 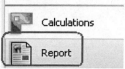 Highlight **Report** under the Results area in the dialog.

15.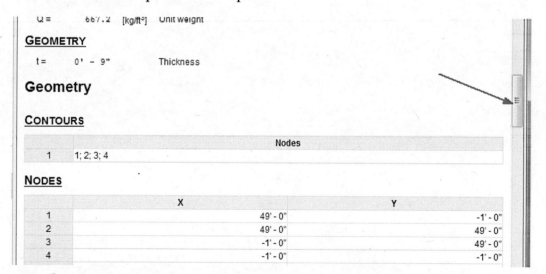

Under Data:
Enable **Geometry**.
Enable **Supports**.

16. Under Load and Results:
Enable **Extreme Values**.
Enable **Detailed Results**.
Enable **Selected load case**.
Select the **LL1** (live load) from the drop down list.

17. Use the scroll bar to preview the report.

q =   667.2   [kg/ft²]   Unit weight

GEOMETRY

t =   0' – 9"   Thickness

Geometry

CONTOURS

	Nodes
1	1; 2; 3; 4

NODES

	X	Y
1	49' - 0"	-1' - 0"
2	49' - 0"	49' - 0"
3	-1' - 0"	49' - 0"
4	-1' - 0"	-1' - 0"

18. File ▾ View ▾
    - Export to Microsoft Word
    - Export to Microsoft Excel
    - Save as ...
    - Print

    Go to the top of the dialog.
    Under File, select **Save as**.

    Note you can also export the report to Word or Excel.

19.   **File name:** load-take-down
    Save as type: HTML (*.html) file
        Browse to your exercises folder to save the file.
Name the file *load-take-down*.
Set the file type to *html*.
Press **Save**.

20.   Press **OK** to close the dialog window.

21.   Level Name with Circle   Browse to the exercises file.
   load-take-down   Locate the html file that was just saved.
   load-take-down_1   Double click on it to open it.

22.   The html file can be attached to an email or printed out for review.

23.   Close the file without saving.

Command Exercise

Exercise 8-5 – Static Analysis of Beams

Drawing Name: **static-beam-tool.rvt**
Estimated Time to Completion: 30 Minutes

Scope

Static Analysis of Beams

Solution

1. 3D Views
    View 1 - Analytical

    Activate **View 1 - Analytical** under 3D Views in the Project Browser.

2. Select the beam indicated.

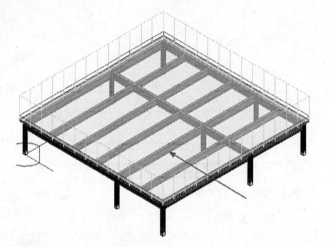

3.

    Activate the **Analyze** ribbon.

    Select the **Loads** tool.

4. Select the **Hosted Line Load** tool.

5.

Select the beam.

6.   The load will be displayed in the window.

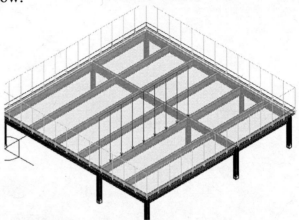

7.

Structural Analysis	
Is Reaction	☐
Load Case	LL1 (2)
Orient to	Project
Fx 1	0.000 kip/ft
Fy 1	0.000 kip/ft
Fz 1	-0.1000 kip/ft
Fx 2	0.000 kip/ft
Fy 2	0.000 kip/ft

In the Properties Pane:

Set the Load Case to **LL1 (2)**. This indicates a live load.

Set Fz1 to **-0.100 kip/ft**.

Press **Apply**.

8.

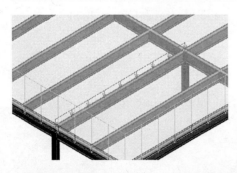

The load display will adjust to indicate the new values.

9.

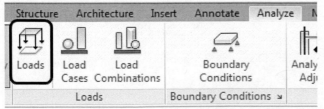

Activate the **Analyze** ribbon.

Select the **Loads** tool.

10.  Select the **Hosted Line Load** tool.

11. 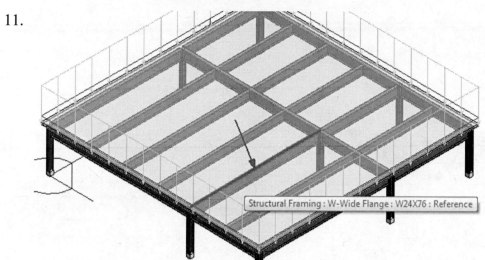 Select the same beam.

Structural Framing : W-Wide Flange : W24X76 : Reference

12.

Structural Analysis	
Is Reaction	☐
Load Case	TEMP1 (7)
Orient to	Project
Fx 1	0.000 kip/ft
Fy 1	0.000 kip/ft
Fz 1	-1.000 kip/ft

In the Properties pane:

Set the Load Case to **TEMP1 (7).**

Set the Fz1 value to **-1.0 kip/ft**.

Press **Apply**.

13.  The display will show both loads applied to the beam.

14.

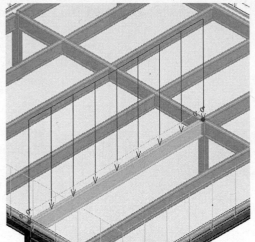

Select the beam so it is highlighted.

15.

| ecture | Insert | Annotate | Analyze | Massing & Site | Collaborate | View | Manage | Extensions | Mo |

Modeling Analysis Import Export Reinforcement AutoCAD Structural Detailing Steel Connections Tools Civil Structures

Autodesk Revit Extensions

Activate the **Extensions** tab.

16.

Analysis Import Export Reinforcement

Composite Design

Conceptual Form Simulation

Floor Vibrations Analyzer

Gravity Column Designer

Load Takedown

Static Analysis of Beams

Select **Static Analysis of Beams** under Analysis.

Remember you need to preselect the elements to be analyzed or you will get an error.

17. 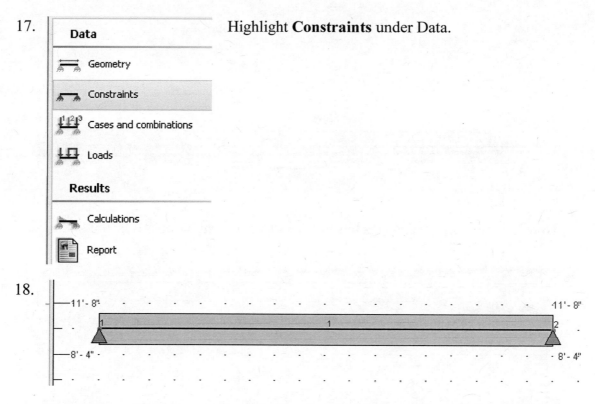   Highlight **Constraints** under Data.

18.

The display will change to show the fixed constraints at each end of the beam.

19. 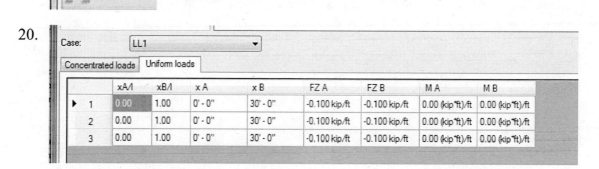   Highlight **Loads** under Data.

20.

Select **LL1** in the Case drop-down list.
Select the **Uniform loads** tab to see the loads.

21.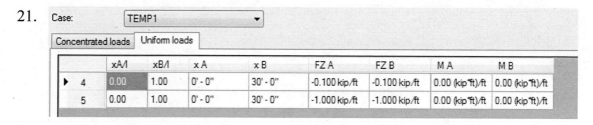

Select **TEMP1** in the Case drop-down list.
Select the **Uniform loads** tab to see the loads.

22. Note how the display changes depending on which load is selected.

23. 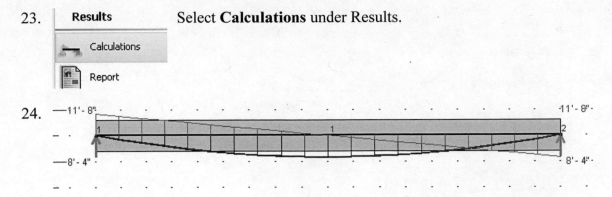 Select **Calculations** under Results.

24.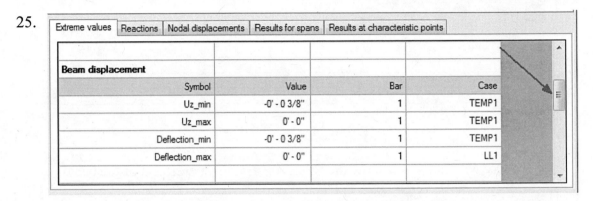

Note how the display changes to show the displacement based on the applied loads.

25.

Extreme values	Reactions	Nodal displacements	Results for spans	Results at characteristic points

Beam displacement			
Symbol	Value	Bar	Case
Uz_min	-0' - 0 3/8"	1	TEMP1
Uz_max	0' - 0"	1	TEMP1
Deflection_min	-0' - 0 3/8"	1	TEMP1
Deflection_max	0' - 0"	1	LL1

Use the scroll bar to scroll down to see the values based on the different case loads.

26. 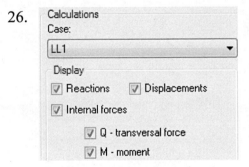 Select **LL1** in the Case drop-down list under Calculations.

27.

Extreme values	Reactions	Nodal displacements	Results

	Uz	Fi
▶ 1	0' - 0"	-0.04 °
2	0' - 0"	0.04 °

Select the Nodal displacements tab.

28. 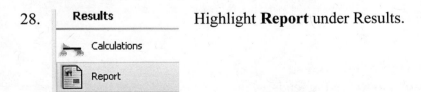 Highlight **Report** under Results.

29.

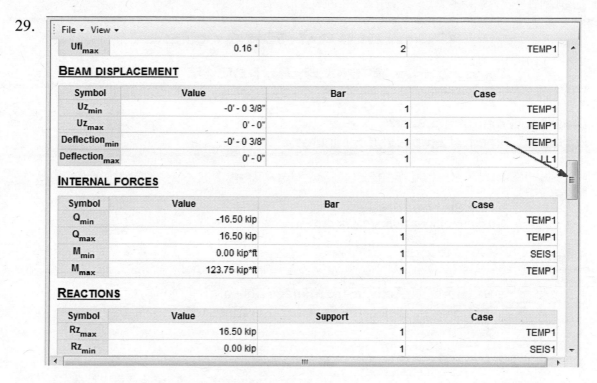

| Ufi_max | 0.16 ° | | 2 | TEMP1 |

BEAM DISPLACEMENT

Symbol	Value	Bar	Case
Uz_{min}	-0' - 0 3/8"	1	TEMP1
Uz_{max}	0' - 0"	1	TEMP1
Deflection$_{min}$	-0' - 0 3/8"	1	TEMP1
Deflection$_{max}$	0' - 0"	1	LL1

INTERNAL FORCES

Symbol	Value	Bar	Case
Q_{min}	-16.50 kip	1	TEMP1
Q_{max}	16.50 kip	1	TEMP1
M_{min}	0.00 kip*ft	1	SEIS1
M_{max}	123.75 kip*ft	1	TEMP1

REACTIONS

Symbol	Value	Support	Case
Rz_{max}	16.50 kip	1	TEMP1
Rz_{min}	0.00 kip	1	SEIS1

Use the scroll bar to preview the report.

30. Close without saving.

Command Exercise

Exercise 8-6 – Analytical Checks

Drawing Name: **checks.rvt**
Estimated Time to Completion: 5 Minutes

Scope

Use Structural Settings
Run Member Support Checks

Solution

1. 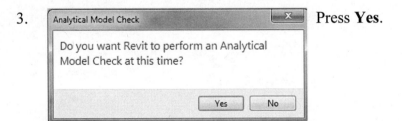 Activate the **Manage** ribbon.
Select the **Structural Settings** tool.

2.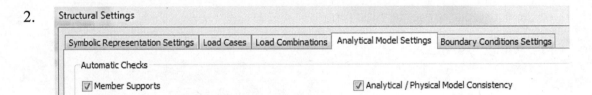

Select the **Analytical Model Settings**.
Enable **Member Supports**.
Enable **Analytical/ Physical Model Consistency**.
Press **OK**.

3.  Press **Yes**.

4. A warning dialog will pop up.
Click the **Expand Warning dialog** button.

5.
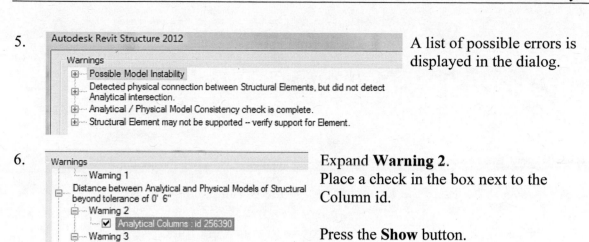

A list of possible errors is displayed in the dialog.

6.
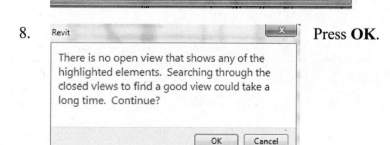

Expand **Warning 2**.
Place a check in the box next to the Column id.

Press the **Show** button.

7.

Error Handling - Viewing Elements

When you view elements, consider the following information:

- You can use standard View commands to see the highlighted elements even while the message dialog is visible.

- The Show command finds views where the relevant elements are visible. Pressing the Show button repeatedly opens each of these views.

- Changing the view to Wireframe might reveal elements unseen in other views.

☐ Do not show me this message again   [Close]

Close the dialog.

8.

Revit

There is no open view that shows any of the highlighted elements. Searching through the closed views to find a good view could take a long time. Continue?

[OK] [Cancel]

Press **OK**.

9.   Zoom into the corner of the model.

                                              Do not close the error dialog.

10. Inspect the model.

11. [Export...]   Press the **Export** button in the warning dialog.

12.   File name: checks_Error Report   Browse to your work folder.
       Files of type: Revit Error Report (*.html)   Save the file.

13.   checks   Locate the file in your work folder and double click to open.
      checks_Error Report
      Column - Grecian
      column

14. The report is displayed.

checks Error Report (1/13/2011 9:39:50 AM)

Error message	Elements
Possible Model Instability	
Detected physical connection between Structural Elements, but did not detect Analytical intersection.	Structural Columns : Concrete-Round-Column : 18" : id 216541 Analytical Beams : id 256464
Detected physical connection between Structural Elements, but did not detect Analytical intersection.	Structural Columns : Concrete-Round-Column : 18" : id 216541 Analytical Beams : id 256496
Detected physical connection between Structural Elements, but did not detect Analytical intersection.	Structural Columns : Concrete-Round-Column : 18" : id 216542 Analytical Beams : id 256462
Detected physical connection between Structural Elements, but did not detect Analytical intersection.	Structural Columns : Concrete-Round-Column : 18" : id 216542 Analytical Beams : id 256463
Detected physical connection between Structural Elements, but did not detect Analytical intersection.	Structural Columns : Concrete-Round-Column : 18" : id 216542 Analytical Beams : id 256507
Detected physical connection between Structural Elements, but did not detect Analytical intersection.	Structural Columns : Concrete-Round-Column : 18" : id 216543 Analytical Beams : id 256461
Detected physical connection between Structural Elements, but did not detect Analytical intersection.	Structural Columns : Concrete-Round-Column : 18" : id 216543 Analytical Beams : id 256462
Detected physical connection between Structural Elements, but did not detect Analytical intersection.	Structural Columns : Concrete-Round-Column : 18" : id 216543

15. Close the warning dialog.

16. Close the file without saving.

Command Exercise

Exercise 8-7 – Boundary Conditions

Drawing Name: **boundary_conditions.rvt**
Estimated Time to Completion: 5 Minutes

Scope

Assign boundary conditions

Solution

1. 3D Views
   View 1 - Analytical
   Activate the **View 1 - Analytical** under 3D Views in the Project Browser.

2. Analyze   Architect & S
   Boundary Conditions
   Boundary Conditions »
   Activate the **Analyze** ribbon.

   Select the **Boundary Conditions** tool.

3. Point   Line   Area
   Boundary Conditions
   Select the **Point** tool from the ribbon.

4. State: Fixed
   Fixed
   Pinned
   Roller
   User
   On the Options bar:

   Select **Fixed**.

5. Select a column.

Structural Columns : W-Wide Flange-Column : W10X49 :
Reference

6. A boundary condition block will appear at the end of the column.

Repeat to add to each column.

7. Close without saving.

Lesson Nine
Roof Project

This is a small portion of a project done by my son for Bill Brown Construction. Each project he works on begins with a set of AutoCAD drawings provided by an architect. So, we will start the same way. Bringing in an AutoCAD drawing and developing our project in Revit.

This project reviews many of the concepts and techniques learned in the text so far.

Command Exercise

Exercise 9-1 – Link an AutoCAD Drawing

Drawing Name: **new**
Estimated Time to Completion: 30 Minutes

Scope

Link to an AutoCAD file
Turn off visibility of layers
Add grid lines
Create Framing Elevation
Add layers

Solution

1. 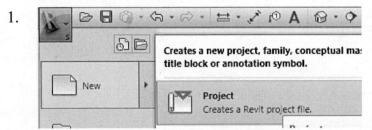 Start a **New Project** using the default template.

2. 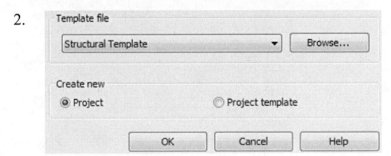 Press **OK** when the dialog appears.

3. Structural Plans
   Level 1
   Level 1 - Analytical
   Level 2
   Level 2 - Analytical

   Activate the **Level 1 Structural Plan** in the Project Browser.

4. Activate the **Insert** ribbon.

   Select **Link CAD**.

5.

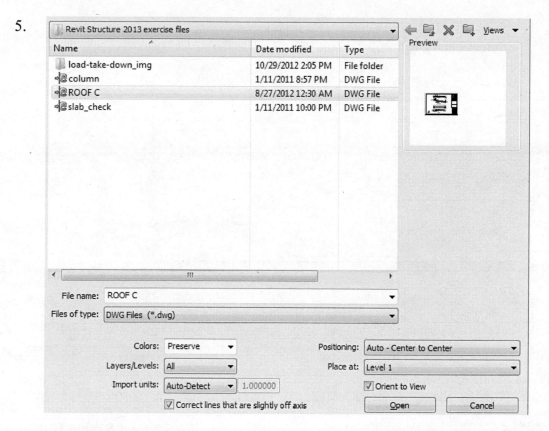

Locate *Roof C.dwg*.
Set Colors to **Preserve**.
Set Layers to **All**.
Set Import Units to **Auto-Detect**.
Set Postioning to **Auto-Center to Center**.
Place at **Level 1**.
Enable **Orient to View**.
Press **Open**.

6.

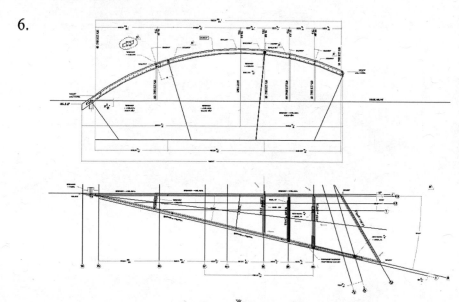

You may need to zoom out and then zoom in to see the drawing.
The top view is an elevation view of the roof.
The bottom view is a plan view.

7. 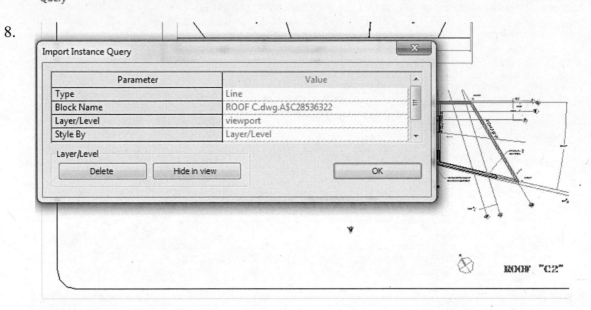 Select the linked CAD file so it highlights.
Select Query from the ribbon.

8.

Select the title block.
Select **Hide in view**.

 If you accidentally hide too many things, select **Reveal Hidden Elements** from the View Display bar.

Select **Unhide in View→By Filter**.

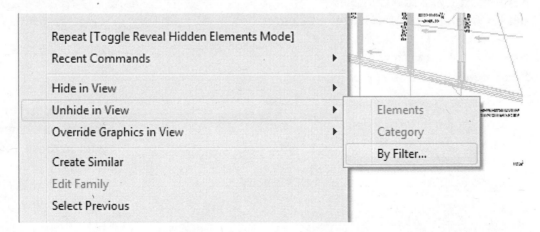

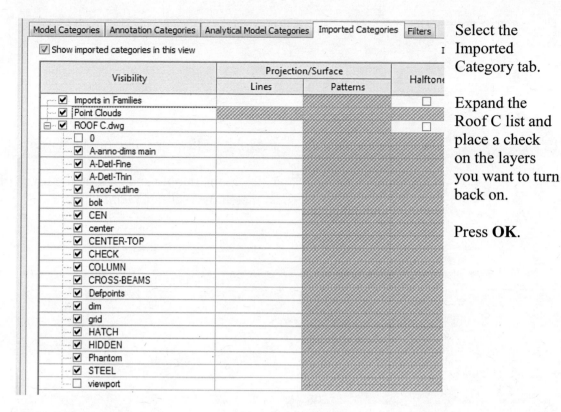

Select the Imported Category tab.

Expand the Roof C list and place a check on the layers you want to turn back on.

Press **OK**.

9.   Focus on the plan view.

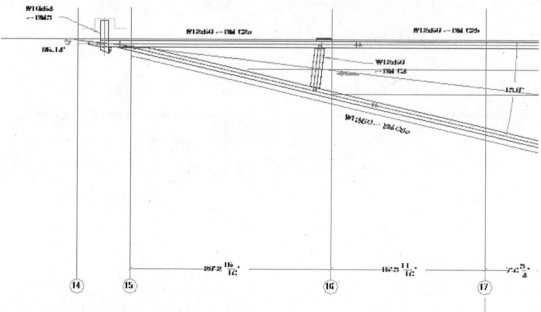

Each black/gray line is a grid line.

10.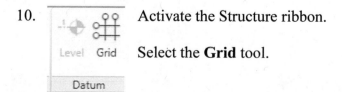

Activate the Structure ribbon.

Select the **Grid** tool.

11.  Select the **Pick** tool.

12. 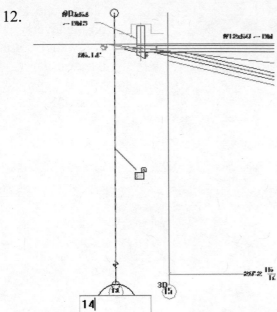 Pick the vertical grid line on the far left.

Click in the bubble and change the text to **14** to match the AutoCAD drawing.

13. Using the Pick tool, place grid lines with numbers as shown.

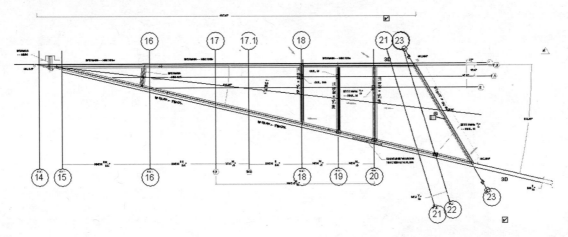

14. Using the Pick tool, place grid lines with letters as shown.

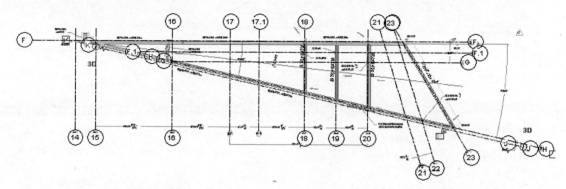

15. 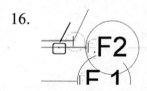 Add jogs to the grid lines to make them easier to read and see.

16. To add a jog, click on the grid to see the Z symbol. Then left click on the Z symbol to place the jog.

17. Reposition the elevation markers so they are oriented around the plan view.

Activate the South elevation.

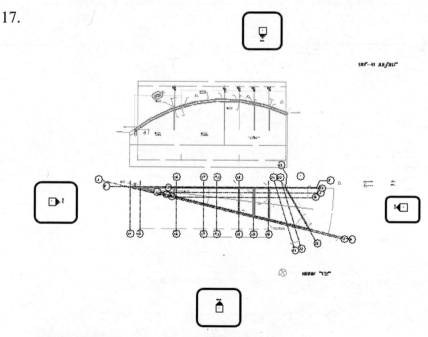

18.  Activate the **Insert** ribbon.

Select **Link CAD**.

19.

File name:	roof c elevation
Files of type:	DWG Files (*.dwg)

☑ Current view only

Colors:	Preserve
Layers/Levels:	All
Import units:	Auto-Detect 1.000000

☑ Correct lines that are slightly off axis

Positioning:	Auto - Center to Center
Place at:	Level 1

☑ Orient to View

Tools ▼   Open   Cancel

Locate *Roof C elevation.dwg*.
Set Colors to **Preserve**.
Set Layers to **All**.
Set Import Units to **Auto-Detect**.
Set Postioning to **Auto-Center to Center**.
Because this is an elevation view, enable **Current view only**.

This will place the view so it is oriented to the elevation.

Press **Open**.

20. Use the MOVE tool to reposition the CAD file so it is aligned with the existing grid lines.

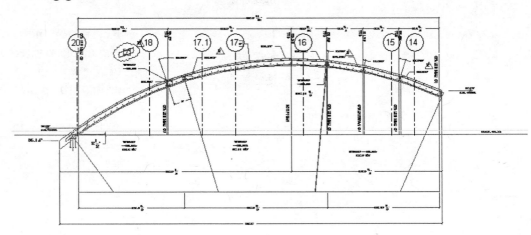

The cyan center line for C7 should be aligned to Grid 20.

21.

Model Categories	Annotation Categories	Analytical Model Categories	Imported Categories	Filters

☑ Show imported categories in this view   If a catego

Visibility	Projection/Surface		Halftone
	Lines	Patterns	
☑ Imports in Families			☐
☑ Point Clouds			
☑ roof c elevation.dwg			☐
☐ ROOF C.dwg			☐

Type VV to access the **Visibilities/Graphics** dialog.

Select the Imported Categories tab.
Uncheck **Roof C.dwg**.

This will hide the imported CAD link that is on Level 1.

This only hides the linked file in the active view..

22.   Activate the Structure ribbon.

   Select the **Level** tool.

23.   Select the **Pick** tool.

24. Place the levels as shown.

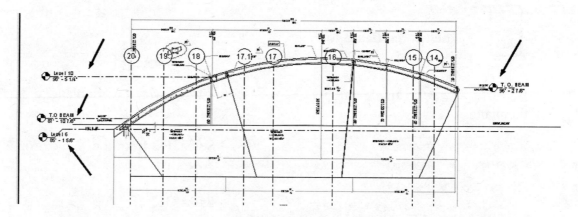

Reposition the CAD link so it is aligned with the grids and levels.

25. Use the PIN tool on the Modify ribbon to fix the position of the CAD link. This will ensure it doesn't move around while you are placing and modifying elements.

26. Save the project as *Roof C.rvt*.

Command Exercise

Exercise 9-2 – Adding Beams

Drawing Name: **Roof C.rvt**
Estimated Time to Completion: 60 Minutes

Scope

Add Beam
Load Beam Family
Modify Beam Properties

Solution

1. Elevations (Building Elevation)   Activate the **South** elevation.
    East
    North
    South
    West

2. Structure   Activate the Structure ribbon.

    Beam   Wall   Select the **Beam** tool.

3. Because you are in an elevation view, you will be asked which work plane to place the plane.

    Specify a new Work Plane
    ○ Name   Grid : F.2
    ○ Pick a plane
    ○ Pick a line and use the work plane it was sketched in

    Select F.2 from the Name drop-down list.

    Press **OK**.

4. Select **Load Family**.

    Load
    Family
    Mode

5. ProgramData   Browse to the *Steel* folder under Structural Framing.
    Autodesk
    RST 2013
    Libraries
    US Imperial
    Structural Framing
    Steel

6.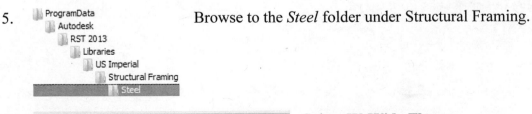

    File name: W-Wide Flange

    Files of type: All Supported Files (*.rfa, *.adsk)

    Select **W-Wide Flange**.

    Press **Open**.

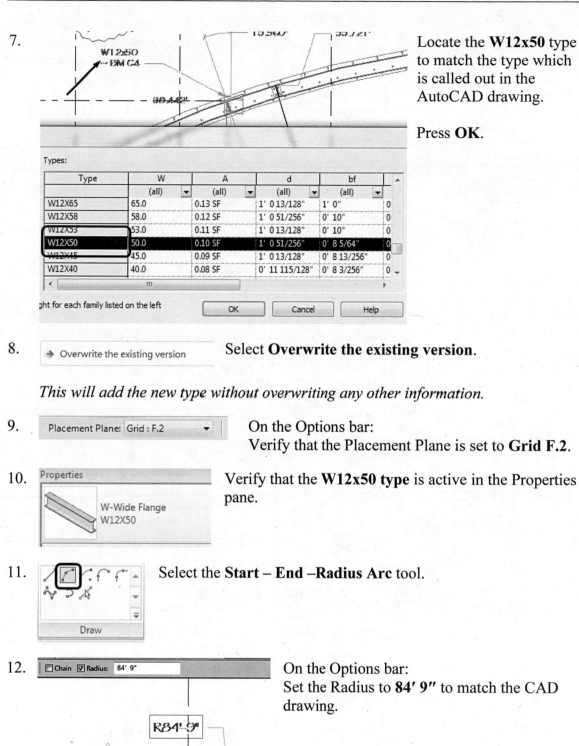

7.
Locate the **W12x50** type to match the type which is called out in the AutoCAD drawing.

Press **OK**.

Type	W	A	d	bf	
	(all)	(all)	(all)	(all)	
W12X65	65.0	0.13 SF	1' 0 13/128"	1' 0"	0
W12X58	58.0	0.12 SF	1' 0 51/256"	0' 10"	0
W12X53	53.0	0.11 SF	1' 0 13/128"	0' 10"	0
W12X50	50.0	0.10 SF	1' 0 51/256"	0' 8 5/64"	0
W12X45	45.0	0.09 SF	1' 0 13/128"	0' 8 13/256"	0
W12X40	40.0	0.08 SF	0' 11 115/128"	0' 8 3/256"	0

ght for each family listed on the left

8.
→ Overwrite the existing version

Select **Overwrite the existing version**.

This will add the new type without overwriting any other information.

9.
Placement Plane: Grid : F.2

On the Options bar:
Verify that the Placement Plane is set to **Grid F.2**.

10.
Properties
W-Wide Flange
W12X50

Verify that the **W12x50 type** is active in the Properties pane.

11.
Draw

Select the **Start – End –Radius Arc** tool.

12.
☐ Chain ☑ Radius: 84' 9"

On the Options bar:
Set the Radius to **84′ 9″** to match the CAD drawing.

13.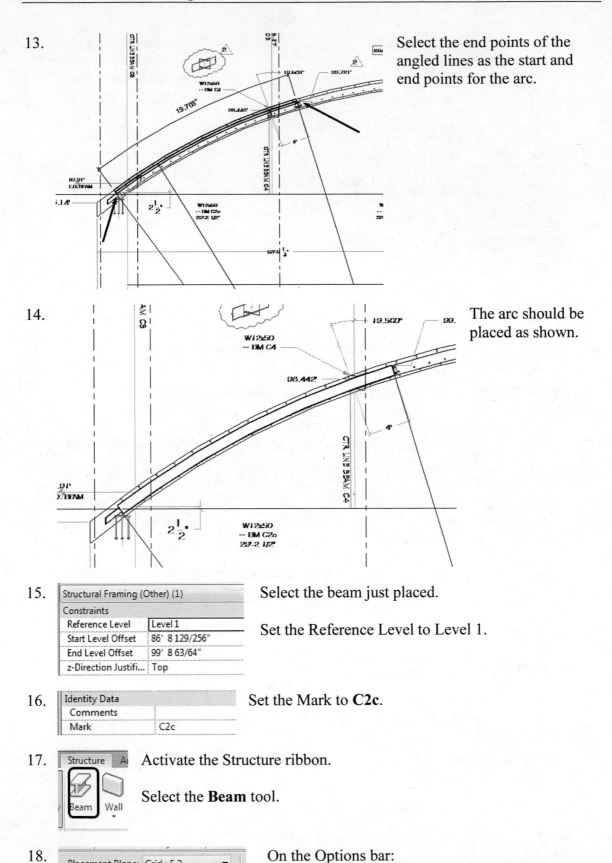

Select the end points of the angled lines as the start and end points for the arc.

14.

The arc should be placed as shown.

15.

Structural Framing (Other) (1)	
Constraints	
Reference Level	Level 1
Start Level Offset	86' 8 129/256"
End Level Offset	99' 8 63/64"
z-Direction Justifi...	Top

Select the beam just placed.

Set the Reference Level to Level 1.

16.

Identity Data	
Comments	
Mark	C2c

Set the Mark to **C2c**.

17. Structure

Beam Wall

Activate the Structure ribbon.

Select the **Beam** tool.

18.

Placement Plane: Grid : F.2

On the Options bar:
Verify that the Placement Plane is set to **Grid F.2**.

19. 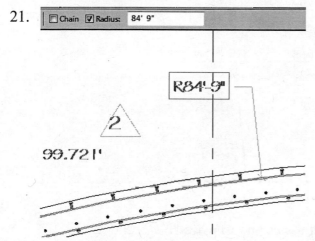 Verify that the **W12x50 type** is active in the Properties pane.

20. Select the **Start – End –Radius Arc** tool.

21. On the Options bar:
Set the Radius to **84′ 9″** to match the CAD drawing.

22. 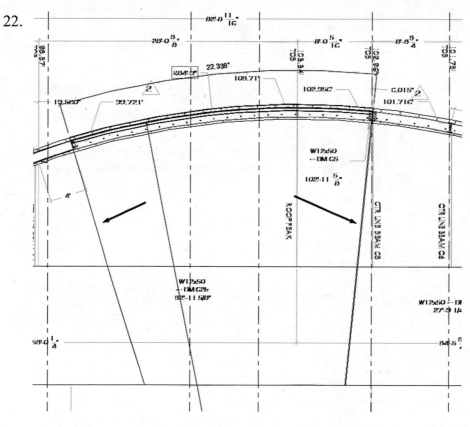 Select the end points of the angled lines as the start and end points for the arc.

23.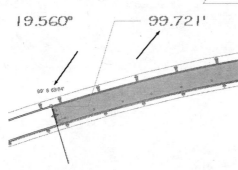

The arc should be placed as shown.

24.

Structural Framing (Other) (1)	
Reference Level	Level 1
Start Level Offset	99' 8 63/64"
End Level Offset	102' 11 137/256"
z-Direction Justifi...	Top
z-Direction Offset...	0' 0"

Select the beam just placed.

Set the Reference Level to Level 1.

25.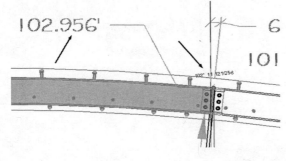

The green dimension in the CAD drawing states that the beam end point should be at 99.721'.
To adjust the value of the endpoint, select the blue dimension and enter the correct value.

26.

Inspect the right end and adjust the elevation of the beam if needed.

27. Set the Mark to **C2b**.

28. Activate the Structure ribbon.

    Select the **Beam** tool.

29. On the Options bar:
    Verify that the Placement Plane is set to **Grid F.2**.

30. Verify that the **W12x50 type** is active in the Properties pane.

    W-Wide Flange
    W12X50

31. Select the **Start – End – Radius Arc** tool.

    Draw

32.  On the Options bar:
    Set the Radius to **84′ 9″** to match the CAD drawing.

33. 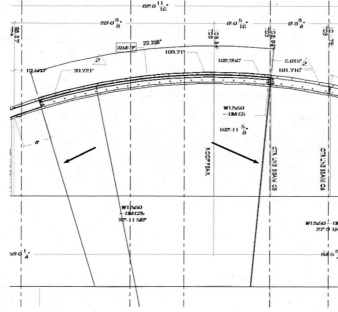 Select the end points of the angled lines as the start and end points for the arc.

34.

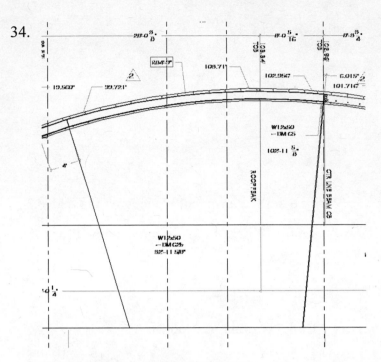

The arc should be placed as shown.

35.

Reference Level	Level 1
Start Level Offset	102' 11 121/256"
End Level Offset	95' 9 139/256"
z-Direction Justifi...	Top
z-Direction Offset...	0' 0"

Select the beam just placed.

Set the Reference Level to Level 1.

36.

The green dimension in the CAD drawing states that the beam end point should be at 102′ 11 5/8″.
To adjust the value of the endpoint, select the blue dimension and enter the correct value.

37.

Inspect the right end and adjust the elevation of the beam if needed.

38.

Identity Data	
Comments	
Mark	C2a

Set the Mark to **C2a**.

39.

```
        I. O. BEAM
   3D Views
        Analytical Model
        {3D}
```

Switch to a 3D view.

40. The beam you placed is floating above Level 1.

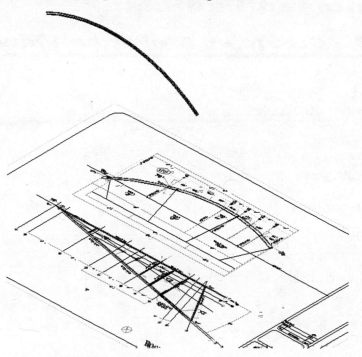

41. Save your project.

Command Exercise

Exercise 9-3 – Create an Elevation View

Drawing Name: **Roof C.rvt**
Estimated Time to Completion: 40 Minutes

Scope

Create an Elevation view.
Link to an AutoCAD file
Add Beams
Change Beam Properties

Solution

1. 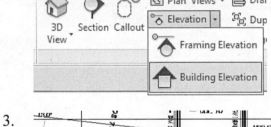   Activate Level 1.

2.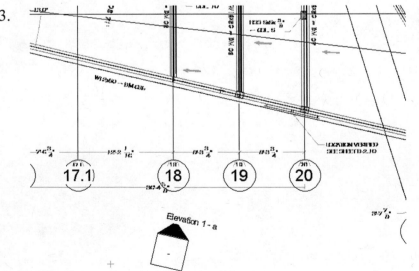

Activate the View ribbon.

Select **Elevation→Building Elevation**.

3. Place an elevation marker perpendicular to Grid J.

4. 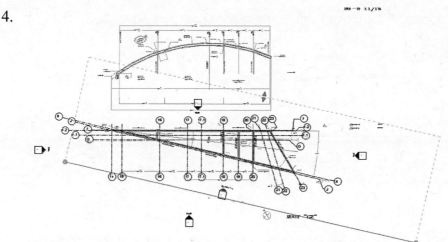 Adjust the clip plane for the elevation view to encompass the entire plan view.

5. 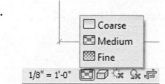 Rename the view **Elevation C3 Beam**.

Rename View

Name: Elevation C3 Beam

OK

6. Set the Detail Level for the view to **Medium**.

☐ Coarse
☒ Medium
☒ Fine

1/8" = 1'-0"

7. Activate the **Insert** ribbon.

Select **Link CAD**.

Structure | Architecture | Insert | Annotate

Link Revit | Link CAD | DWF Markup | Decal | Point Cloud | Manage Links

Link

8.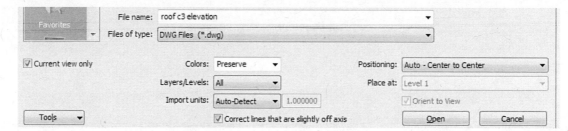

File name: roof c3 elevation
Files of type: DWG Files (*.dwg)

☑ Current view only

Colors: Preserve
Layers/Levels: All
Import units: Auto-Detect   1.000000

Positioning: Auto - Center to Center
Place at: Level 1
☑ Orient to View

Tools

☑ Correct lines that are slightly off axis

Open   Cancel

Locate *Roof C3 elevation.dwg*.
Set Colors to **Preserve**.
Set Layers to **All**.
Set Import Units to **Auto-Detect**.
Set Postioning to **Auto-Center to Center**.
Because this is an elevation view, enable **Current view only**.

This will place the view so it is oriented to the elevation.

Press **Open**.

9. You may need to adjust the Crop Region in order to see the imported CAD file.

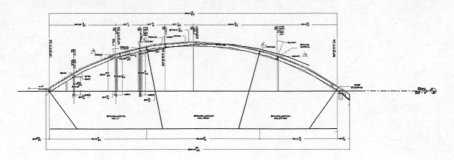

Use the MOVE tool to reposition the CAD file so it is aligned with the Elev. Level.

10. Activate the Structure ribbon.

Select the **Beam** tool.

11. Set the Placement Plane to **Grid H**.

Specify a new Work Plane

◉ Name   Grid : H

○ Pick a plane

○ Pick a line and use the work plane it was sketched in

Press **OK**.

12. Modify | Place Beam   Placement Plane: Grid : H

Properties

W-Wide Flange
W12X50

Verify that W12x50 is selected on the Properties pane.
Set the Placement Plane to Grid H.

13. 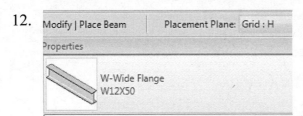 Select the **Start – End – Radius Arc** tool.

Draw

14. ☐ Chain ☑ Radius: 84' 9"

On the Options bar:
Set the Radius to **84′ 9″** to match the CAD drawing.

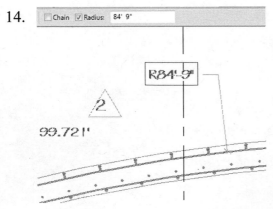

15.

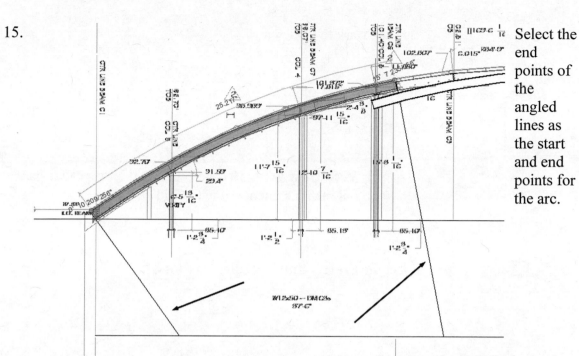

Select the end points of the angled lines as the start and end points for the arc.

16.

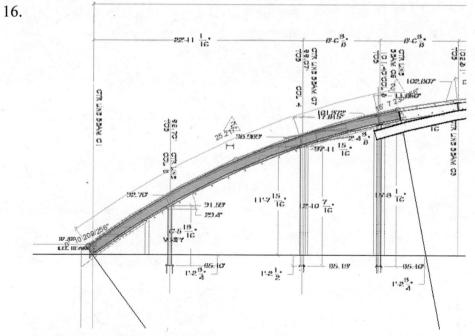

The arc should be placed as shown.

17.

Constraints	
Reference Level	Level 1
Start Level Offset	87' 2 99/128"
End Level Offset	101' 11 225/256"
z-Direction Justifi...	Top
z-Direction Offset...	0' 0"
Lateral Justification	Center
Cross-Section Ro...	0.000°

Select the beam just placed.

Set the Reference Level to Level 1.

18. Set the Mark to **C3a**.

13. 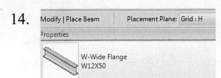 Activate the Structure ribbon.

    Select the **Beam** tool.

14. 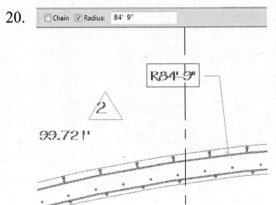 Verify that W12x50 is selected on the Properties pane. Set the Placement Plane to Grid H.

19. 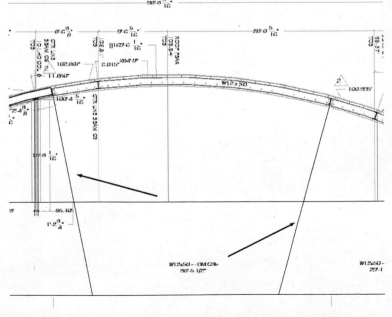 Select the **Start – End – Radius Arc** tool.

20. On the Options bar:
    Set the Radius to **84′ 9″** to match the CAD drawing.

21. Select the end points of the angled lines as the start and end points for the arc.

22.

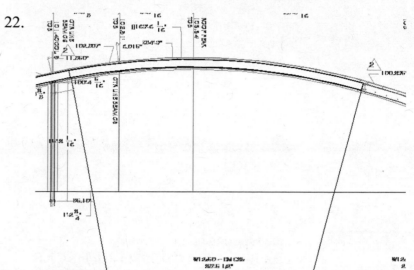

The arc should be placed as shown.

23.

Constraints	
Reference Level	Level 1
Start Level Offset	87' 2 99/128"
End Level Offset	101' 11 225/256"
z-Direction Justifi...	Top
z-Direction Offset...	0' 0"
Lateral Justification	Center
Cross-Section Ro...	0.000°

Select the beam just placed.

Set the Reference Level to Level 1.

24.

Check the elevation values of the end points.

$\triangle$ 2

100.395'

25.

Identity Data	
Comments	
Mark	C3b

Set the Mark to **C3b**.

26. Structure

Activate the Structure ribbon.

Beam   Wall

Select the **Beam** tool.

27.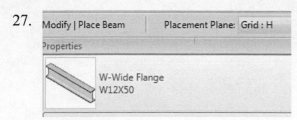

Verify that W12x50 is selected on the Properties pane.
Set the Placement Plane to Grid H.

28.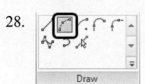

Select the **Start – End – Radius Arc** tool.

29.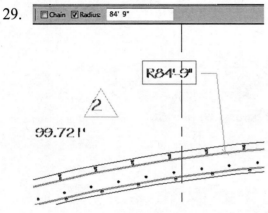

On the Options bar:
Set the Radius to **84′ 9″** to match the CAD drawing.

30.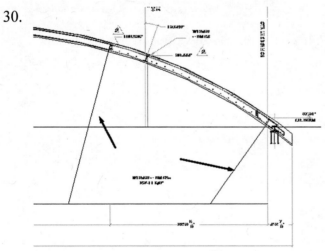

Select the end points of the angled lines as the start and end points for the arc.

31.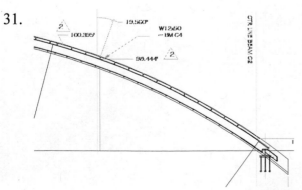

The arc should be placed as shown.

32.

Constraints	
Reference Level	Level 1
Start Level Offset	100' 4 189/256"
End Level Offset	87' 7 205/256"
z-Direction Justification	Top
z-Direction Offset Value	0' 0"

Select the beam just placed.

Set the Reference Level to Level 1.

33.

Identity Data	
Comments	
Mark	C3c
Phasing	

Set the Mark to **C3c**.

34.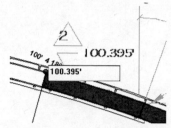

Check the beam ends and verify that the end elevations match the callouts.

35.

3D Views
— Analytical Model
— {3D}

Switch to a 3D view.

36. Both beams are visible.

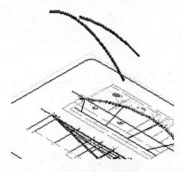

We will adjust their positions once the model is more developed.

Save the project.

Command Exercise

Exercise 9-4 – Add Columns

Drawing Name: **Roof C.rvt**
Estimated Time to Completion: 10 Minutes

Scope

Add Column
Load Column Family

Solution

1.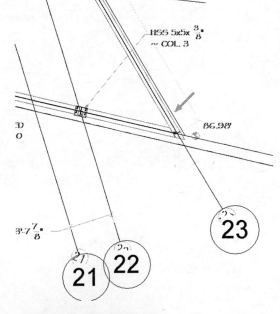

   Structural Plans
      Level 1
      Level 1 - Analytical
      Level 2
      Level 2 - Analytical
      Level 6
      Level 10
      Site
      T. O. BEAM

   Activate **Level 1**.

2. Zoom into Grids 21~23.

   Note the column callout.

   HSS 5x5x $\frac{3}{8}$
   ~ COL. 3

   86.98

   3'-7 $\frac{7}{8}$

   21 **22** **23**

3. Select the **Column** tool from the Structure ribbon.

   Structure | Architecture | Inser
   Beam | Wall | Column | Floor
   Structure

4. Select **Load Family** from the ribbon.

Load
Family
Mode

5. 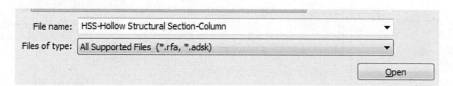 Browse to the *Steel* folder under Structural Columns.

ProgramData
Autodesk
RST 2013
Libraries
US Imperial
Structural Columns
Steel

6. Locate *HSS-Hollow Structural Section-Column.*

| File name: | HSS-Hollow Structural Section-Column |
| Files of type: | All Supported Files (*.rfa, *.adsk) |

Open

Press **Open.**

7.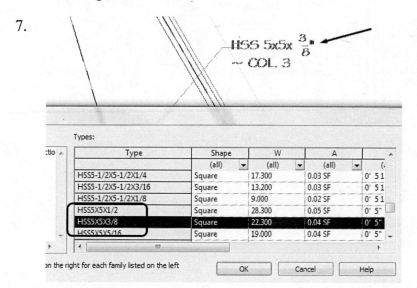

Locate the HSS5X5X3/8
Type as called out in the
AutoCAD drawing.

Press **OK.**

Types:

Type	Shape	W	A	(.
(all)	(all)	(all)	(all)	
HSS5-1/2X5-1/2X1/4	Square	17.300	0.03 SF	0' 5 1
HSS5-1/2X5-1/2X3/16	Square	13.200	0.03 SF	0' 5 1
HSS5-1/2X5-1/2X1/8	Square	9.000	0.02 SF	0' 5 1
HSS5X5X1/2	Square	28.300	0.05 SF	0' 5"
HSS5X5X3/8	Square	22.300	0.04 SF	0' 5"
HSS5X5X5/16	Square	19.000	0.04 SF	0' 5"

on the right for each family listed on the left   OK   Cancel   Help

8. On the Options bar:

 Set the Height **Unconnected 100′ 0″.**

Rotate after placement   Height ▼   Uncon ▼   100' 0"

We can adjust the height later.

9.  Use the ALIGN and MOVE tools to orient the column.

10. Change the Mark value to match the callout value.

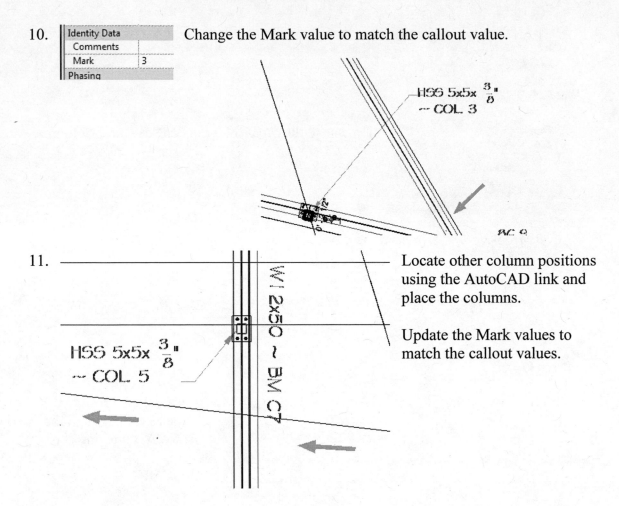

Identity Data	
Comments	
Mark	3
Phasing	

11. Locate other column positions using the AutoCAD link and place the columns.

Update the Mark values to match the callout values.

12. Save the project.

Command Exercise

Exercise 9-5 – Create a 3D Model View Template

Drawing Name: **Roof C.rvt**
Estimated Time to Completion: 15 Minutes

Scope

Duplicate a 3D View
Create a View Template
Assign a view template to a view

Solution

1.

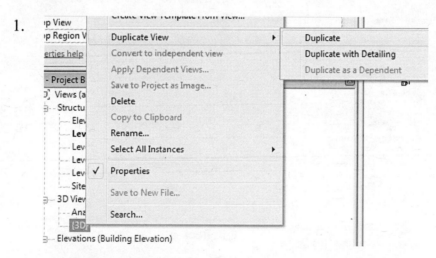

Highlight the {3D} view.

Right click and select **Duplicate View→ Duplicate**.

2.

Rename the view **3D-Model**.

Press **OK**.

3.

Activate the **View** ribbon.

Select **View Template→Manage View Templates**.

4.
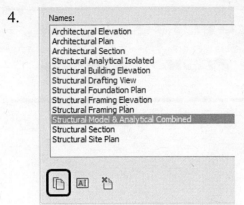

Highlight **Structural Model & Analytical Combined**.

Select **Duplicate**.

5.

Name: 3D- Structural Model

OK

Type **3D-Structural Model** for the name.

Press **OK**.

6.

View Properties

Number of views with this template assigned: **0**

Parameter	Value	Incl
View Scale	1/8" = 1'-0"	
Scale Value 1:	96	
Detail Level	Medium	
Parts Visibility	Show Original	
V/G Overrides Model	Edit...	
V/G Overrides Annotation	Edit...	
V/G Overrides Analytical Model	Edit...	
V/G Overrides Import	Edit...	
V/G Overrides Filters	Edit...	
Model Display	Edit...	
Shadows	Edit...	
Lighting	Edit...	
Photographic Exposure	Edit...	

Select Edit next the **V/G Overrides Analytical Model**.

7.
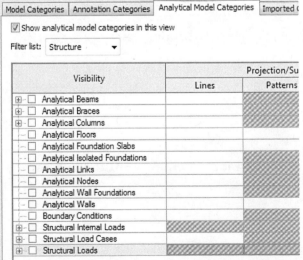

Uncheck all the categories.

Press **Apply** and **OK**.

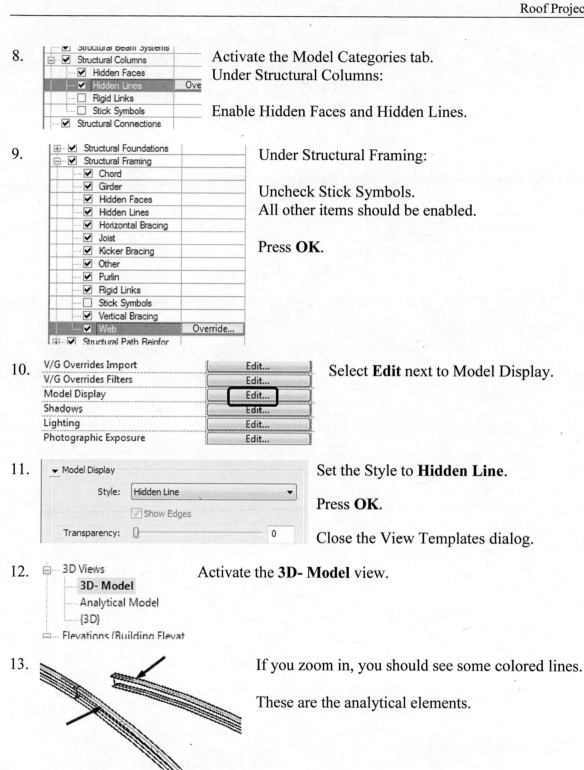

8. Activate the Model Categories tab.
Under Structural Columns:

Enable Hidden Faces and Hidden Lines.

9. Under Structural Framing:

Uncheck Stick Symbols.
All other items should be enabled.

Press **OK**.

10. Select **Edit** next to Model Display.

11. Set the Style to **Hidden Line**.

Press **OK**.

Close the View Templates dialog.

12. Activate the **3D- Model** view.

13. If you zoom in, you should see some colored lines.

These are the analytical elements.

14. Activate the **View** ribbon.

Select **View Templates→Apply Template Properties to Current View**.

15.

Sun Path	☐
Identity Data	
View Template	3D- Structural Model
View Name	3D- Model
Dependency	Independent
Title on Sheet	
Extents	
Crop View	☐

In the Project Browser, set the Default View Template to **3D-Structural Model**.

16. The stick elements are no longer visible.

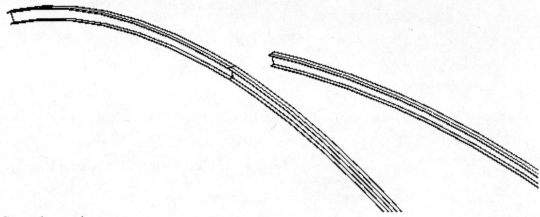

Save the project.

Command Exercise

Exercise 9-6 – Add Cross Beams

Drawing Name: **Roof C.rvt**
Estimated Time to Completion: 60 Minutes

Scope

Change Display Settings
Change Project Units
Add Beam
Modify Beam Properties

Solution

1. Structural Plans
   - **Level 1**
   - Level 1 - Analytical
   - Level 2
   - Level 2 - Analytical
   - Level 6
   - Level 10
   - Site
   - T. O. BEAM

   Activate **Level 1**.

2. 1/8" = 1'-0"   Set the Detail Level to **Medium**.
   Set the Display to **Hidden Lines**.

3. Analyze   Massing & Site   Collaborate   View   Manage

   Project Units   Shared Parameters   Transfer Project Standards   Purge Unused   Structural Settings

   Settings

   Activate the **Manage** ribbon.
   Select **Project Units**.

4.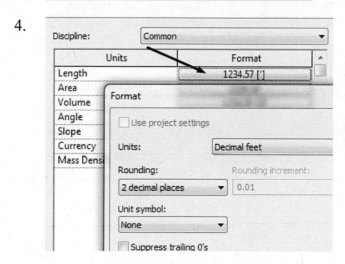

   Discipline: Common

Units	Format
Length	1234.57 [']
Area	
Volume	
Angle	
Slope	
Currency	
Mass Dens	

   Format

   ☐ Use project settings

   Units: Decimal feet

   Rounding:
   2 decimal places   Rounding increment: 0.01

   Unit symbol:
   None

   ☐ Suppress trailing 0's

   Select the **Length Format** button.
   Set the Units to **Decimal Feet**.
   Set the Rounding to **2 decimal places**.

   Press **OK**.

9-33

5. 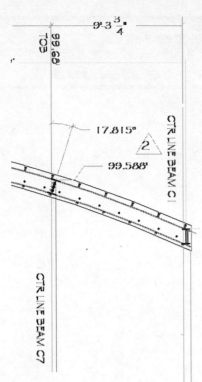   Note that the top of Beam C7 is set to 99.68'.

6. 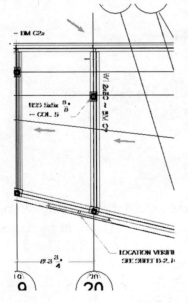   Beam C7 is located on Grid 20.

7. 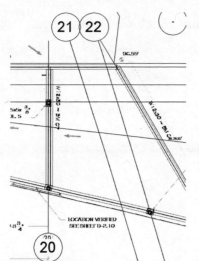 Locate Beam C7 on Grid 20.

8.  Select the **Beam** tool on the Structure ribbon.

9. Verify the beam type is set to W12x50.

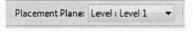 On the Options bar: Set the Placement Plane to Level 1.

10.  Check in the Properties pane that the z-direction Justification is set to Top.

11. Use the Pick tool and pick the line indicating the beam to place.

Cancel out of the command.

12.

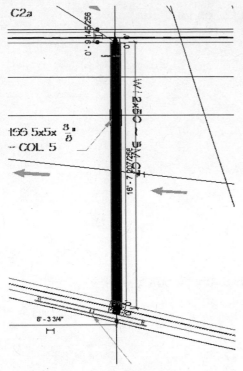

Select the beam which was just placed.

13.

Structural Framing (Other) (1)	
Constraints	
Reference Level	Level 1
Start Level Offset	99.680
End Level Offset	99.588
z-Direction Justification	Top

Change the Start Level Offset to **99.68'**.
Change the End Level Offsets to **99.588'**.

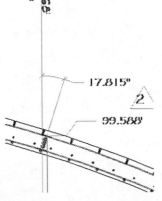

The C7 beam has a rotation of 17.815°.

14.

Constraints	
Reference Level	Level 1
Start Level Offset	99.680
End Level Offset	99.588
z-Direction Justification	Top
z-Direction Offset Value	0.000
Lateral Justification	Center
Cross-Section Rotation	17.815°

Change the Cross-Section rotation to 17.815°.

15. 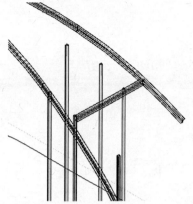 Update the Mark to **C7**.

16. Switch to a 3D view and you will see the beam.

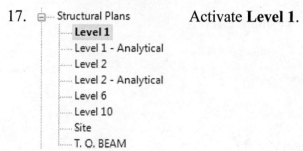

17. Structural Plans
    Level 1
    Level 1 - Analytical
    Level 2
    Level 2 - Analytical
    Level 6
    Level 10
    Site
    T. O. BEAM

    Activate **Level 1**.

18. Locate Beam C1 on Grid 23.

    Note that the elevation on the top is 96.55′ and the elevation on the bottom is 86.98′.

    The beam type is W12x30.

19. Select the **Beam** tool on the Structure ribbon.

20. 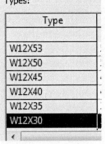 Select **Load Family** from the ribbon.

21. Browse to *Steel* under *Structural Framing*.

ProgramData
    Autodesk
        RST 2013
            Libraries
                US Imperial
                    Structural Framing
                        Steel

22. File name: W-Wide Flange

Files of type: All Supported Files (*.rfa, *.adsk)

Select the **W-Wide Flange** family.

Press **Open**.

23. Types:

Type
W12X53
W12X50
W12X45
W12X40
W12X35
W12X30

Locate the **W12x30** type and press **OK**.

24. Verify the beam type is set to W12x30.

Placement Plane: Level : Level 1

On the Options bar: Set the Placement Plane to Level 1.

25. Properties

W-Wide Flange
W12X30

New Structural Framing (<Automatic>)

Reference Le...	
z-Direction J...	Top
z-Direction ...	0' 0"
Lateral Justifi...	Center

Check in the Properties pane that the z-direction Justification is set to Top.

26.  Use the Draw tool and trace over the line indicating the beam to place.

Cancel out of the command.

27. 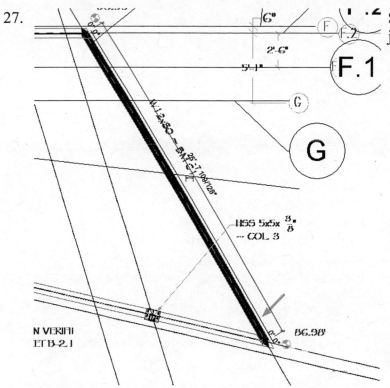 Select the beam which was just placed.

28.

Constraints	
Reference Level	Level 1
Start Level Offset	96.550
End Level Offset	86.980
z-Direction Justification	Top

Change the Start Level Offset to **96.55′**.

Change the End Level Offsets to **86.98′**.

29.

Identity Data	
Comments	
Mark	C1
Phasing	

Update the Mark to **C1**.

30. Switch to a 3D view and you will see the beam.

One end position needs to be adjusted.

31. 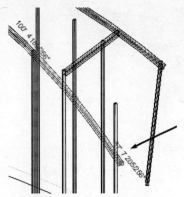 Select the C3c beam.

32.

Structural Framing (Other) (1)	
Constraints	
Reference Level	Level 1
Start Level Offset	100.395
End Level Offset	87.715
z-Direction Justification	Top
z-Direction Offset Value	0.000

In the Properties pane:
Highlight the End Level Offset.

Press **Ctl+C** on the keyboard to copy the value.

33.

Structural Framing (Other) (1)	
Constraints	
Reference Level	Level 1
Start Level Offset	96.550
End Level Offset	87.715
z-Direction Justification	Top
z-Direction Offset Value	0.000

Type **Ctl+V** to paste the value into the End Level Offset.

Press **Apply**.

34. 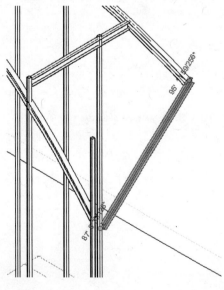 The beam position will update.

35. 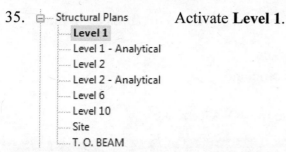 Activate **Level 1**.

36. 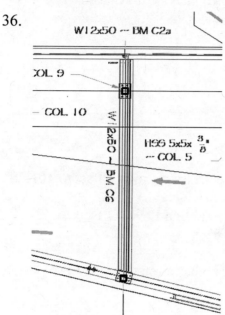 Locate Beam C6 on Grid 19.

Note that the end elevation is 101.716′ and the start elevation is 101.75′. The beam has a rotation of 11.85°.

The beam type is W12x50.

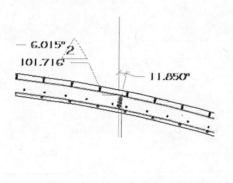

37. Select the **Beam** tool on the Structure ribbon.

38. Verify the beam type is set to W12x50.

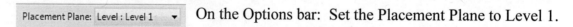

On the Options bar: Set the Placement Plane to Level 1.

39. 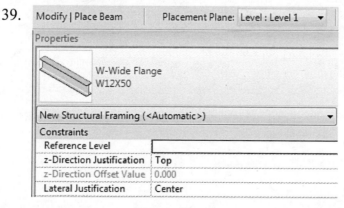 Check in the Properties pane that the z-direction Justification is set to Top.

40.  Use the Draw tool and trace over the line indicating the beam to place.

Cancel out of the command.

41. 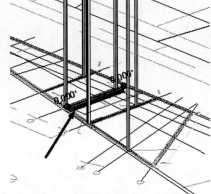 Activate the 3D- Model view.

Select the beam which was just placed.

42.  Change the Start Level Offset to **101.75′**.

Change the End Level Offsets to **101.716′**.

The beam has a rotation of **11.85°**.

43. 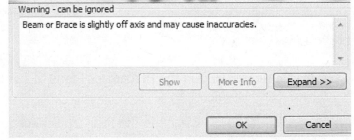 Press **OK** if you see this warning.

44. 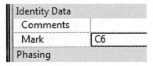 Update the Mark to **C6**.

45. 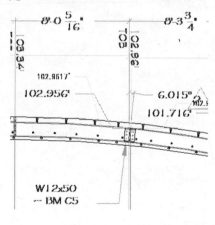   *Inspect the model*

46. 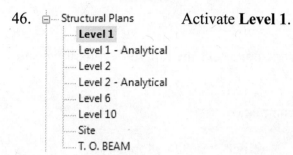   Activate **Level 1**.

47. 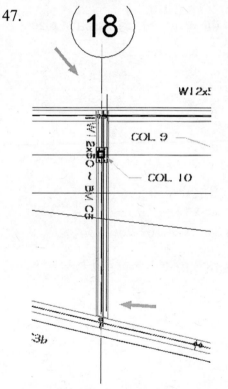   Locate Beam C5 on Grid 18.

Note that the end elevation is 102.956′ and the start elevation is 102.96′. The beam has a rotation of 6.015°.

The beam type is W12x50.

48.   Select the **Beam** tool on the Structure ribbon.

49.   Verify the beam type is set to W12x50.

Placement Plane: Level : Level 1 ▼   On the Options bar: Set the Placement Plane to Level 1.

50.

Modify | Place Beam	Placement Plane:	Level : Level 1 ▼

Properties

W-Wide Flange
W12X50

New Structural Framing (<Automatic>) ▼

Constraints	
Reference Level	
z-Direction Justification	Top
z-Direction Offset Value	0.000
Lateral Justification	Center

Check in the Properties pane that the z-direction Justification is set to Top.

51.

Draw

Use the Draw tool and trace over the line indicating the beam to place.

Cancel out of the command.

52.

Activate the 3D- Model view.

Select the beam which was just placed.

53.

W-Wide Flange
W12X50

Structural Framing (Other) (1)	
Constraints	
Reference Level	Level 1
Start Level Of...	102.960
End Level Off...	102.956
z-Direction Ju...	Top
z-Direction O...	0.000
Lateral Justifi...	Center
Cross-Section...	6.015°

Change the Start Level Offset to **102.96′**.

Change the End Level Offsets to **102.956′**.

The beam has a rotation of **6.015°**.

54.

Warning - can be ignored

Beam or Brace is slightly off axis and may cause inaccuracies.

Show	More Info	Expand >>

OK	Cancel

Press **OK** if you see this warning.

55.  Update the Mark to **C5**.

56. *Inspect the model*

57.
```
Structural Plans
    Level 1
    Level 1 - Analytical
    Level 2
    Level 2 - Analytical
    Level 6
    Level 10
    Site
    T. O. BEAM
```
Activate **Level 1**.

58. 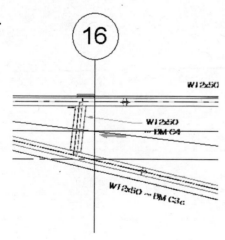 Locate Beam C4 near on Grid 16.

Note that the end elevation is 98.442′ and the start elevation is 98.57′. The beam has a rotation of 19.56°.

The beam type is W12x50.

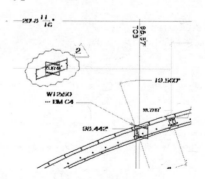

59. Select the **Beam** tool on the Structure ribbon.

60. Verify the beam type is set to W12x50.

On the Options bar: Set the Placement Plane to Level 1.

61.

Modify	Place Beam		Placement Plane: Level : Level 1 ▾

Properties

W-Wide Flange
W12X50

New Structural Framing (<Automatic>) ▾

Constraints	
Reference Level	
z-Direction Justification	Top
z-Direction Offset Value	0.000
Lateral Justification	Center

Check in the Properties pane that the z-direction Justification is set to Top.

62.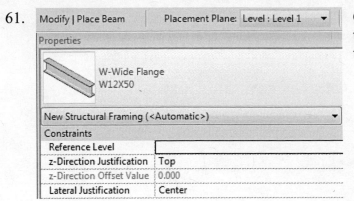

Use the Draw tool and trace over the line indicating the beam to place.

Cancel out of the command.

63.

Activate the 3D- Model view.

Select the beam which was just placed.

64.

Reference Level	Level 1
Start Level Offset	98.570
End Level Offset	98.442
z-Direction Justification	Top
z-Direction Offset Value	0.000
Lateral Justification	Center
Cross-Section Rotation	19.560°

Change the Start Level Offset to **98.57'**.

Change the End Level Offsets to **98.442'**.

The beam has a rotation of **19.56°**.

65.

Warning - can be ignored

Beam or Brace is slightly off axis and may cause inaccuracies.

Show	More Info	Expand >>

OK	Cancel

Press **OK** if you see this warning.

66.

Identity Data	
Comments	
Mark	C4
Phasing	

Update the Mark to **C4**.

67.   *Inspect the model*

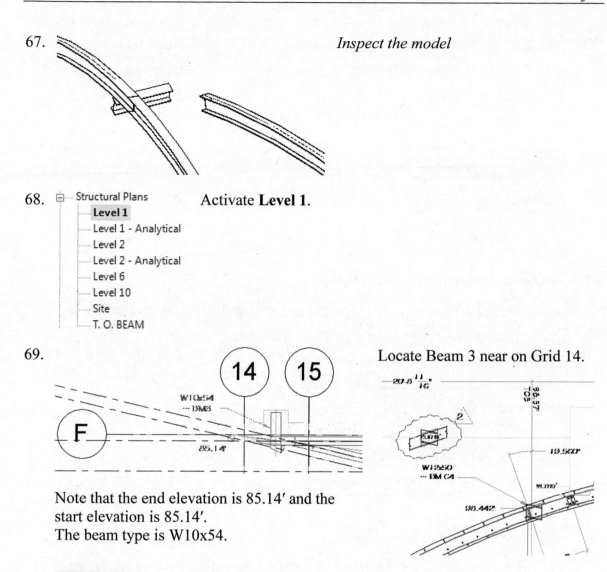

68.   Structural Plans
      Level 1
      Level 1 - Analytical
      Level 2
      Level 2 - Analytical
      Level 6
      Level 10
      Site
      T. O. BEAM

Activate **Level 1**.

69.   Locate Beam 3 near on Grid 14.

Note that the end elevation is 85.14′ and the
start elevation is 85.14′.
The beam type is W10x54.

70.   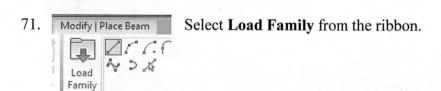 Select the **Beam** tool on the Structure ribbon.

71.   Select **Load Family** from the ribbon.

72.   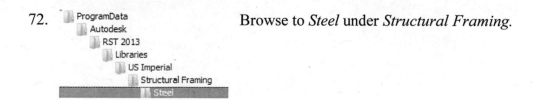 Browse to *Steel* under *Structural Framing*.

73. 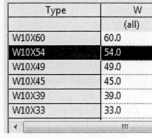 Select the **W-Wide Flange** family.

Press **Open**.

74. Locate the **W10x54** type and press **OK**.

Type	W
	(all)
W10X60	60.0
W10X54	54.0
W10X49	49.0
W10X45	45.0
W10X39	39.0
W10X33	33.0

75. Verify the beam type is set to W10x54.

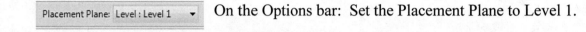 On the Options bar: Set the Placement Plane to Level 1.

76. 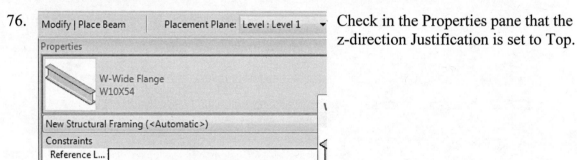 Check in the Properties pane that the z-direction Justification is set to Top.

77. 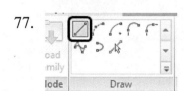 Use the Draw tool and trace over the line indicating the beam to place.

Cancel out of the command.

78. Activate the 3D- Model view.

Select the beam which was just placed.

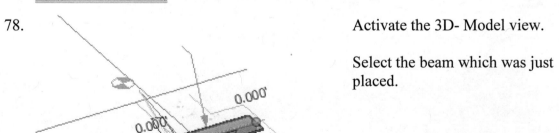

79.

Structural Framing (Other) (1)	
Constraints	
Reference Level	Level 1
Start Level Offset	85.140
End Level Offset	85.140
z-Direction Justification	Top
z-Direction Offset Value	0.000
Lateral Justification	Center
Cross-Section Rotation	0.000°

W-Wide Flange
W10X54

Change the Start Level Offset to **85.14′**.

Change the End Level Offsets to **85.14′**.

The beam has a rotation of **0.0°**.

80.

Identity Data	
Comments	
Mark	3

Update the Mark to **3**.

81.

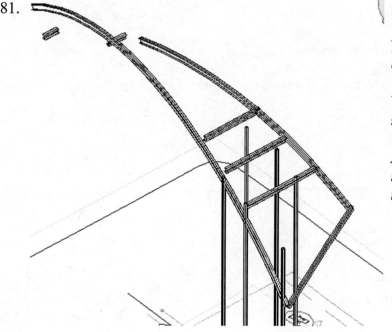

Switch to a 3D view.

Note that the end points display the elevations.

Verify that the end points are not swapped.

Add Mark information to the beams to help identify them.

82. Save the project.

Command Exercise

Exercise 9-7 – Modifying Columns

Drawing Name: Roof C.rvt
Estimated Time to Completion: 10 Minutes

Scope

Modify Columns

Solution

1. ⊟— 3D Views
        — **3D - Model**
        — Analytical Model
        — {3D}

    Activate the **3D-Model** view.

2. Select a column.

    Note which beams each column is aligned with.

3. Select **Attach Top/Base**.

    Select the beam it attaches to.

4. The column updates.

5. Repeat for all the columns.

6. Save the project.

Command Exercise

Exercise 9-8 – Adding a Scope Box

Drawing Name: **Roof C.rvt**
Estimated Time to Completion: 20 Minutes

Scope

Add a scope box to control visibility of grids

Solution

1. 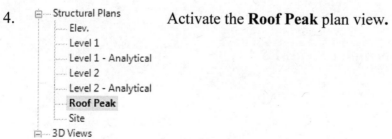 Activate the North Elevation

2. Activate the **Level** tool.

3. **Roof Peak** 103.34   Name the Level **Roof Peak**.
   Adjust the Elevation to **103.34**.

4. Activate the **Roof Peak** plan view.

   - Structural Plans
     - Elev.
     - Level 1
     - Level 1 - Analytical
     - Level 2
     - Level 2 - Analytical
     - **Roof Peak**
     - Site
   - 3D Views

5. Set the Underlay to **None**.

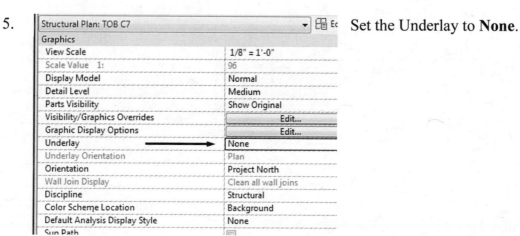

6.

We see vertical gridlines but no horizontal grid lines.

7.

Structural Plans
 Elev.
 Level 1
 Level 1 - Analytical
 Level 2
 Level 2 - Analytical
 Roof Peak
 Site

Activate **Level 1**.

8.

On the view ribbon:

Select **Scope Box**.

9.

Name: Horizontal Grids-F&J Height: 100.0

On the Options bar:
Name the scope box: **Horizontal Grids-F&J**.

Set the Height to **100′**.

10.

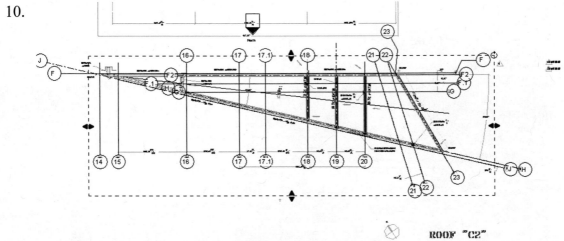

Position the scope box so it overlays the plan view.

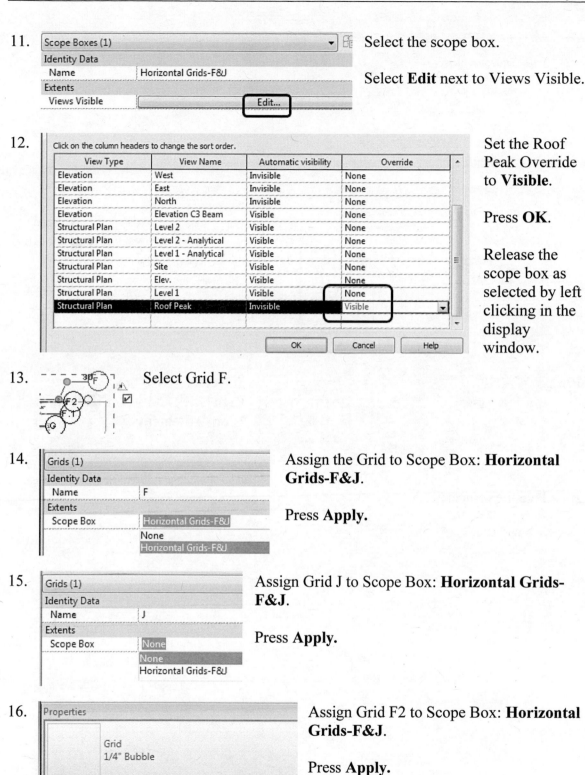

11. Select the scope box.

Select **Edit** next to Views Visible.

12. Set the Roof Peak Override to **Visible**.

Press **OK**.

Release the scope box as selected by left clicking in the display window.

13. Select Grid F.

14. Assign the Grid to Scope Box: **Horizontal Grids-F&J**.

Press **Apply.**

15. Assign Grid J to Scope Box: **Horizontal Grids-F&J**.

Press **Apply.**

16. Assign Grid F2 to Scope Box: **Horizontal Grids-F&J**.

Press **Apply.**

17. Activate the **Roof Peak plan.**

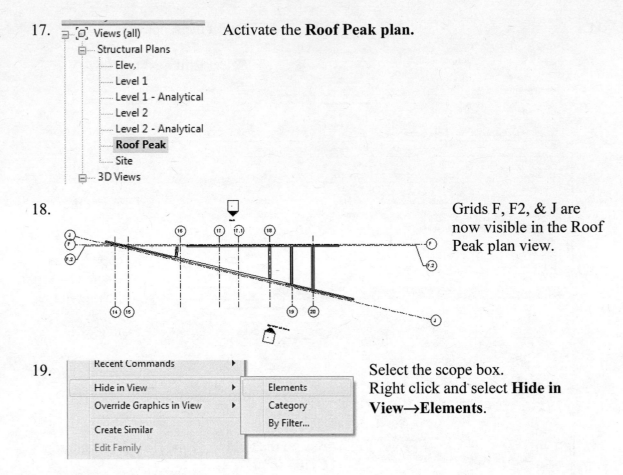

18. Grids F, F2, & J are now visible in the Roof Peak plan view.

19. Select the scope box. Right click and select **Hide in View→Elements.**

20. Save the project.

Command Exercise

Exercise 9-5 – Create a Framing Elevation

Drawing Name: **Roof C.rvt**
Estimated Time to Completion: 60 Minutes

Scope

Create a Framing Elevation view

Solution

1.
   - Structural Plans
     - **Level 1**
     - Level 1 - Analytical
     - Level 2
     - Level 2 - Analytical
     - Level 6
     - Level 10
     - Site
     - T. O. BEAM
     - TOB C7
   - 3D Views

   Activate **Level 1**.

2.

   View | Manage | Extensions | Modify
   3D View | Section | Callout | Plan Views | Draftin | Elevation | Duplica | Framing Elevation | enc

   Activate the View ribbon.

   Select **Elevation→Framing Elevation**.

3.
   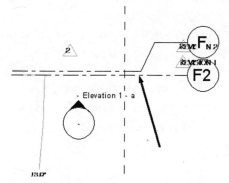

   - Elevation 1 - a

   Select **Grid F2**.

   Place the symbol so it is below F2 and oriented up/North.

4.
   - Elevations (Framing Elevation)
     - Elevation 1 - a
   - Legends

   The elevation is listed in the browser.
   Rename to **Beam C2 Elevation**.

5.
     - West
   - Elevations (Framing Elevation)
     - **Beam C2 Elevation**
   - Legends

   Activate **Beam C2 Elevation**.

6.

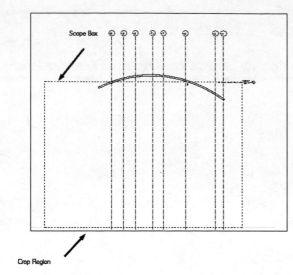

There are two rectangles.

One rectangle is the Scope Box.

One rectangle is the Crop Region.

Note you only see one level in the elevation view.
We can control visibility of levels with a scope box.

7.

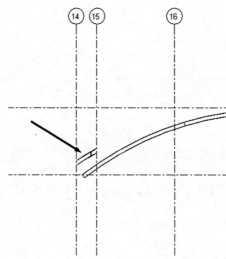

You may see portions of other beams.

Select these and Hide Elements in View.

8.

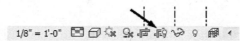

Turn off the visibility of the Crop Region using the toggle on the Display bar.

9.

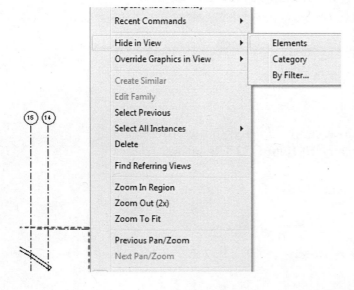

Select the scope box.
Right click and select **Hide in View→Elements**.

10.

Activate the **Insert ribbon.**

Select **Load Family.**

11.
| File name: | Level - Decimal Feet |
| Files of type: | All Supported Files (*.rfa, *.adsk) |

Load the *Level-Decimal Feet* family.

12.

Activate the Structure ribbon.

Select the **Level** tool.

13.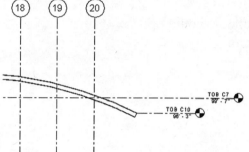

Place a level on the right side of the beam.

14.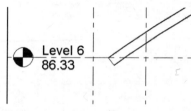

Place a level on the left side of the beam.

15.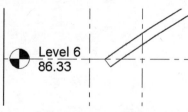

Select the Level call out you just placed.

16.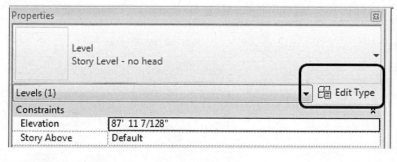

Select **Edit Type** from the Properties pane.

17.

Select **Duplicate.**

18.

Name: Level - Elevation Only

OK   Cance

Rename **Level – Elevation Only**.

Press **OK**.

19.

Type Parameters	
Parameter	Value
Constraints	
Elevation Base	Project Base Point
Graphics	
Line Weight	1
Color	■ Black
Line Pattern	Grid Line 1/4"
Symbol	Level - Decimal Feet : Elevation Only
Symbol at End 1 Default	☐
Symbol at End 2 Default	☑

In the Symbol field:
Select the **Level – Decimal Feet: Elevation Only** family.

Press **OK**.

20.

86.33

The Level callout should update.

21.

95.92

Repeat on the other side.

22.

| sert | Annotate | Analyze | Massing & Site | Collaborate | View | Manage | Extensions | Modify |

I Diameter   Arc Length   Spot Elevation   Spot Coordinate   Spot Slope   Detail Line   Region   Component

🔄 Revision Cloud
[A] Detail Group ▾
⊗ Insulation

Detail Component

Dimension ▾

☐ Rotate after placement

Activate the Annotate ribbon.

Select **Component→Detail Component**.

23.

Load
Family
Mode

Select **Load Family**.

24.

ProgramData
  Autodesk
    RST 2013
      Libraries
        US Imperial
          Detail Items
            Div 05-Metals
              050500-Common Work Results for Metals
                050523-Metal Fastenings
System Reserved (D:)

Browse to the *Metal Fastenings* folder under *Detail Items/Metals/Common Work Results for Metals*.

25. | File name: | A325 Bolts-Side |
     | Files of type: | All Supported Files (*.rfa, *.adsk) |

Open the *A325 Bolts-Side* family.

26.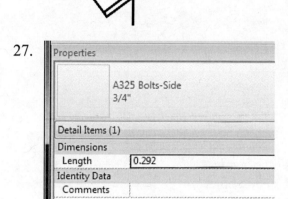

Place on the beam.

27.

Properties	
	A325 Bolts-Side 3/4"
Detail Items (1)	
Dimensions	
Length	0.292
Identity Data	
Comments	

Set the Bolt Type to ¾″.

With the bolt selected, change the Length in the Properties pane to **3 ½″**.

28. Use the ROTATE tool to orient to the beam flange.

29. Place a radial dimension for the beam.

This will place a center point for the arc.

30.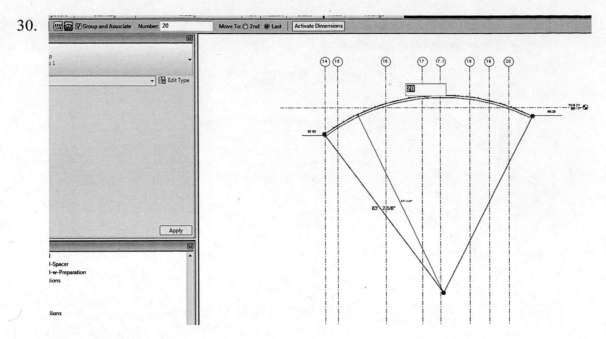

Select the bolt.
Select the radial array option.
Drag the center point of the array to align with the center point displayed by the radial dimension.
Select the left end point of the beam as the start angle.
Select the right end point of the beam as the end angle.
Enable Group and Associate.
Set the Number to 20.
Enable Move to Last.
You will see a preview of the array.
Press ENTER or left click in the display window to accept.

31.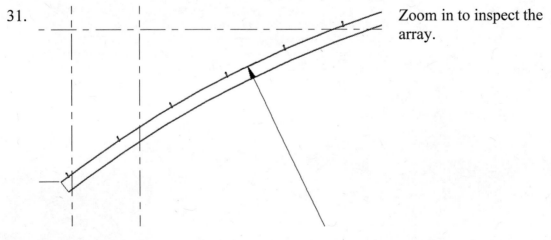

Zoom in to inspect the array.

32. Adjust the position of the far right top bolt to about 6 inches from the end.

33.

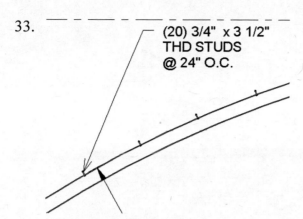

(20) 3/4" x 3 1/2"
THD STUDS
@ 24" O.C.

Add a text note to call out the studs.

34.

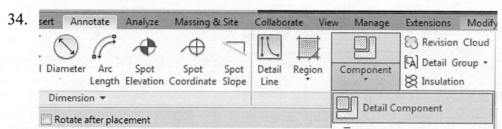

Activate the Annotate ribbon.

Select **Component→Detail Component**.

35.

Properties

A325 Bolts-Side
3/4"

Detail Items

Set the Bolt Type to ¾″.

36.

Place a bolt on the underside flange.

With the bolt selected, change the Length in the Properties pane to **3 ½″**.

Use the ROTATE tool to orient to the beam flange.

37.

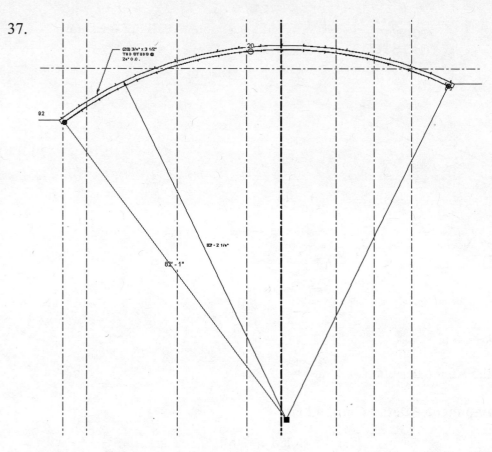

Create a radial array of the bottom bolt.

Select the radial array option.

Drag the center point of the array to align with the center point displayed by the radial dimension.

Select the center of the left bottom bolt as the start angle.

Select the center of the right top bolt as the end angle.

Enable Group and Associate.

Set the Number to 20.

Enable Move to Last.

You will see a preview of the array.

Press ENTER or left click in the display window to accept.

38.

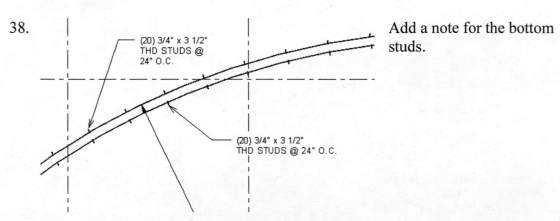

Add a note for the bottom studs.

39.    Select the **Detail Line** tool.

Detail
Line

40. 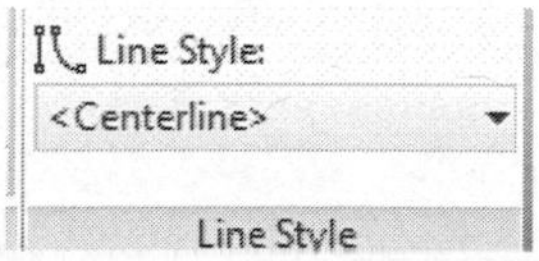   Line Style:
<Centerline>

Line Style

Set the Line Style to **Centerline.**

41. 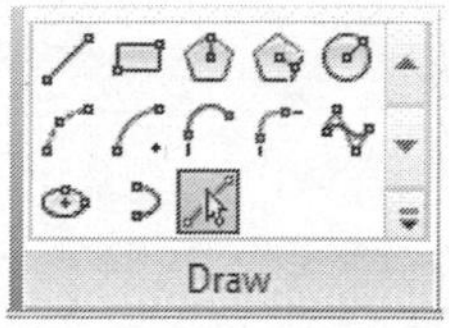   Select the **Pick** tool.

Draw

42. 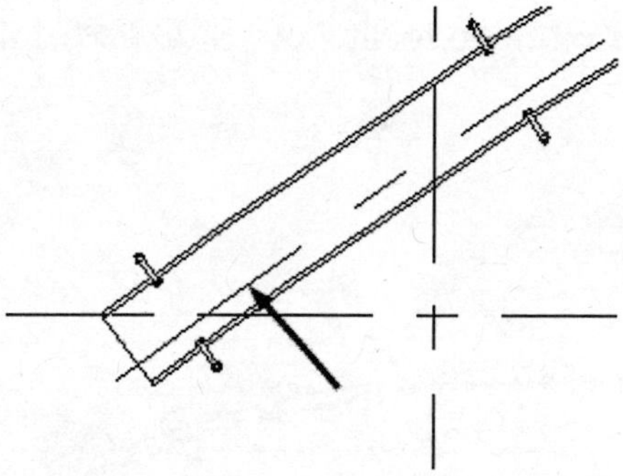   Place the centerline so it is offset 4″ into the beam.

43.    Select the **Detail Line** tool.

Detail
Line

44. 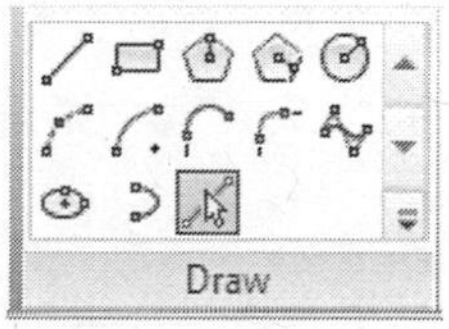   Select the Pick tool.

Draw

45. 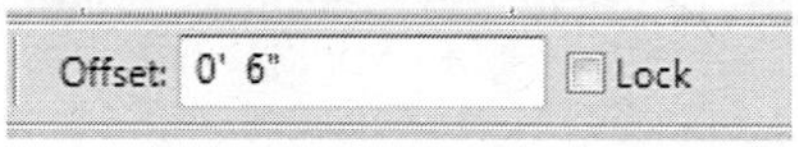   Offset: 0' 6"   ☐ Lock   Set the Offset to **6″**.

46. 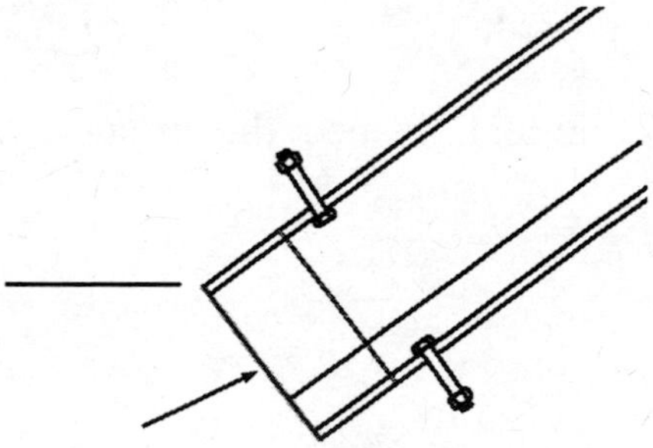   Select the end edge to place the offset line.

Use the Preview to confirm placement of the offset line.

47. 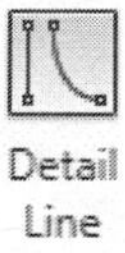   Select the **Detail Line** tool.

Detail
Line

48. 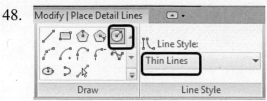 Select the **Circle** tool.
Set the Line Style to **Thin Lines**.

49. 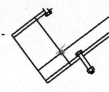 Set the Radius to **15/32″**.

50. 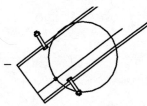 Place the circle at the intersection of the offset line and the centerline arc.

Delete the offset line.

51. Draw a 1′ 6″ diameter circle to locate an 18″ O.C. from the placed circle.

52.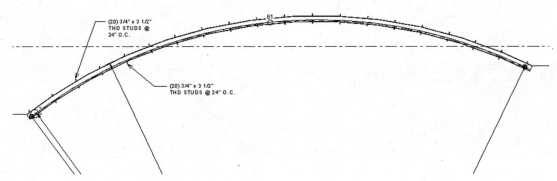

Create a radial array of the circle.
Set the center of the array to the centerline arc center.
Set the Spacing to 2nd and use the 1′ 6″ diameter circle to set the spacing distance.
Set the number to 60.

Delete the 1′ 6″ diameter circle once the array is placed.

53. 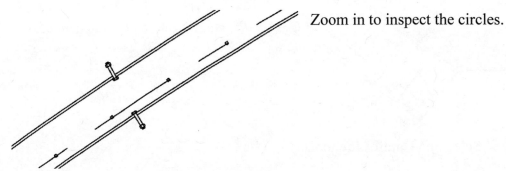 Zoom in to inspect the circles.

54.

(60) 15/16" HOLES
@ 18" O.C.

86.33

Add a text note for the holes.

55.

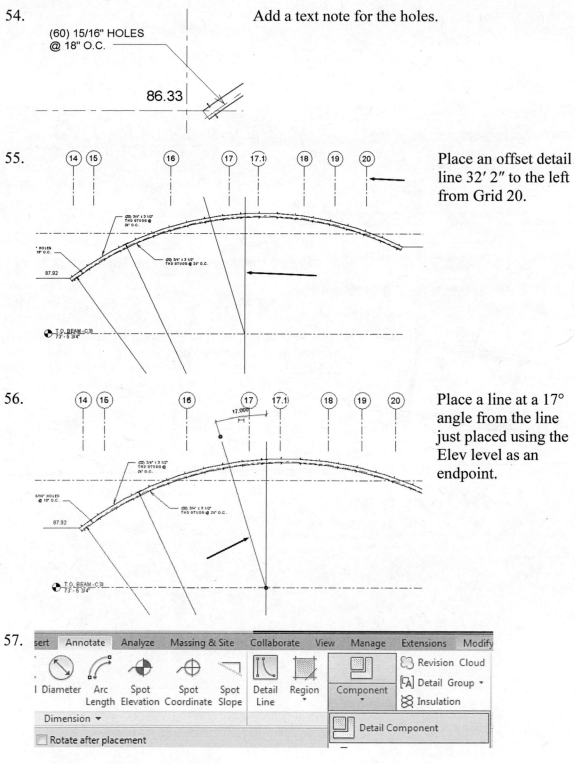

Place an offset detail line 32′ 2″ to the left from Grid 20.

56.

Place a line at a 17° angle from the line just placed using the Elev level as an endpoint.

57.

sert   Annotate   Analyze   Massing & Site   Collaborate   View   Manage   Extensions   Modify

Diameter   Arc Length   Spot Elevation   Spot Coordinate   Spot Slope   Detail Line   Region   Component   Revision Cloud   Detail Group   Insulation

Dimension ▼

Detail Component

☐ Rotate after placement

Activate the Annotate ribbon.

Select **Component→Detail Component**.

58. 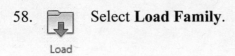 Select **Load Family**.

59. 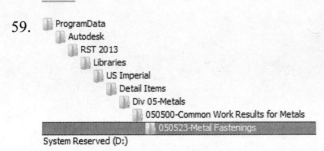   Browse to the *Metal Fastenings* folder under *Detail Items/Metals/Common Work Results for Metals*.

60. 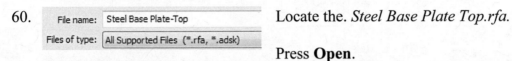   Locate the. *Steel Base Plate Top.rfa.*

Press **Open**.

61. 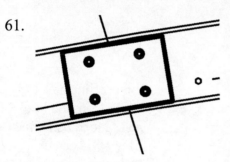   Position the plate so it is between the flanges and centered on the angled line.

62. Save the project.

Challenge Exercises:

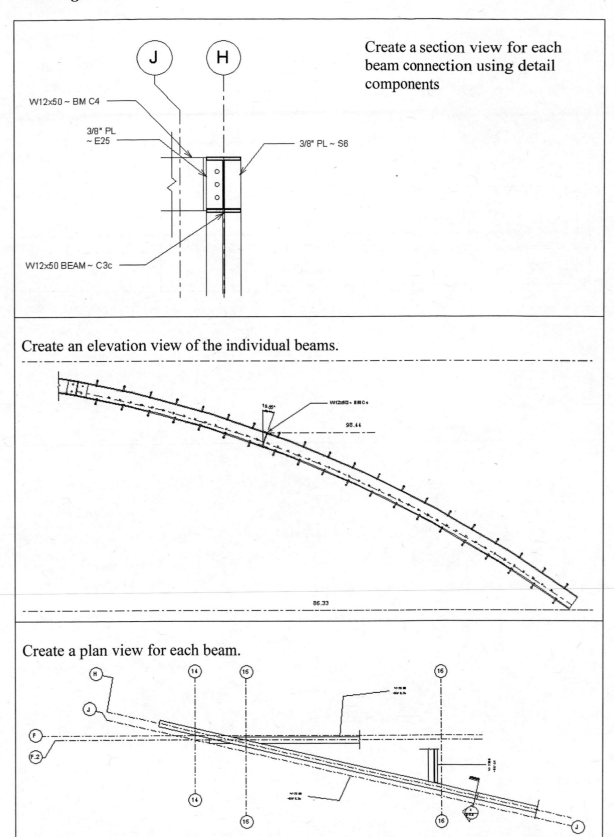

Create a section view for each beam connection using detail components

W12x50 ~ BM C4

3/8" PL ~ E25

3/8" PL ~ S6

W12x50 BEAM ~ C3c

Create an elevation view of the individual beams.

Create a plan view for each beam.

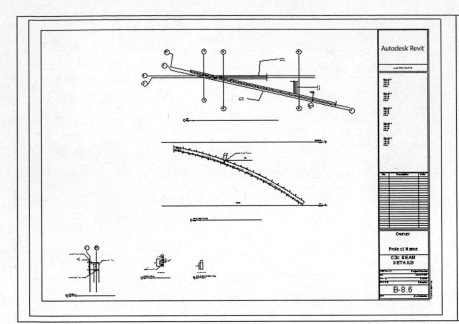

Create a sheet for each beam.
Add an elevation and plan view.
Add drafting and section views as needed.

About the Author

Autodesk
Certified Instructor

Elise Moss has worked for the past thirty years as a mechanical designer in Silicon Valley, primarily creating sheet metal designs. She has written articles for Autodesk's Toplines magazine, AUGI's PaperSpace, DigitalCAD.com and Tenlinks.com. She is President of Moss Designs, creating custom applications and designs for corporate clients. She has taught CAD classes at DeAnza College, Silicon Valley College, and for Autodesk resellers. She is currently teaching CAD at SFSU, in the College for Extended Learning campus and at Laney College in Oakland. Autodesk has named her as a Faculty of Distinction for the curriculum she has developed for Autodesk products. She holds a baccalaureate degree in Mechanical Engineering from San Jose State.

She is married with three sons. Her older son, Benjamin, is an electrical engineer. Her middle son, Daniel, works with AutoCAD Architecture in the construction industry. His designs have been featured in architectural journals. Her youngest son, Isaiah, is starting high school, but shows signs of being a budding engineer. Her husband, Ari, has a distinguished career in software development.

Elise is a third generation engineer. Her father, Robert Moss, was a metallurgical engineer in the aerospace industry. Her grandfather, Solomon Kupperman, was a civil engineer for the City of Chicago.

She can be contacted via email at elise_moss@mossdesigns.com.

More information about the author and her work can be found on her website at www.mossdesigns.com.

Other books by Elise Moss
AutoCAD Architecture 2013 Fundamentals
Autodesk Revit Architecture 2013 Basics